The Perennial Gardener's Design Primer

The Perennial Gardener's Design Primer

Stephanie Cohen & **Nancy J. Ondra**

FOREWORD BY **ALLAN M. ARMITAGE**
PHOTOGRAPHS BY **ROB CARDILLO**

Storey Publishing

The mission of Storey Publishing is to serve our customers by publishing practical information that encourages personal independence in harmony with the environment.

Edited by Gwen Steege and Sarah Guare

Art direction, and cover and text design by Kent Lew

Text production by Cynthia McFarland

Photographs © Rob Cardillo, with the exception of the following: © Adam Mastoon, back cover authors photo; © Gary Campbell, p. 226; MACORE, Inc., p. 71 (#1); © Nancy J. Ondra, pp. 71 (#6), 76 (#4, #5), 124 right, 205 right, 223 right, 225 right

Watercolor illustrations © Lois Lovejoy

Garden plans created by the authors and drawn by Alison Kolesar

Indexed by Susan Olason, Indexes + Knowledge Maps

Printed in Hong Kong by Elegance Printing

10 9 8 7 6 5 4 3

LIBRARY OF CONGRESS CATALOGING-IN-PUBLICATION DATA

Cohen, Stephanie, 1937–
    The perennial gardener's design primer / Stephanie Cohen and Nancy J. Ondra.
        p. cm.
    Includes bibliographical references and index.
    ISBN-13: 978-1-58017-543-2; ISBN-10: 1-58017-543-0 (PBK. : ALK. PAPER)
    ISBN-13: 978-1-58017-545-6; ISBN-10: 1-58017-545-7 (HARDCOVER : ALK. PAPER)
    1. Perennials. 2. Gardens—Design. 3. Landscape gardening. I. Ondra, Nancy J.
II. Title.

SB434.C63 2005
635.9'32—dc22

2004020306

Dedication

*To my husband, Dick, who encouraged me every step of the way in my career;
I thank him for helping to create a true plantaholic.
To my long-suffering children, Abby, Doug, and Rachel,
who were dragged to more gardens as children than they ever cared to see.
And to my new granddaughter, Chelsea, who I have visions
of making into a gardener and nature lover.*

— STEPHANIE COHEN

*To my aunt and uncle, Nona and Mike Ondra.
Who knew that three people with a pot of coffee and a couple of hours to kill
could come up with solutions to all of the world's problems?
If only we had kept notes!*

— NANCY J. ONDRA

contents

foreword

ALTHOUGH I AM SELDOM CALLED UPON for assistance with garden design, I do enjoy the topic. Both Stephanie and Nancy know that I am somewhat design-challenged and books on the subject usually leave me cold. Not so with this one! It is not only a pleasant read, but also informative and educational, making it easy even for someone like me to put its basic tenets into practice.

From Getting Started to It's All in the Details, Stephanie and Nancy keep things simple but informative. One of the things I most appreciate is that although this book is about perennials, the authors understand that man does not live by perennials alone. Including a chapter on Exploring Perennial Partners shows that while they appreciate perennials in the design, they acknowledge that a fine garden consists of more than one group of plants. Readers will also be pleased with the diverse palette of perennials they discuss, which reflects their attitude that not all gardeners

are master gardeners, nor are they witless garden novices. It is obvious that a good deal of thought about the diversity of plant material appropriate for American gardens went into their choices.

The "before and after" sections in part 3 are another plus for so many of us as our gardens get older or shadier or simply more tired. I am ready to steal Stephanie's and Nancy's ideas with the hope that my "after" will be half as good as theirs. This book should make you smarter and happier: What else is there?

— Allan M. Armitage
Author and Professor of Horticulture
University of Georgia

introduction

WE HAVE TO CONFESS IT at the beginning of our book: We're both obsessed by gardens and gardening. Gardens are our work and our play, and we love to share our passion, along with what we've learned from years of gardening and teaching others about gardening. We recognize that people garden for many different reasons, from the fun of simply being outdoors and getting fresh air and exercise, to watching things grow, to treasuring a quiet time to just think about things. Gardening helps us beautify our homes, enhance our environment, and make our communities better places in which to live. Gardens even add to the value of our homes, though for most gardeners that's just a side benefit. Our hope is that what we offer in the pages that follow will give you the confidence to experiment and explore. Although we believe you'll soon be able to create your own beautiful gardens, we hope that you'll also understand that you can't really fail, for even garden mistakes can turn into opportunities to learn. After all, you don't really know a plant until you've killed it!

part one

Perennial Design Demystified

1 Getting Started

WHETHER YOU'RE A BRAND-NEW GARDENER or a veteran of the spade-and-trowel brigade, starting a perennial garden project can be both exhilarating and overwhelming. The key to making the process go smoothly is knowing the right questions to ask yourself, because when you ask the right questions, the answers are sure to follow. Let's take a look at the basics of getting any design off to a great start, from identifying your wants and needs to evaluating your site and soil.

What's on My Wish List?

THE BEST WAY TO BEGIN the creative process is to think about what you want from your perennial garden. Sounds obvious, perhaps, but when you concentrate on all of the potential purposes your planting can serve, you can get lots of helpful design clues. Not sure of the possibilities? Here are some ideas to get you started.

Make an Enticing Entrance. All of us want the front of our house to be attractive and inviting. Placing a perennial garden anywhere in your front yard — by your main door, along the walkway, against the foundation, or next to your parking area, for example — is a perfect opportunity to give family and friends a warm welcome. Color plays a major role here, and four-season interest is important too. Low-maintenance features help ensure that your planting looks good without taking up all of your free time. And, if possible, pick up style clues from your home's architecture, so that the garden and house complement each other.

Face the Challenge. Most of us have some problem area in our yard: dry shade under mature trees; a site that's wet in spring and dry in summer and fall, or that stays wet all year long; or a steep slope that defies mowing. Instead of struggling to grow lawn grass in these trouble spots, save time and money by growing perennials there instead. Be sure to choose plants that are naturally adapted to the conditions.

Create a Green Screen. A property-line perennial planting is an effective and neighbor-friendly way to delineate the boundaries of your yard without the expense of a fence or formal hedge. Eye-high perennials can also provide summer and fall privacy screening for areas within your yard, such as around a swimming pool. Because screen plantings require tall plants, your design palette will focus mostly on perennials and grasses that are at least 5 feet. It's important that they be self-supporting, too, unless you don't mind staking them. By their nature, screen plantings are primarily summer and fall gardens, because it takes a few months for them to grow tall enough to provide privacy.

Extend Your Living Space. Nothing brightens a bad day quicker than seeing a beautiful garden. Even in winter, a well-planned design provides a view worth admiring against an otherwise bleak landscape.

A WARM WELCOME. Massed plantings overflow the wide pathway of this colorfully gracious front entrance.

Take advantage of perennials with year-round interest around a deck or other outdoor living space, or give them a site you easily see from indoors; either way, you'll double the pleasure you get out of both your home and your gardens.

Get Crafty. If you enjoy bringing Mother Nature's bounty indoors, plan a perennial garden filled with suitable flowers, foliage, and seedheads. Color is critical, so choose perennials that complement colors you use inside your home. In addition, select a variety of flower forms, such as daisies, spikes, and fine-textured fillers, as well as plenty of green and variegated foliage to set off those beautiful blooms. And don't forget fragrance. To have a steady supply of flowers for cutting, drying, or pressing, include perennials that bloom at different times of the year. You may want to site your crafter's garden in a side- or backyard, so that you won't hesitate to cut blooms for fear of spoiling a showcase garden.

Welcome Wildlife. One of the great delights in gardening is observing the abundance of life that comes to visit. Besides the usual array of songbirds, hummingbirds drawn by bright flowers provide a special touch of magic. Butterflies delight young and old alike, and beneficial insects like lady beetles, ground beetles, and praying mantids help keep bad bugs to a minimum. Any garden will provide some shelter and food for wild creatures, but you can make a planting more welcoming by including perennials with lots of seeds (like daisies and ornamental grasses) for birds and plants with many small, nectar- and pollen-rich flowers, such as yarrows (*Achillea*), for butterflies and beneficial insects. Hummingbirds love the color

red, but the shape of blossoms is just as important, so plant lots of tubular-flowered perennials, such as penstemons. Remember to include a water source, too, and your beautiful perennial garden will do double duty as a wonderful wildlife habitat.

Nan's Notebook

What's Your Style?

IF YOU'RE STILL NOT SURE WHAT KIND of perennial garden you'd be happy with, take a look around the inside of your home for clues. Maybe you enjoy displaying lots of knickknacks and family photos, or you think of yourself as a laid-back, easygoing kind of person. If so, consider a casual-style garden, such as a naturalistic planting or a cottage garden. Do you prefer to keep clutter to a minimum and maintain a nice, tidy house? A manicured formal garden might be more to your liking.

A particular color or color combination can also be a fun starting point for a new garden. I have to catch myself each time I think about a new planting, because I always want to start with chartreuse foliage as the key element. There's nothing wrong with using similar colors in different gardens, of course, but sometimes it's a good idea to break out of your comfort zone and try something different.

Another place to look for inspiration is the outside of your home. If the architecture evokes a certain historical time period, that can be a great basis for creating a complementary garden design. Rustic features such as picket or split-rail fences, for instance, lend themselves to a Colonial look, while brick paths and wrought-iron fences provide a perfect setting for a Victorian-style garden.

For more ideas and inspiration, check out photos in books and magazines, and take every opportunity to "try on" gardens for yourself: Watch your local newspaper for garden tours in your area, join local plant societies to get an "in" for activities at members' homes, and generally keep an eye out for appealing gardens as you walk and drive around town. Always have a notebook handy, and jot down ideas of plants, features, and general styles that you like and (just as important) don't like. These notes will be helpful when it comes time to fine-tune your personal gardening style and invaluable when you actually start drawing the design.

Set the Mood.
Each time you create a perennial planting, you are an artist as well as a gardener, painting a living picture that will rival any masterpiece on canvas. Use your favorite colors to create a feeling of playfulness, joy, serenity, or wildness. Each part of the garden can evoke a different mood. A pastel-flowered planting or a peaceful woodland garden provides a soothing setting for reading or birdwatching; a vibrant, hot-color border or flower-packed cottage garden is a great backdrop for lively summertime cookouts. Both color and style play important roles in designing a perennial garden that creates a particular mood.

Putting It All Together.
You're at the wishful-thinking stage here, so there are no bad ideas; just jot down whatever comes to mind. Don't be dismayed if you have a half-dozen or so seemingly different ideas but want to put in only one garden right now. With some imagination, you'll be able to create a single planting that meets many, if not all, of your needs. A garden based on tall, brightly colored perennials, for example, can serve as screening for your pool, provide ample summer and fall color, create a vibrant setting for summer picnics, attract birds and butterflies, *and* provide a solution for a troublesome wet spot, all at the same time. Identifying several functions for a single garden is a tremendous help in focusing its overall design, and your plant choices in particular. The result? A garden that works almost as hard as you do.

CREATE A MOOD.
Perennials and roses not only screen this backyard pool, but they create a colorful, yet serene setting, as well.

What's My Site Like?

Now that you've thought about what you want to design in terms of your dream garden, it's time for a reality check. Even what seems like a perfect plan is doomed to fail if it doesn't take into account the growing conditions your site has to offer. Perhaps you've fallen in love with pictures of expansive English borders awash with early-summer perennials and roses, but the only space you have is a small side yard that's heavily shaded by a big maple tree for most of the year. You can still have a formal border, but you may decide to base it on spring-blooming flowers and shrubs instead, or to fill it mostly with colorful foliage to create a lush summer look. It's certainly possible to modify just about any site — by cutting down trees to get more light or by building lattice-covered structures to provide shade, for instance — but these kinds of modifications require a significant investment of time and money. In most cases, working *with* the conditions you have, instead of trying to change them to match the plants you want, is the surest way to create a good-looking and naturally healthy garden.

Let There Be Light. One of the most important features of any garden site is the amount of sunlight it receives. Unless your property is set in the middle of a dense grove of evergreen trees (in which case you know you have deep shade and can move on to the next section), every property has areas with different light levels. Even where there are no trees at all, buildings and walls cast shade at certain times of the day. Light levels can also change dramatically throughout the year. A wooded lot with deciduous trees, for example, may get full sun in winter and spring, then be cast in full shade once the trees leaf out.

Because light is such a changeable factor, looking at your potential site just once won't give you a true picture of the light levels. Ideally, you should check it out over the course of an entire growing season, but if you're not willing to wait that long, the best way is to observe it over the course of one sunny summer day. Check the site first thing in the morning, around noon, and again in mid-afternoon (more often if you like) and note whether it is in sun or shade. At the end of the day, you can then make your best guess about how many hours of sun the site receives during the course of the day. Now, turn to Getting a Handle on Shade on page 98 to determine just what kind of light levels you are working with. Add the results to your design notes so you'll remember them when it comes time to choose the perennials for your new garden.

SIGNS OF SPRING.
Primroses tumble over rocks in this woodland garden each spring.

RIGHT PLACE, RIGHT PLANT. Ensure that each plant's needs are met by site conditions. For instance, butterfly weed *(Asclepias tuberosa)* ① thrives in dry, sunny spots, whereas pitcher plants *(Sarracenia* 'Dana's Delight') ② and Siberian iris *(Iris sibirica* 'Caesar's Brother') ③ prefer moisture.

Working with "Off-the-Shelf" Designs

Taking the time to do an honest and thorough analysis of your site is the biggest favor you can do for yourself during the garden-planning process. And that goes double when you're thinking of planting a design you've seen in a magazine or book — such as one of the sample plans we've included in Part Two — on your own property. "Premade" designs can be a useful starting point for your own plantings, especially if you're attempting your very first perennial garden. But don't expect to reproduce them exactly and have them succeed unless you're sure that the size, shape, and plant choices are all appropriate for the site and growing conditions you have to work with.

Getting Down and Dirty.

What's going on under your feet is just as important to the future success of your garden as what's going on over your head. The many aspects of soil that influence plant growth — its fertility, texture, structure, and drainage, to name just a few — are sciences unto themselves, but you don't need years of advanced studies to get a basic idea of what your site has to offer. The vast majority of common garden perennials will adapt to a wide range of growing conditions (that's how they get to *be* common, after all), so it's mostly just extremes that you need to be concerned about.

If there is any existing landscaping near the site you're considering for a garden, take a good look at the plants there. Does the lawn look pretty good, and are the trees and shrubs growing all right? If so, it's likely that you have the so-called average soil that will suit most perennials just fine.

If your soil is at one extreme or another — you have either dry, infertile sand or heavy wet clay — that will probably be obvious too, from signs like stunted growth, rotting, wilting, and long-lasting puddles. To confirm this, you can test your soil by feel: Simply scoop up a handful of soil and rub some of it between your fingers. A gritty feeling is a sure sign of sand. This generally means that drainage is good, so roots will get plenty of the air they need, but you'll have to either supply water when rain is lacking or look for perennials that are naturally drought-tolerant. If your handful of soil seems sticky, or if it makes a tight ball when you squeeze it and doesn't crumble when you tap it with your finger, your soil is likely high in clay. Clay soils tend to hold lots of moisture, which is fine when plants are actively growing in the summer; during the colder months, though, constantly moist roots can be susceptible to rotting. Once again, the trick is to choose plants that are naturally adapted to the conditions you have, so you won't need to go to great lengths to modify the site. For more details on dealing with these challenges, see Dry-Soil Sites (page 113) and Solutions for Soggy Sites (page 92).

Battling Breezes. A factor many folks don't think about when choosing a garden site is how windy the area is. Constant breezes will dry out the soil quickly, so gardens in exposed sites may need extra irrigation. You'll probably also have to stake tall perennials to keep them upright, unless you look for those with extra-strong stems or cut them back by about half in early summer to promote bushier growth. Strong winds can make your yard unpleasant for you as well as for your perennials, so this is one case where it's worth contemplating some site alterations, such as installing fences or evergreens to create a windbreak. If that's not an option, consider siting your garden on the sheltered side of your home or a garage, shed, or other outbuilding.

Making the Grade. While you're investigating a possible garden site, make a note of whether it is flat or sloping. A gentle slope is fine, but a steep slope (one that's difficult to mow safely) can be a real challenge; water will run off the surface faster than it can soak in, often carrying away good topsoil with it. Establishing a garden on a slope like this can be tricky, but it will pay off in the long run, because the garden will need a lot less maintenance than will frequently mowed turf. Another option is to build low walls across the slope to create broad, flat "steps": These terraces look great and make maintenance even easier. You'll find more information on your options in Coping with Slopes on page 113.

Flat sites offer a wide range of planting possibilities, as well as the readiest access for gardeners of all ages and physical abilities. Stephanie's knees aren't what they used to be, for instance, so she finds her current, mostly flat property much easier to navigate than was her previous, sloping yard. An entirely level site may have drainage problems, though; Solutions for Soggy Sites (page 92), covers lots of possibilities if that's an issue for you. Raised beds, which are an excellent option for counteracting poor drainage, also make tasks like planting, weeding, and grooming much more pleasant for gardeners with physical challenges.

Keep in mind, too, that a perennial garden plunked down in the middle of a flat, open area will look out of place, particularly if it doesn't include any trees or shrubs to give it some height. In that case, consider incorporating a wall, fence, trellis, or arbor into your design to give the planting some structure and "verticality."

HEIGHTENED INTEREST. Flat sites can be made more interesting if you provide height in the form of trellises for plants to scramble on.

Getting to Know You

Creating a beautiful perennial garden is more than just choosing the right colors and proportions: It's also a matter of developing a good "mental encyclopedia" of plants. There are plenty of on-paper plant encyclopedias, of course, and they're an invaluable reference for gardeners of all levels. But let's face it: Plants don't read books, so they don't know where the books say they are supposed to grow, how tall they are supposed to get, and so on. Seeing for yourself how plants perform in real-life situations is the best way to develop an internal database that you can draw on when designing your dream gardens.

One of the best ways to get acquainted with locally-adapted plants is visiting other people's gardens ①. Watch your local newspaper for announcements of garden tours, and consider joining a garden club or plant society in your area; most offer visits to members' gardens as a benefit. When you go visiting, be sure to take a notebook so you can write down the names of plants and ideas that appeal to you.

A good local nursery ② is another invaluable resource for learning about plants. Look for one with well-labeled, well-maintained plants, and display beds where you can see the plants actually growing in the ground. Feel free to ask questions of the staff, but be considerate, too. It's not fair to monopolize their time for hours, or expect them to design your whole garden for you.

Arboreta and botanical gardens ③ with well-labeled display gardens are yet another super place to see plants that are well adapted to your climate, and to get design ideas that appeal to you. Keep in mind, though, that these plantings tend to be rather larger than a typical home garden setting — and that they have a whole staff to maintain them!

Bringing New Life to Tired Gardens

SO FAR WE'VE EXPLORED the many possibilities of establishing a brand-new garden on an "empty" site. But unless you've just bought a house in a new development with absolutely no landscaping, you probably have some existing gardens that could use some help. Maybe you've neglected a garden you put in a few years ago, or you inherited someone else's poor choices when you moved into an older home; either way, the prospect of turning chaos into a well-ordered planting can seem daunting.

What's Up? The best way to start the process is with a site inventory — figuring out what's already growing there. If you planted the original garden yourself, you can probably identify most of the perennials, either from memory or with the help of the original plan, remaining plant labels, or nursery receipts. If the garden is new to you, try to watch it over the course of one growing season. Otherwise, it's easy to overlook small early-flowering perennials and spring-flowering bulbs, as well as perennials that go dormant after flowering (that is, they die back to the ground and won't be apparent in summer or fall). If you rush to redo a garden, you may accidentally dig up these "surprises" and end up ruining some very nice plants in the process.

As you watch the garden's progress through the season, keep notes of all the plants that are visible at various times. If there are some you can't identify, talk to the former owner, if possible, or ask for help from an experienced gardening friend. Or take pictures or samples of your mystery plants (a leaf and flower or a flower cluster, too, if possible) to your local Cooperative Extension office, a botanical garden, or your local garden center. Flipping through plant catalogs and photographic perennial encyclopedias is another way to identify mystery plants.

Once you know what you're starting with, it's time to decide what will stay and what will go. When a garden is left to its own devices for a few years, the weakest plants tend to die out and the sturdier survivors spread out to fill in the spaces. Make a note of which plants are particularly abundant, and do some research to determine if they are troublesome spreaders or simply a bit overgenerous with their seedlings. Plants that self-sow are worth keeping if you're willing to pinch off their spent flowers regularly from now on, but think twice about keeping those that spread quickly by creeping roots, unless the site is so difficult that few other perennials will grow there. For more on identifying and coping with these overenthusiastic plants, see Watch Out for Thugs on page 13.

A Quick Refresher. If you think that the garden is basically worth keeping — in other words, you like the current size, shape, and placement, and the plants just need some tidying up — you can perform a little minor surgery. First, thoroughly weed out everything you don't want, then divide any remaining overgrown clumps (those that look crowded and are blooming poorly). Before you replant any of the divisions, add a shovelful or two of compost to each planting hole to help rejuvenate the soil. If you have leftover divisions, use them in another part of your yard or find a good home for them with friends, neighbors, or family.

Now fill any remaining empty spaces with a few new perennials to add a complementary or contrasting color, additional seasonal interest, or some needed height variation. If the garden is bordered by turf, use a spade or edging tool to cut a sharp new edge around the planting; you won't believe the difference this will make! Finish up with a fresh layer of mulch, and perhaps add a garden ornament, to give your old planting a new lease on life.

GET EDGY.
A sharply delineated, neatly maintained edge goes a long way toward transforming garden beds in need of attention.

A Full-Scale "Facelift."

If weeds or overly vigorous perennials have taken over the garden, if it's too large or small, or if it otherwise doesn't meet your needs, it's time for a full-scale renovation. Dig up any perennials and bulbs you want to save and move them to a holding bed (an out-of-the-way spot where they can grow until you are ready to replant them) or plant them in pots. Then remove any remaining vegetation and create an all-new design for the site. This is a perfect opportunity to learn from any mistakes you or the previous owner made: You can easily change the size and outline, and you can replace any poor plant choices with perennials that are better suited to the site. If the previous planting was often affected by disease, do some research to see if there are newer, disease-resistant selections. If the garden was too wide to allow for easy weeding and maintenance, change the shape or add a path behind or through the area for better access.

Redoing a garden may sound like a lot of work, and, to be honest, it is. But you also have a head start over someone beginning with a brand-new site, because you already have a good idea of which perennials will thrive there. Plus, you can use the mature plants you kept as the basis for the new design, which will save you a significant amount of money. Best of all, most of the soil preparation work has already been done; simply spread a 2- to 3-inch-deep layer of compost over the area and dig or till it in, and you're set to plant.

Looking for more information on the process of renovating an old perennial garden? Turn to Reworking an Old Garden (page 257) for an in-depth analysis of a planting we renovated at Nan's parents' house.

Watch Out for Thugs

No matter how many years you've been gardening, it's all too easy to be tempted by impulse plant purchases. Beware — many turn out to be serious mistakes. They look so pretty and harmless in their nursery pots, but when you bring them home and let them loose in your good garden soil, they may take over before you know it. This happened to me recently with an 'Oriental Limelight' wormwood (*Artemisia vulgaris*). I planted it in June, and in the spring of the following year I had to dig up half the border to get rid of it.

The best defense against all garden thugs is to do your research ahead of time (by checking with your local Cooperative Extension Service office, for instance), so you'll know whether they're a potential problem in your area and won't be lured by their charms. If you're tempted by a potted perennial and aren't sure about its potential for being invasive, check the label for verbal clues such as "vigorous," "strong grower," "quick spreader," and "fills in rapidly." Other clues to watch for are shoots growing out of the drainage holes at the base of the pot, as well as thick white roots that are visible on the outside of the root-ball when you slip the plant out of its pot. Different plants are problems in different regions, so those that are true thugs in one area may be perfectly well behaved in others. But to get you started, here's a list (at right) of spreaders that Stephanie vows she'll never plant directly in her southeastern Pennsylvania garden.

If you really want to grow a confirmed spreader, or if you want to test a new plant and aren't sure of its spreading habits, try growing it in a pot or planter. Make sure there is a saucer underneath, though, or set the pot on an impervious surface, so the roots can't escape through the drainage holes and root into the soil. You can consider planting it in the ground if you have a difficult site where you can't get anything better to grow, but if it takes over that spot and begins to run amok in other parts of your yard, you'll have learned a tough lesson: These spreaders really spread.

In any case, don't plant purple loosestrife (any non-native species, hybrids, or cultivars of *Lythrum*) under any circumstances. Its proven ability to seed into the wild, choking out native plants and destroying valuable wildlife habitat, has made this pretty but pernicious perennial the poster child for plant thuggery.

INVASIVES TO AVOID

Aegopodium podagraria 'Variegata' (variegated bishop's weed — and the all-green species too)

Allium tuberosum (garlic chives)

Artemisia vulgaris (mugwort)

Cerastium tomentosum (snow-in-summer)

Convallaria majalis (lily of the valley)

Coronilla varia (crown vetch)

Corydalis ophiocarpa (corydalis)

Euphorbia cyparissias (cypress spurge)

Houttuynia cordata (chameleon plant)

Lamiastrum galeobdolon (yellow archangel — except for 'Herman's Pride')

Lysimachia clethroides (gooseneck loosestrife)

Lythrum (purple loosestrifes — banned in many states)

Macleaya cordata (plume poppy)

Oenothera speciosa (showy evening primrose)

Physalis alkekengi (Chinese lantern)

Physostegia virginiana (obedient plant — except for 'Miss Manners')

Ranunculus ficaria (creeping buttercup) — photo above left

Salvia lyrata (lyre-leaved sage)

Saponaria ocymoides (rock soapwort)

Sedum acre (gold moss sedum)

Selecting Your Perennials

2

Deciding what you want your new garden to be like and figuring out where you want to put it are two key steps in the perennial design process. But for most of us, the heart of the experience is choosing the specific plants that will turn our paper plan into the garden of our dreams. So let's dive right into the subject of perennial selection, because there's a lot to cover.

Matching Plants to Your Site

SOME LIKE IT WET. **Spring-blossoming Japanese primrose** *(Primula japonica)* **thrives in very wet sites.**

W E'VE SAID IT BEFORE, but we'll say it again: If you want a beautiful, healthy garden, concentrate on perennials that are naturally adapted to the growing conditions your site has to offer. Yes, it's possible to grow just about any plant just about anywhere if you work hard enough — so if you're willing to take extraordinary measures to grow alpines in Alabama or Himalayan blue poppies *(Meconopsis)* in Mississippi, more power to you. But Stephanie likes to sum up the situation this way: "Pampered plants are like pampered pets — they're beautiful to look at, but they can be hard to live with." For most of us, the ideal is a lovely, lush garden that thrives with a minimum of weeding, watering, staking, and other boring maintenance chores. Making a thorough assessment of your climate, available sunlight, and soil conditions, and then making the best match you can from among the perennials that meet your other needs (color, height, and so on), is the surest way to reach that goal.

Climate Considerations. Before

you start looking at site specifics like drainage and exposure, you should have a good idea of the overall year-round weather conditions in your area. These conditions consist of a wide variety of factors, including average annual high and low temperatures, humidity, and rainfall. When you read plant descriptions, however, the only specific climate-related information you're likely to find is the *hardiness zone*. This rating is based on the USDA Plant Hardiness Zone Map, which divides the country into zones based on average annual low temperatures. If you don't already know what zone you live in, we've included a copy of the USDA map in the Appendix on page 273 for easy reference.

Some plant descriptions give hardiness zone ratings as a single number; others give a range. If you see Zone 5, for example, that means the perennial in question should survive an average winter outdoors in Zone 5. It doesn't *guarantee* the plant will survive, as it doesn't take into account factors like unusually low temperatures or extended cold snaps. Drainage plays an important role in hardiness too. Lavenders, for instance, may survive the winter in Zone 4 if their soil is exceptionally well drained, but where the soil is on the clayey side and tends to stay moist all winter, they may not survive north of Zone 6 or 7. Snow also makes a big difference. A thick blanket of snow that stays all winter does a great job insulating perennials from extreme cold, so the same perennial may survive in a colder zone with dependable snow but die in a warmer zone without snow. Despite the weaknesses of the hardiness zone ratings, they are still undeniably useful as a starting point for matching perennials to your climate.

By the way, when you see a plant description with a range of hardiness zones (Zones 4–7, for example), it means the plant is likely to perform well in Zones 4, 5, 6, and 7 but it probably won't thrive in Zones 8, 9, and 10.

Stephanie Says

Finding Your Niche

THE HARDINESS ZONE MAP is a good place to start in predicting whether a perennial will thrive in your yard, but it doesn't have all the answers. Nearly every property has *microclimates*: areas that are warmer or colder than the average conditions. In a low spot (where cold air settles) or in a site that tends to collect water, a perennial that would usually overwinter in your area may not survive. In gardens right next to your home's foundation (especially on the south side) or on the sheltered side of a hedge, solid fence, or stone wall, you may have success with plants that normally overwinter only in a zone warmer than yours.

If you're a beginning gardener, play it safe with your plant choices: Look for those that are rated to a zone or two colder than yours. (If you live in Zone 5, for example, choose perennials that are hardy to Zones 3 and 4.) As your gardening prowess increases, you'll develop a good idea of the microclimates on your property, and you'll be able to experiment with marginally hardy perennials to expand your planting options. Plants make up their own rules about where they want to grow, and sometimes they'll thrive where you'd never expect them to. If you try a plant and have luck with it, you get special bragging rights; if it dies, no one but you will be the wiser. My own rule is to give any plant three tries: If I still can't find a site to suit it, I move on to something else! ✳

Sun and Shade.

In your site analysis, you determined whether you have full sun, partial shade, or full shade, based on the number of hours of sunlight the area receives (see also Getting a Handle on Shade, page 98.) Many perennials can adapt to a range of light levels, and most will survive just about anywhere, although they probably won't thrive if they get far more or less sunlight than they prefer. The recommended light levels given in catalog descriptions and on plant tags are a help, but they generally don't take regional differences into account.

✳ In southern gardens, plants that typically thrive in full sun may actually need light shade, especially in the afternoon.

✳ In the North, perennials that most gardeners farther south grow in shade may perform just fine in full sun.

Soil moisture levels can also have a significant influence on light preferences: Some shade-loving plants grow quite well in full sun as long as their soil is constantly moist. (The reverse doesn't seem to be true, though, so don't expect perennials that thrive in full sun and dry soil to adapt to moist shade.)

Once again, our advice is to start out with perennials that seem the best match for your site. Observe how they perform before you start experimenting with them under less-than-ideal conditions. How will you know if a plant is not getting the right light? Sun-lovers that get too much shade tend to flower poorly and have weak stems; shade lovers may be stunted and have browned, scorched-looking leaves if they are placed in the sun. In both

MEET THE SHADE-LOVERS.
Ferns and hostas combine with a colorful caladium to light up this shady garden.

Wondering about Wind?

Few folks take wind into account when selecting their perennials, but if you live where stiff breezes and sudden gusts are common and you aren't interested in extensive staking, it's worth thinking ahead. When you read plant descriptions, look for species and cultivars that are touted as having naturally strong stems and/or a compact growth habit. If that's not an option, consider giving your tall plants a good hard pinch in early summer to make their stems branch out from the base; this will make them bushier but shorter, so they'll be less likely to get knocked over. After planting, keep irrigation and fertilizing to a minimum to encourage sturdier, self-supporting stems. Here, butterfly weed (*Asclepias tuberosa*) paired with lavender (*Lavandula*) sturdily resists the abuse of its windy site.

cases, the plants will be stressed and more susceptible to pest and disease problems. If you notice any of these symptoms after planting, consider moving the affected perennials into more or less light to see if that solves the problem.

Soil Matters.

The third main factor in getting a good match between a plant and a site is the soil conditions. You'll have luck with the widest variety of perennials if you have "average" soil — that is, neither so clayey that water ponds there for days after a rain, nor so sandy that water drains before plant roots can use it, and fertile enough that other plants grow there satisfactorily without frequent feeding. Fertility is relatively easy to improve, first by digging ample amounts of

compost, chopped leaves, or other forms of organic matter into the soil before planting and then using organic mulches afterward. Extremely slow or fast drainage, however, is an issue not so easily remedied, so you'll need either to consider major improvements or — preferably — to choose perennials that are naturally adapted to those conditions. See Solutions for Soggy Sites (page 92) and Dry-Soil Sites (page 113) for design and plant-selection tips that can turn even these challenges into stunning garden features.

Creative Color Concepts

OLOR IS EVERYWHERE in our world, but there's no place where it thrills us as much as in the garden. We all have favorite colors as well as those we dislike, and these preferences are a natural jumping-off point for creating a pleasing garden design. But if you make the same color choices for every planting you create, you're missing out on exciting effects that are possible with a broad color palette. If you're ready to expand your horizons or you're simply not sure where to start, here are some basics of choosing and combining flower and foliage colors.

Keep Your Cool. The many characteristics of colors, and the terminology to describe them, is a science unto itself. Fortunately, it's possible to create beautiful gardens without getting bogged down in a lot of detailed definitions. But it *is* helpful to keep a few basics in mind — especially the issue of "cool" and "hot" colors. Artists typically consider greens, blues, and violets to be cool colors, because these hues make you feel calm and cool when you see them. Many gardeners expand their definition of cool colors to include light yellow and pale pink flowers, along with silvery foliage, because these pastels have a similar effect on viewers.

Beginning gardeners often like to use these colors because they feel "safe," and with good reason — they look great together! There's also a good deal of historical precedence: The Taj Mahal, the great old gardens of France and England, and the earliest perennial gardens in the United States all had cool color palettes. Think you'd like to use soft colors in your new perennial garden? Turn to Pastel Plantings (page 153) for tips on getting the best from these calming colors.

SINGIN' THE BLUES. The violet-to-blue family creates a welcome cool-and-calm ambience on a hot summer day.

Turn Up the Heat.

As you might guess, "hot" or "warm" colors like red, orange, and yellow create a stimulating effect that makes us feel excited. In a garden, these colors seem to perk up our spirits and delight our senses. It takes a lot of confidence — and a willingness to move plants around if clashing combinations occur — to base a whole garden on these vibrant colors. Some folks garden quite happily without ever using orange or red blooms; others would never be without them. Adventurous gardeners often expand their hot-color palette to include a wide range of really vivid bloom color, such as vibrant violet-purple and intense bright blue, as well as the glowing chartreuse and moody purple of a number of foliage plants. Ready to take the plunge yourself? See Handling Hot Colors (page 140).

Mixing It Up.

Basing your garden on either cool or hot colors is one way to go, but there's no law banning the use of both in one

PICK IT UP. Provide a jolt of lively color with a garden scheme based on yellows, oranges, and reds.

planting. You can even use the whole range in one garden, if that's what pleases you. Unless you're going for a free-for-all, cottage-style effect, however, a rainbow of colors can make a garden look unfocused. Narrowing your palette to a few main colors gives your design a well-thought-out appearance, and simplifies the plant selection process as well. The color theme you choose can be the same from spring through fall or change with the season. In spring, for example, you might choose baby blue and pale pink, warm things up with yellow and purple in summer, and finish the year with scarlet and gold. In most climates, the winter palette is more limited, but you can still carry through color themes with evergreen, ever-gold, and ever-purple foliage, as well as with the bark and berries of shrubs and trees.

So which colors do you want to use as your main theme? The more similar the colors you choose, the more harmonious the planting will appear. A garden of blue, purple, and violet flowers, for instance, will appear quiet and soothing, whereas an area of orange and yellow blooms with lots of green foliage will impart a cheerful, uplifting mood. Other examples of harmonious pairings are yellow, blue, and green; red, blue, and purple; and yellow, orange, and red.

We're all for harmony in the garden, but sometimes there's a little too much of a good thing. Adding some contrast can give your planting a bit of edginess and save it from being predictable. Silver foliage and white and pale yellow flowers pep up cool blues and purples; intense violets and blues add pizzazz to orange and yellow companions. A little contrast can go a long way, however, so you probably won't want to base a garden on equal amounts of two opposing colors. Unless you really want a dramatic (and possibly jarring) design, it's best to choose one or two main colors and use smaller amounts of contrast as accents.

THE SPICE OF LIFE. Variety and contrast can add just the lift a garden needs. Here are some surprising color combinations that you may like to explore. If you can't find the exact plants shown here, select other similarly colored plants. Shown here are blue-violet catmint *(Nepeta)* and orange wallflower *(Erysimum)* 1 ; violet spiderwort *(Tradescantia)* and yellow green-and-gold *(Chrysogonum virginianum)* 2 ; scarlet Maltese cross *(Lychnis chalcedonica)* and silvery green Scotch thistle *(Onopordum)* 3 .

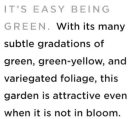

IT'S EASY BEING GREEN. With its many subtle gradations of green, green-yellow, and variegated foliage, this garden is attractive even when it is not in bloom.

Narrowing the Field.

Getting confused by harmonies and contrasts? You might be tempted to try a monochromatic, or "one-color," garden. An all-white garden, for example, is a classic choice for gardeners of all skill levels. Creating a pleasing monochromatic planting isn't quite as simple as it sounds, though. First, there is no such thing as a truly one-color garden: Even if all the flowers are in shades of the same color, the foliage (in its endless varieties of green) always adds another color. And unless you're using a mass planting of one perennial, the flowers you combine *won't* be exactly the same color. Blues range from pale lilac to indigo to deep navy blue, for example, while yellow ranges from light yellow to gold to brassy orange-yellow. Flowers within the blue and yellow ranges can make compatible partners, but be careful with reds: Orangey reds (like scarlet and peach), true red, and bluish reds (including mauve and burgundy) are less compatible and can make very uneasy companions.

Stephanie Says

Keeping the Peace

WHEN YOU'RE WORKING WITH BRIGHT COLORS, or with gradations of one color, you may find situations in which you need a "neutral" to separate two plants that clash. I like to think of neutral colors as garden peacemakers. Their mellow ambience and sense of tranquillity give your eye a resting place as it moves between more obvious colors, thus preventing jarring contrasts. In that way, placing a neutral shade in between warring factions eventually brings a peaceful coexistence to these colorful skirmishes.

In the garden, green, usually in the form of foliage, is the most obvious neutral; gray or purple foliage is also a useful peacemaker. For years I have used white flowers as a neutral, although there is some disagreement here. Some people consider white a "negative" color that punches holes in your floral canvas, and I agree that one large block of white in the garden can be too dominant or startling. If the white is repeated, however, and used with variegated foliage of white and green and off-white, it seems to work well for me. ✻

Perhaps the simplest reason to think twice about a monochromatic garden is the very real likelihood of getting bored with your border. It may be nice to look at for a few minutes, or to visit in someone else's yard, but the sameness all through the growing season may make a one-color garden a bit monotonous in a site you see every day. Still think you'd like to give one a try? Turn to Working with White (page 147) and have fun.

Other Sources of Inspiration.

If you still can't decide which colors would work best in your design, look for clues in the setting you've chosen for your new garden, both in your yard and in any "borrowed land-scape" — that is, in something that's visible from your site but not an immediate part of it. A grouping of purple-leaved trees in a neighbor's yard, a snow-capped mountain, a sparkling blue pond, or some other promi-nent feature can provide great inspiration for color themes. Repeating the colors used in a man-made object, such as your house, a fence, or a shed, is another trick professional designers use to give the entire yard a uni-fied look.

When you can't pick up any obvious color clues that way, consider the site itself and the time of day you'll most often see the garden. In shady sites and in gardens viewed in the evening, white and pastel flowers and silvery foliage tend to be most visible. Blues, purples, and intense reds and oranges, on the other hand, usually look their best in sun-drenched sites, holding their colors even in strong afternoon sunlight.

REPEAT THAT, PLEASE. **The soft rose shade of the bold sedum perfectly echoes the aged stones of the nearby home.**

Testing Your Color Theories.

One advantage of using actual plants to "test-drive" combinations is that you are seeing their true colors. If you look only at plant-tag or catalog photographs, which may be color-enhanced, you may experience major disappointments under real-life conditions. It is far better to see your choices growing in someone else's garden or in bloom at the garden center. (If you buy plants in bloom, you are also ensured that you're getting exactly the color you want, even if some careless shopper has accidentally switched the label that provides all the plant information.)

If you are basing a design on vegetatively propagated cultivars (plants that are propagated by cuttings or division to produce identical offspring), you can expect the color to be consistent from plant to plant. Seed-grown perennials often vary in color, however, and may not look exactly like the picture that's on the packet. If an exact color match is not critical to your design, seed-grown plants are a far more economical way to acquire perennials. Be cautious of seeds that come in mixed colors; planting too many of these can create a muddy, jumbled effect. Just as with perfume or aftershave, a little dab of color variety goes a long way.

Nan's Notebook

A "Garden" in Miniature

ONE OF MY FAVORITE WAYS to come up with new color combinations is to snip bits of flowers and foliage from my gardens, then try to put them together into little bouquets. It's a simple matter to add, remove, or rearrange any of the pieces to try new effects. When I find a pairing I particularly like, I jot down the overall color theme and the specific plants for future reference.

Last fall, for instance, I ended up with a smashing bouquet of hot pink Knock Out roses with a deep blue monkshood (*Aconitum*), an unnamed orange chrysanthemum, and the bright yellow foliage of 'All Gold' lemon balm (*Melissa officinalis*). It definitely was not a combination I would have considered on paper, but when I saw the actual blooms and leaves together, I was sure I had found a winner. By spring, though, I lost a bit of my nerve to try this color theme with a permanent planting, so I committed to the roses but used annuals for the other colors: blue mealycup sage (*Salvia farinacea*), chartreuse 'Sweet Caroline Light Green' sweet potato vine (*Ipomoea batatas*), and orange cosmos (*Cosmos bipinnatus*). The combination looked just as great in a border as it did in the bouquet, so next year I'll replace the sage with monkshood and the sweet potato vine with chartreuse-leaved perennials. I'll add the orange mum too, but I'll keep the cosmos as well, for summer color. ✳

SPARK IT UP.
White-edged variegated foliage and white-flowering plants make this a garden to enjoy well into the evening.

All Shapes and Sizes

ONCE YOU'VE CHOSEN the basic color palette for your design, you're ready to narrow down your choices by height (how tall the plant's foliage is, as well as how tall it is in full bloom) and by habit (the overall shape of the plant).

Sizing Things Up. The most pleasing gardens include perennials of varying heights. A general rule of thumb is that the shortest plants go near the front and the tallest near the back (or the shortest near the edge and the tallest in the middle, if you see the garden from all sides). That way, the plants in front won't cover up those behind them. But it's best not to follow this rule slavishly, or your garden will look like a series of steps. Here are some exceptions to keep in mind:

* Some perennials, such as 'Husker Red' foxglove penstemon (*Penstemon digitalis* 'Husker Red') ①, produce a flush of attractive new leaves if you cut them back when flowers are spent. This makes them good candidates for near the front or edge of your garden.

* "See-through" perennials, including many ornamental grasses, as well as the *Verbena bonariensis* ② shown here, have fine-textured foliage and wispy stems that allow plants behind them to be visible. That makes them a great option for bringing some height toward the front without covering up shorter plants.

* Some spring-flowering perennials and bulbs, such as tulips ③ and bleeding heart (*Dicentra spectabilis*) ④, die back to the ground after they bloom. These usually work best near the middle or back of a garden where later-blooming companions can cover up their declining foliage and fill in the gaps they leave.

* If you have a shorter perennial that looks ratty once it's done flowering, such as early bellflowers (*Campanula*), plant it behind a taller, later-flowering companion that will cover it up.

* You can't make short plants significantly taller, but you can make many tall perennials shorter, with judicious pruning. If you love the clear yellow daisies of the perennial sunflower 'Lemon Queen' (*Helianthus*), for instance, but you'd like them near the middle of your border instead of at the back, cut back the stems by about half in late spring and again by a third or so in midsummer to get a very bushy, 4-foot-tall plant instead of a 6- to 7-foot-tall one. This approach takes careful planning and a good memory to time the trimmings, though, so you won't want to rely on it too much.

A Place for Everything

When designing a border set against a fence or wall, start by placing the tallest plants toward the back and the shortest toward the front. In an island bed, the tallest plants are typically toward the middle, with the shortest around the edges.

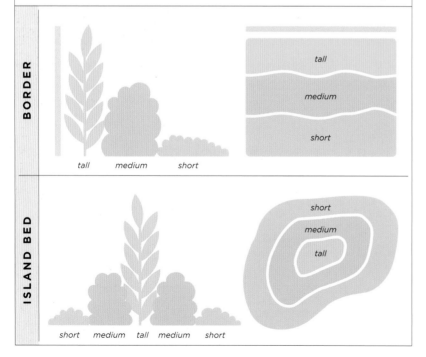

BORDER

tall   medium   short

tall

medium

short

ISLAND BED

short   medium   tall   medium   short

short

medium

tall

Good Habits Are Easy to Find.

Plants themselves assume a variety of shapes. Some of them are creepers: short plants that hug the soil and have a flat appearance. Other plants are equally low but grow in tidy-looking balls, buns, or mounds. Taller perennials may have a loose, open habit that makes them look cloudlike, or a narrow, upright habit that makes them look like exclamation points. Still others have an amorphous form: They often sprawl into or weave among their companions. Using a variety of plant shapes, and making sure you don't have several similar habits right next to each other, adds interest and diversity to your design.

Just as the plants have an overall shape, each flower has its own form. The shape of a daisy, with a central disk and oval petals around it, is one of the most common forms. It's so prevalent among perennials, in fact, that it's easy to end up with way too many daisies, especially in summer and fall. To avoid that, take advantage of the many other available blossom shapes, such as bells, bowls, cups, circles, spikes, stars, and plumes, and mix them up throughout your design. Remember, flat flowers like daisies and yarrows provide resting spots for your eyes, vertical spikes and fluffy plumes draw your attention upward, and other shapes provide dots of accent color. This visual roller coaster ride makes your eyes look at the entire garden and allows for lots of visual impact.

Not only do flowers have their own distinct shapes, but leaves, too, are diverse in their form. For example, they may be narrow or broad, pointed or blunt, and rounded,

FORMING HABITS. The examples at left demonstrate some of the basic shapes of plants: upright torch lily *(Kniphofia)* 1 ; cloudlike crambe *(Crambe cordifolia)* 2 ; ground-hugging 'Burgundy Glow' ajuga *(Ajuga reptans)* 3 ; and mounding sedums 4 .

arrowhead-shaped, heart-shaped, or sword-shaped. They also come in a wide range of sizes, edging patterns (smooth, toothed, lobed, scalloped, etc.), and surfaces (from smooth to crinkled). Some leaves are simple — in one solid piece — while others are cut or dissected into two or more parts.

Depending on their overall size and shape, leaves are roughly classed as having a coarse, medium, or fine texture. Coarse-textured leaves, such as those of ligularias and common rose mallow (*Hibiscus moscheutos*), are large and broad. Medium textures are usually somewhat smaller and narrower. Foliage with fine texture can be long and narrow, like iris leaves, or delicate and lacy, like fern fronds. Coarse leaves tend to be the most noticeable, so you don't want to plant too many of them;

GETTING IN SHAPE. Two purple-blue "spikes" — the very narrow, upright salvia in back and the looser false indigo *(Baptisia australis)* in front — combine effectively with the rosy blooms of painted daisy *(Tanacetum coccineum).*

Common Flower Forms

Pairing perennials with different bloom shapes is a key part of creating attractive combinations and a great overall garden design.

STAR	DAISY	CUP	BELL
EXAMPLES	EXAMPLES	EXAMPLES	EXAMPLES
Amsonia	*Aster*	*Anemone*	*Adenophora*
Belamcanda	*Chrysanthemum*	*Geranium*	*Campanula*
Gaura	*Coreopsis*	*Oenothera*	*Kirengeshoma*
Gillenia	*Echinacea*	*Papaver*	*Mertensia*
Sisyrinchium	*Rudbeckia*	*Potentilla*	*Polygonatum*

GLOBE	SPRAY	UMBEL	SPIKE	PLUME
EXAMPLES	EXAMPLES	EXAMPLES	EXAMPLES	EXAMPLES
Allium	*Alchemilla*	*Achillea*	*Baptisia*	*Aruncus*
Armeria	*Crambe*	*Eupatorium*	*Cimicifuga*	*Astilbe*
Echinops	*Gypsophila*	*Foeniculum*	*Kniphofia*	*Filipendula*
Monarda	*Thalictrum*	*Lychnis chalcedonica*	*Liatris*	*Macleaya*
		Sedum	*Salvia*	*Rodgersia*

A Few Foliage Forms

Combining plants with a variety of leaf shapes, such as these examples, adds ample interest to your garden, even when blooms are scarce.

ROUNDED	HEART-SHAPED	STRAP-LIKE
EXAMPLES	**EXAMPLES**	**EXAMPLES**
Alchemilla	*Epimedium*	*Allium*
Asarum	*Hosta*	*Camassia*
Ligularia	*Lunaria*	*Crocosmia*
Lysimachia nummularia	*Pulmonaria saccharata*	*Iris*
Podophyllum	*Rheum*	*Yucca*

NARROW VS. BROAD		POINTED VS. BLUNT	
EXAMPLES	**EXAMPLES**	**EXAMPLES**	**EXAMPLES**
Amsonia	*Angelica*	*Echinacea*	*Ajuga*
Armeria	*Digitalis*	*Liatris*	*Bergenia*
Aster	*Hosta*	*Nepeta*	*Heuchera*
Dianthus	*Ligularia*	*Phlox*	*Origanum*
Gaura	*Verbascum*	*Veronica*	*Sedum*

Leaf Textures

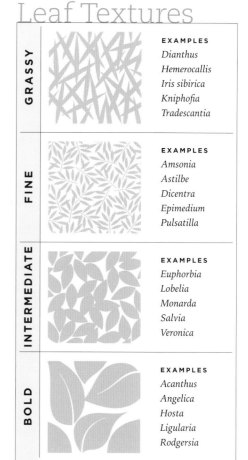

	EXAMPLES
GRASSY	*Dianthus*
	Hemerocallis
	Iris sibirica
	Kniphofia
	Tradescantia
FINE	*Amsonia*
	Astilbe
	Dicentra
	Epimedium
	Pulsatilla
INTERMEDIATE	*Euphorbia*
	Lobelia
	Monarda
	Salvia
	Veronica
BOLD	*Acanthus*
	Angelica
	Hosta
	Ligularia
	Rodgersia

OPPOSITES ATTRACT. From a bold-leafed caladium through a medium-sized coleus to the delicacy of a maidenhair fern, this garden sample dramatizes the value of textural contrast.

a few clumps scattered throughout the garden may be all you need. Fine textures provide lots of visual interest when you see them up close, but several different fine-textured perennials next to each other will probably look busy. Medium textures are so common that they pretty much take care of themselves in a design.

Keep in mind that you can use foliage textures to make your garden appear larger or smaller. In a small space, using lots of fine- to medium-textured plants makes the garden appear larger. (You still need some broad leaves for contrast, but keep them to a minimum.) In a large garden, using bold foliage generously throughout your design helps to bring the space down to a more comfortable scale. For more ideas on how to use foliage, see pages 32–33.

WE'VE COVERED A LOT OF GROUND in this chapter on selecting the perfect perennials for your garden. But just how are you supposed to use this information in creating your design? You have a couple of options. Some folks keep a running list of perennials they'd like to try someday, then review the list and pick out those with the colors, heights, habits, and growing conditions they need when it's time to start a garden. Others choose their colors first, generate lists of possible choices by paging through books and catalogs, then narrow them down by crossing out any that aren't a good match for the site conditions. Or you could do the reverse: Identify the perennials that are the best match for your site, then narrow them down to your chosen colors.

Which of these ways will work best for you? You won't know for sure until you try them for yourself. Or you may decide to skip list-making altogether and jump ahead to drawing your design, then look for the perennials that fit into your vision for the garden. This approach will work if you already have a good mental encyclopedia of perennials; otherwise, you may end up doing a lot of research to seek out something that isn't readily available, such as a tall, spiky, yellow flower for shade or a creeping perennial with red flowers and silver-spotted leaves that thrives in full sun. That isn't to say that you might not eventually find just what you want if you're patient, but in the meantime, you'll be left with either an unfinished design or an empty space in your garden.

PUTTING IT ALL TOGETHER.
With many different heights and textures represented, and all in good proportion to each other as well as to the accessories, Stephanie's garden demonstrates well-executed balance and scale.

Leafy Thoughts

We couldn't finish a chapter on selecting perennials without taking a little time to talk more about foliage. It's easy to get distracted by the in-your-face beauty of flowers, but in many cases, blossoms last only for a few weeks each season. Leaves, on the other hand, are generally around from spring through fall, and their appearance can make or break a design at times when the flowers aren't at their peak. Back when Stephanie was working in a garden center, customers often asked her whether they should buy a certain perennial. Her advice to them was to forget the flowers and look at the leaves; if they still liked the plant, it was probably a good choice for them.

In their colors alone, some leaves rival the showiest blooms. Besides the many shades of green, perennial leaves come in rich red, rusty orange, coppery brown, silver, gray, pink, burgundy, and even black. They may be one solid color, or they may have one or more base colors that are edged, centered, streaked, splashed, striped, or spotted with another. With a little research, you can create an eye-catching garden where the flowers are actually incidental to the foliage.

Another often overlooked foliage feature is fall color. This phenomenon isn't limited to trees and shrubs; many perennials put on an excellent fall show too. This trait is typically very weather-dependent, so you probably wouldn't want to base an entire border on perennials with good autumn color. Think of them as additional accents for gardens that have a good showing of late-blooming flowers. To get you started, here's a list of some of our favorite perennials for fall-foliage color:

Aconitum (monkshoods): Yellow

Amsonia (bluestars): Yellow to yellow-orange

Bergenia (bergenias): Reddish purple

Dictamnus albus (gas plant): Yellow

Geranium (hardy geraniums, especially 'Brookside' and *G. wlassovianum*): Many shades of red and orange

Hosta (hostas): Bright yellow

Liatris spicata (spike gayfeather): Maroon

Miscanthus 'Purpurascens' (flame grass): Orange, red, and yellow in sun; pink, peach, and yellow in light shade

Molinia caerulea subsp. *arundinacea* (purple moor grass): Yellow

Mukdenia rossii (mukdenia): Maroon and red

Oenothera fruticosa (sundrops): Bright red

Paeonia (peonies): Maroons and reds

Panicum virgatum (switch grass): Yellows, oranges, and reds, depending on the cultivar

Platycodon grandiflorus (balloon flower): Gold, sometimes with orange

Polygonatum (Solomon's seals): Yellow

Schizachyrium scoparium (little bluestem): Bronze to orange

Sporobolus heterolepis (prairie dropseed): Orange

1

These perennials contribute not only lovely leaves to spring and summer gardens, but also glowing fall color as well.

1. Bonanza Gold barberry *(Berberis thunbergii* 'Bogozam'), *Epimedium* x *versicolor,* and heuchera
2. Peony *(Paeonia* hybrid)
3. Arkansas bluestar *(Amsonia hubrectii)*
4. 'Brigadoon' hypericum *(Hypericum calycinum)*
5. Moor grass *(Molinia),* flame grass *(Miscanthus* 'Purpurascens'), and switch grass *(Panicum virgatum)*
6. Switch grass and big bluestem *(Andropogon gerardii)*

Exploring Perennial Partners

W E'D BE REMISS if we didn't remind you of the many plants that make super bedmates for perennials, including annuals, biennials, bulbs, grasses, and shrubs. Strictly speaking, a perennial garden incorporates only perennials; adding other plants makes the garden into a mixed border. But we don't see any point in getting bogged down in terminology when the issue is simply to create pleasing plantings that beautify your home. To that end, let's look at the wide variety of excellent perennial partners you can use to expand your plant possibilities.

Annuals and Biennials for Perennial Gardens

Perennial gardeners who are attempting to be one up on their fellow gardeners are often heard to say with disdain that they never use annuals. This snobbery hearkens back to Victorian times when "bedding out" was the style. Wealthy people crammed as many annuals into a design as possible — sometimes thousands — in all sorts of geometric and unusual patterns. In order to do so, they had to have multiple gardeners, greenhouses, and lots of land. (You sometimes still see examples of this style of bedding out around commercial establishments or in public gardens.) In some respects, perennial gardening became the reaction to this example of gardening excess. But there's no good reason to reject growing any annuals next to perennials; in fact, there are plenty of benefits to be gained from giving annuals a try.

Long-Lasting Color. Many annuals bloom for several months at a time, which is more than can be said for many perennials. Tucking a few of these short-lived-but-long-flowering plants among your perennials helps give your design continuity throughout much of the growing season. Our favorite use for annuals, though, is to get color at specific times when perennials aren't at their best. In late spring, for example, most of the early bloomers are finished and the summer perennials haven't yet hit their stride; this is a

AN ANNUAL MIXER. Dependable, richly orange-and-rust-colored marigolds form a streamlike movement through this large perennial bed.

prime time for using cool-season annuals like love-in-a-mist *(Nigella damascena)*, snapdragon *(Antirrhinum majus)*, and sweet alyssum *(Lobularia maritima)*. Heat-loving annuals, such as cosmos, mealycup sage *(Salvia farinacea)*, and zinnias, come into their glory in late July and August — just when the summer perennials are looking a bit tired and the fall bloomers are still a few weeks from flowering.

All-Around Versatility.
Annuals will keep the color coming all season, but that's just the beginning. Here are some other ideas for making the most of adaptable annuals:

✻ Test a new color in your garden, without committing to a perennial. Try an annual in that color, and if you like the effect, replace the annual with a similar-color perennial next year; if not, toss the annual on your compost pile and try a different one next season.

✻ Is your newly planted perennial garden looking a little sparse? Look for annuals to use as fillers for the first year or two, until the perennials are large enough to knit together and fill the gaps.

✻ Do you enjoy cutting flowers to bring indoors? Including annuals in your borders will give you a bounty of blooms to pick without weakening your perennials.

✻ Need something to fill gaps left when early bloomers and bulbs go dormant, or when spring-flowering perennials look a bit ratty? Annuals are a perfect solution for these spots.

✻ Want a particular color or flower form you just can't get with perennials? Annuals might be a good alternative. In our southeastern Pennsylvania climate, for instance, we usually don't have luck with delphiniums, so we like to use annual larkspurs *(Consolida)* to get a similar spiky blue flower.

If you've deliberately left space in your design for annuals, or if you're using them as fillers around newly planted perennials, you can have good luck by sowing seeds directly where you want them to grow. But when you're tucking them in to cover up early bloomers or to fill gaps left by dormant bulbs and perennials, transplants may be a better choice, because it could take too long for direct-sown seeds to grow up enough to make an impact. Just be very careful when you're planting over dormant bulbs or perennials; you don't want to cut into them with your trowel.

Love These Tenders. Technically

speaking, annuals are plants that sprout from seed, produce flowers, set seed, and die in the course of one year. But many classic "annuals" are actually tender perennials: that is, plants that live from year to year in warmer climates but die during the winter in yours. (A plant rated as hardy in Zone 7, for example, is considered a tender perennial in Zone 6 but a hardy — or true — perennial in Zones 7–10.) Coleus (*Solenostemon scutellarioides*) and impatiens (*Impatiens wallerana*) are just two examples.

Treat tender perennials like true annuals and buy new ones each spring, or bring them indoors for the winter and plant them outside when the weather warms up again. Digging and potting up tenders before the first fall frost is one way to keep them, but if your indoor space is limited, take just a few cuttings in late summer and root them indoors. Either way is worth the extra effort when you're dealing with uncommon or expensive tenders you really treasure, or if you enjoy the extra impact made by large clumps. Usually, however, it's easier to buy starter plants every year.

Many tender perennials absolutely hate frost, so make sure nighttime temperatures stay well above freezing before you set them outdoors (that's usually late May or early June in Zone 6). This late planting obviously makes them impractical for late-spring interest in most climates; still, tenders can serve all the functions of true annuals — and they'll do it with style. For a rundown of some must-have tender perennials, see Awesome Annuals and Top-Notch Tenders (facing page).

PURPLE PASSION. The striking purple-and-green leaves of tender Persian shield (*Strobilanthes dyerianus*) provide a dependable presence through the growing season, while hardy perennials such as sedum can change dramatically from month to month.

Awesome Annuals and Top-Notch Tenders

Once you expand your plant possibilities to include annuals and tender perennials, it's easy to get carried away. Trust us, we've done it! The effect can be spectacular in the garden — but so can the amount of work when you consider all the time spent planting, digging up, potting up, taking cuttings, and replanting. If you find yourself getting immersed in these beauties, think about setting aside a separate area for most of them and using only a few as perennial partners. Otherwise, your borders will be full of craters and bare spots after you dig or pull out the annuals and tenders in fall. If you promise to follow our advice, we'll share some of our favorites to get you started:

Abutilon (flowering maples): *A. megapotamicum* 'Variegatum'; *A. pictum* 'Thompsonii'

Alternanthera dentata (alternanthera): 'Purple Knight', 'Rubiginosa'

Angelonia angustifolia (angelonia)

Anisodontea x *hypomandarum* (cape mallow)

Antirrhinum majus (snapdragon): 'Madame Butterfly Hybrids', 'Rocket Hybrids'

Asclepias curassavica (blood flower)

Begonia (begonias): 'Escargot'; *B. pedatifida*; *B. sutherlandii*

Browallia americana (browallia)

Brugmansia (angel's trumpets): *B. arborea* [*B. versicolor*]; *B. suaveolens*

Calibrachoa (million bells)

Consolida (larkspurs)

Cosmos bipinnatus (cosmos): 'Seashell' and 'Sonata' series

Cuphea x *purpurea* (cuphea): 'Firefly'

Diascia (diascia): 'Sun Chimes Coral'

Dicliptera suberecta (king's crown)

Euphorbia cotinifolia (red spurge)

Fuchsia (fuchsias): 'Firecracker', 'Gartenmeister Bonstedt'

Hebe (hebes): 'Purple Pixie'; *H.* x *franciscana* 'Variegata'

Heliotropium arborescens (heliotrope)

Hibiscus acetosella (hibiscus): 'Red Shield'

Ipomoea batatas (sweet potato vine): 'Blackie', 'Margarita', 'Sweet Caroline' series

Lantana camara (lantana): 'Patriot' series

Leonotis leonurus (lion's ear)

Mirabilis jalapa (four-o'clocks): 'Baywatch', 'Limelight'

Musa (bananas): 'Dwarf Red', 'Zebrina'

Nicotiana (flowering tobaccos): *N. langsdorffii*; *N. sylvestris*

Petunia integrifolia (violet-flowered petunia)

Phormium (phormiums)

Phygelius x *rectus* (phygelius): 'Devil's Tears', 'Moonraker'

Plectranthus argentatus (plectranthus)

Salvia greggii (Gregg's sage)

Salvia leucantha (Mexican bush sage): 'Santa Barbara'

Solenostemon scutellarioides (coleus): 'Alabama Sunset', 'Exhibition Lime', 'Inky Fingers', 'Kiwi Fern', 'Palisandra'

Strobilanthes dyerianus (Persian shield)

Tagetes (signet marigold): 'Lemon Gem', 'Tangerine Gem'

Verbena (verbenas): *V. bonariensis*; *V. canadensis*; *V. tenuisecta*

Zinnia (narrow-leaved zinnias): 'Profusion' and 'Star' series

Biennials to Try

When you see a garden where biennials are used properly, you're looking at the work of a well-organized gardener. If you're willing to expend a little effort to get similar results, here's a list of our favorite biennials to get you started:

Alcea rosea (hollyhock): 'Barnyard' series, 'Nigra'

Campanula medium (Canterbury bells)

Dianthus barbatus (sweet William): 'Heart Attack', 'Sooty'

Digitalis purpurea (common foxglove; shown here): Stephanie particularly likes the dwarf 'Foxy'

Lunaria annua (honesty, money plant)

Myosotis sylvatica (forget-me-not)

Verbascum (mulleins)

Beautiful Biennials. Biennials are plants that sprout and grow leaves one year, then flower, produce seed, and (usually) die in the next. This odd life cycle makes them a challenge to use effectively in the garden. The first-year foliage is typically low, so it seems like it should belong at the front of a border, but the taller, second-year-flowering stems can look way out of place there. The first-year foliage also tends to form large, broad rosettes that take up a lot of space without adding much color to the garden for that growing season.

Biennials are so beautiful in bloom, however, that many of us think they'll repay a little extra effort. To grow your own, sow the seed in pots in summer, transplant the seedlings to a holding bed or a corner of your vegetable garden, then move them in fall or early spring to where you want them to flower. Or, if you can find already started biennials for sale, plant them in your garden in fall or spring. Once your plants are done flowering, pull them out and replace them with annuals; just leave one or two of the biennials to produce seed, so you'll have replacement seedlings the following year. Another option is to try this trick Stephanie uses: Cut off all the spent flower stalks and then give the plants a generous dose of high-nitrogen fertilizer. If they regrow, they'll usually flower again the next year, or the year after, on extra-large plants. She has kept some biennials going 5 or 6 years this way!

Bulbs to Light Up Beds & Borders

PAIRING BULBS WITH PERENNIALS is a sure way to get the most out of every bit of garden space. From the last days of winter to the last days of fall, these versatile beauties add a bounty of cheerful color and seasonal interest, all wrapped up in one easy-care package.

The Early Birds. Spring is prime time for the most well-known bulbs, including crocus, daffodils, hyacinths, and tulips. These classics are just the tip of the iceberg, though. There are also many so-called minor bulbs, such as checkered lily (*Fritillaria meleagris*), glory-of-the-snow (*Chionodoxa*), and snowdrops (*Galanthus*). These lesser-known lovelies often have smaller flowers and more natural-looking forms, which make them more comfortable perennial partners than are their highly hybridized cousins, especially in informal settings such as woodland walks and cottage gardens.

You can choose bulbs that match the overall color theme for your garden, or you can do something completely different. For an elegant effect, consider a monochromatic theme, such as all-white or all-pink bulbs. Alternatively, you can celebrate spring's return with a cheerful combination of colors; it's tough to make a bad combination with early-spring bulbs. As the season progresses and your perennials start coming into bloom, you'll need to be more careful about avoiding color clashes.

To get the best effect with spring bulbs, be generous with the size of the clumps: Plant 6 to 12 bulbs in each, depending on their size. Spotting single bulbs here and there — or worse yet, planting them in straight lines like soldiers — is guaranteed to produce disappointing results.

Whichever spring bulbs you choose, remember that the leaves will wither and die after flowering, leaving a bare space in your garden by midsummer. One of Stephanie's favorite tricks is to tuck bulbs around daylilies (*Hemerocallis*) and hostas, which will cover up the declining bulb foliage and readily fill in the gaps. Tall or bushy perennials can

TURN ON SPRING. Tulips are many gardeners' bulb of choice when it comes to spring favorites.

perform the same function, especially if you keep bulb clumps near the back of the border. (At the time the bulbs are in full bloom, the perennials are just coming up, so they won't block your spring bulb display.) If you're still left with gaps once the bulbs die back, you can always tuck in a few annuals as fillers for the rest of the season.

Whatever you decide, please don't be tempted simply to cut off the dying leaves or to braid or fold them into tidy, rubber-banded bundles. Your bulbs need all of their leaves for as long as possible to produce energy to store for next year's flowers. One exception is hybrid tulips. They often die out in a year or two in perennial gardens, because they prefer hot, dry conditions in summer — not the moist, mulched soil that most perennials like. If you really want to grow hybrid tulips with your perennials, you may have to pull out the tulip plants as soon as the flowers drop and put in new bulbs each fall.

Summer Sizzle.

True lilies *(Lilium)*, foxtail lilies *(Eremurus)*, and other summer bulbs that pop up among your perennials give the garden an extra dimension of drama and excitement. They generally look best in small groups of three or five plants (an uneven number is best) rising out of or behind other perennials. Like spring bulbs, hardy summer-flowering bulbs will die back to the ground once they've finished blooming, so you need to make sure their companions will cover up the yellowing foliage. This can be particularly tricky with lilies, which bear foliage all the way up their flowering stems. Planting a 3-foot-tall lily and making it disappear is easy, but with 5- to 6-foot-tall lilies, you're left with the ugly post-bloom stems for several weeks. An interesting solution is to plant seeds or starts of an annual vine, such as hyacinth bean *(Lablab purpureus)*, around the base of the lily stems in late spring or early summer. Once the lilies have flowered, their stems serve as natural supports for the climber.

FLOWERS WITH FLAIR. **Cannas are guaranteed to introduce exuberance into any garden.**

Just like tender perennials, tender summer bulbs can be invaluable for adding color and flair to mid- and late-summer gardens. With their bright flowers and bold foliage, cannas provide a tropical look that perfectly suits the season. If you prefer bulbs that are a smidge more subtle, dahlias might be more to your liking. (We're not talking about the dinner-plate-size flowers that are used for exhibition, but rather the medium- to small-flowered dahlias, especially those with dark foliage, such as 'Bishop of Llandaff' and 'Ellen Huston'.) Dahlias come in a very wide range of interesting flower shapes, from pompon to cactus-style, and their colors range from palest pastel to vividly vibrant. Many of them have more than one color in their blossoms, making it simple to create exciting combinations with other flowers and foliage.

Hardy summer bulbs stay in the ground year-round and come back season after season. If you're growing bulbs that aren't winter-hardy in your area, either treat them like annuals and buy new ones each year or dig them up in fall and store them indoors for the winter.

The Late Show.
Fall has its own special bulb repertoire, from the exquisite to the downright odd. Hardy cyclamen (*Cyclamen hederifolium*) is a gorgeous choice for shady gardens, with silver-mottled foliage and dainty pink or white flowers. The foliage is so beautiful that the flowers are hardly necessary (although they're certainly a nice accompaniment). The strangest of the fall bulbs are autumn crocuses (*Colchicum*), fall crocus (*Crocus sativus*), hardy amaryllis (*Amaryllis belladonna*), and spider lilies (*Lycoris*). It takes a good bit of trial and error to use these bulbs effectively because of their unusual life cycle: Their leaves emerge in spring and disappear by early summer, then the flowers come up without leaves in fall. If you plant them

PREPARE FOR A SURPRISE. **This autumn crocus (*Colchicum* 'Waterlily') bears its blossoms in fall, long after its spring foliage has disappeared.**

Stephanie Says

ONCE YOUR BULBS ARE DORMANT, it can be difficult to tell exactly where they are. If you like to move plants around as much as I do, or if you need to divide some of your perennials, it's all too easy to accidentally skewer your best bulbs with a spading fork or slice them in half with a spade. It's a sickening feeling. My secret is to use green golf tees to mark the perimeter of each bulb clump before the leaves die back (if you borrow too many tees from your golfer buddies, do replace them). The tees blend in from any distance but are easy to see when you're really looking for them, so they definitely help take the guesswork out of avoiding buried bulbs. ✳

Say No to Bulb-kebabs

From left, clockwise: Star of Persia *(Allium christophii)* **1**; Lily *(Lilium)* **2**; blackberry lily *(Belamcanda chinensis)* **3**.

Best Bulbs for Perennial Gardens

Although we're relentless in our pursuit of the latest and greatest perennials, we tend to fall back on old favorites when it comes time to choosing bulbs for our gardens. Here's a list of some tried-and-true bulbs we'd hate to be without:

Allium (alliums, ornamental onions): *A. aflatunense, A. christophii* **1**, *A. karataviense, A. moly, A. tanguticum* 'Summer Beauty'

Anemone blanda (Grecian windflower)

Belamcanda chinensis (blackberry lily) **3**

Camassia (camassias, quamash)

Colchicum (autumn crocus): 'Waterlily'

Crocus (crocus): *C. chrysanthus* 'Ladykiller', *C. medius, C. speciosus*

Dichelostemma ida-maia (firecracker flower)

Eremurus (foxtail lilies)

Galanthus (snowdrops)

Ipheion (spring starflower): 'Rolf Fiedler'

Iris (bearded iris): Reblooming cultivars, such as 'Immortality'

Lilium (lilies): 'Black Dragon', 'Casa Blanca', 'Lollypop' **2**

Muscari (grape hyacinths)

Narcissus (daffodils): 'Actaea', 'February Gold', 'Jack Snipe', 'Mount Hood', 'Thalia'

Sanguinaria canadensis (bloodroot)

Scilla siberica (Siberian squill)

Tulipa (tulips): Hybrids — 'Negrita', 'Orange Emperor', 'Queen of the Night', and 'Red Riding Hood'; species — *T. kaufmanniana; T. praestans* 'Fusilier' and 'Unicum'; *T. saxatilis* 'Lilac Wonder'

among taller or bushy perennials to hide their dying spring foliage, their fall flowers may not be visible. But if you don't give them *any* companions, you're stuck with looking at beautiful flowers atop bare stems (in the case of autumn and fall crocuses, directly against bare soil). To solve this dilemma, plant them among relatively low-growing ground covers, such as ajuga and plumbago *(Ceratostigma plumbaginoides)*. Because the bulbs generally bloom in a different season, you'll get twice the color from your ground covers in the same amount of space.

Planting Pointers. Most bulbs thrive under typical garden conditions, as long as the soil is well drained. To add early-flowering bulbs to your perennial plantings, you must get them in the ground in fall, or else buy already started bulbs in pots in spring (a much more expensive proposition). The same goes for most hardy summer bloomers, although some, such as many lilies, can also be planted in spring. With bulbs that are tender in your area, either start them indoors in pots in spring, and then set them out after all danger of frost has passed, or else plant them directly in your garden after the last frost. Fall bulbs are typically planted in mid- to late summer, while they are dormant. Remember: With any bulbs, it's important to get them in the ground with their pointy side (the bud) facing up. If they are on their side (and sometimes even if they're upside down), they'll usually correct themselves eventually, but that takes some time and energy away from the flower display.

Gardening with Grasses

ORNAMENTAL GRASSES are starting to share the spotlight that fancier-flowered perennials have enjoyed for well over a century. Maybe it's because observant gardeners are beginning to appreciate the way grasses both complement and contrast with many classic border perennials. Or perhaps it's because grasses adapt to just about any site or purpose. Let's take a look at some of these benefits and see whether grasses can work their magic in your garden, too.

Terrific Textures and Elegant Habits.

Grasses typically have slender, fine-textured foliage, which makes a subtle but pleasing contrast with the many common medium-textured perennials. The same goes for grasses' airy flower plumes and seedheads, which complement delicate pastel blooms and add a touch of restfulness to plantings of bold, bright flowers.

Grasses come in all shapes and sizes, but those that are especially upright, such as 'Northwind' switch grass (*Panicum virgatum*), make exciting vertical accents among rounded, bushy perennials. Even short grasses have a spiky look that contrasts prettily with many front-of-the-border perennials, which tend to have a creeping or mounded habit.

Eye-Catching Color.

For many years, the few available grasses had primarily all-green foliage, but nowadays, colorful new offerings are appearing on the market every year. Besides the typical variety of greens and blue-greens, today you can find grasses with bright yellow, orange, burgundy, red, silvery blue, and even near black foliage, as well as with vertical stripes or horizontal bands of white, cream, or yellow. This makes for lots of exciting possibilities when it comes to creating dramatic plant combinations. You can also get color from the flower plumes, which are usually green (often tinged with pink or purple) but may also be silver, bronze, or coppery orange.

VERTICAL ACCENT. The verticality of the grasses at the back forms a strong punctuation mark that balances the richly colored purple phlox in the foreground.

Seasonal Interest. Grasses add excitement to your beds and borders just about any time of year, but they're particularly prized for their dramatic fall color and long-lasting winter structure. Not all grasses are created equal in this respect, so you need to choose carefully to find those that will work best in your climate and under your growing conditions. If you live where winter usually brings heavy wet snow, for example, you'll be better off selecting lower-growing grasses, because tall, somewhat sprawling ones may get flattened by the first storm. Some grasses just naturally tend to break down by midwinter; others, such as many miscanthus, will hold their foliage until spring returns.

WINTER WHITES (above left). An early light snowfall clings to each stem of grass to create a natural sculpture in this winter garden.

MAKING A STATEMENT (above right). Dwarf pampas grass (*Cortaderia selloana* 'Pumila') is at its showy best with sunlight streaming through its plumelike flowerheads in this fall garden.

Versatility. You name the purpose and we'll bet there's a grass to fit it. You can plant single grasses alone as specimens, in masses as a landscape accent, or in rows or groups to provide summer and fall screening. Shorter grasses also look great massed, as well as scattered throughout beds and borders. Grasses with very upright or vase-shaped habits work well in formal plantings; those with looser forms lend themselves to naturalistic, meadowlike plantings. Grasses of all heights and habits can adapt well to life in containers, too, making for some of the most interesting potted plantings you'll ever create.

Adaptability. Grasses and their relatives are invaluable when your goal is to add multi-season interest, and they work under just about any growing conditions. Their moisture demands range from wet to dry, depending on the particular grass, and though most will thrive in full sun, you can find kinds that grow in shade, too. (Many of the shade lovers are not actually true grasses, but instead are close relatives called sedges. Because true grasses and sedges — as well as a similar group called rushes — look so similar, most gardeners use the general term *grasses* to apply to all of them.)

THROUGHOUT THIS SECTION, WHEN WE TALK about "grasses," we're using that as shorthand for "hardy perennial grasses and their relatives." But there's another group of grasses worth considering for your garden: namely, the annual and tender perennial types.

Now, annual grasses can be a little tricky, because they have to make seed to reproduce themselves, and the fear of having self-sown grasses all over the place is enough to turn away many gardeners for good. Two annual grasses I've had luck with are hare's tail grass (*Lagurus ovatus*) and 'Purple Majesty' millet (*Pennisetum glaucum*). You'll know how hare's tail grass got its name when you see its short, white, tufted flower heads bobbing 6 to 12 inches above the soil. I sow the seeds directly in the garden in mid- to late spring around later-emerging perennials to get flowers in early to midsummer; then the grass dies off and the perennials fill in. I usually get a few self-sown seedlings but nowhere near as many as I'd like, so I sow fresh seed each year to be sure I have the plants. 'Purple Majesty' millet is a newer favorite, with strappy, deep purple leaves and near black, cattail-like seedheads on 3- to 5-foot-tall plants. This heat lover looks

Annual Grasses with Wow Power

great from midsummer to frost and is fantastic with all shades of pink, as well as with bright red, orange, and yellow flowers and chartreuse foliage. At the time I'm writing this, it's too early to predict whether self-sown seedlings will be a problem; only time will tell.

Among tender perennial grasses, the popular vote goes to purple fountain grass (*Pennisetum setaceum* 'Rubrum,' shown here). The common form has arching maroon foliage to about 4 feet tall, with pink-tinged, foxtail-like flower heads up to 5 feet tall. If your space is limited, look for the shorter cultivar 'Eaton Canyon', which reaches only about 30 inches in flower. If a bolder effect is what you're after, try the wider-leaved 'Burgundy Giant'. The only downside to these beauties is that it's tough to overwinter them indoors, so it's usually best to buy new plants each year. Still, you need just small starter plants, because they grow quickly once summer's heat sets in. ✳

FALL INTO GRASSES. The brushy spikes of Oriental fountain grass *(Pennisetum orientale)* make a striking contrast to fall daisies, as well as to the arching form of pink bush clover *(Lespedeza thunbergii)*.

Selecting Grasses. To get the best from the grasses you choose, it's important to understand the difference between "cool-season" and "warm-season" varieties. The cool-season grasses, such as blue fescue *(Festuca glauca),* flower in early summer, then take a rest during the hottest part of the summer before showing fresh foliage in fall and spring. The warm-season grasses, like switch grass *(Panicum virgatum),* start several weeks later in spring but then grow steadily until they reach their maximum height and then flower in late summer or fall. Gardeners in the middle hardiness zones (roughly Zones 5–7) can generally have good luck with both kinds of grasses. North of that, warm-season grasses will grow but may not have enough time to flower before frost. And in southern areas, cool-season grasses tend to rot or "melt out" during hot, humid periods. To get the best matches for your climate, look for grasses that are native to your area, and for cultivars of those species. (See Recommended Reading in the Appendix for excellent references for this information.)

Some grasses pose an ecological threat (see What's This about Invasives?, left); others can be a serious threat to your mental health. We're talking about those botanical menaces, such as blue Lyme grass *(Leymus arenarius)* and gardener's garters *(Phalaris arundinacea* var. *picta),* that spread by creeping roots. They look pretty in nursery pots and they stay in nice clumps for the first year or two in your garden, but then watch out! Once they're established, these cute little grasses will send out creeping roots (called rhizomes) in all directions. New plants will pop up where you

What's This about Invasives?

Before you choose any nonnative grasses, please do your research to make sure they are not considered invasive in your area. Miscanthus, for example, has long been a favorite grass for perennial gardens, but it has the potential to seed into wild areas and crowd out native vegetation, especially south of Zone 6. Today, the thinking is that cultivars selected for early flowering are the most serious threats; late-flowering classics such as 'Morning Light' seldom have time to produce seed before frost, at least in the cooler parts of their range. Still, many gardeners don't think it's worth the risk, so they avoid planting them at all. Although we occasionally use miscanthus in our designs, we're now using switch grasses far more often, because they come in a similar height range and are native in our region.

least expect them and crowd out their more delicate companions. Getting rid of these thugs involves digging up whole sections of the border, painstakingly removing all traces of the rhizomes from the soil and the root masses of the perennials, and replanting the perennials, then keeping your fingers crossed that the grass is gone. Again, do your research before planting any grass in your garden, and when in doubt, leave it out!

A Few Grass-Growing Guidelines.

Let's hope we haven't scared you off from growing grasses, because well-chosen types really are a joy in the garden. They don't need your best soil; in fact, many grow quite well where the soil is on the lean, dry side. (They'll be taller and lusher in rich, evenly moist soil, but you may need to stake them to keep them upright there.) Large grasses can form big clumps quickly, and they're a lot of work to dig up and divide or move if they've been left in place for more than 2 or 3 years. Thus, if you want to control the size of a clump, or if you plan to dig it up for any other reason, do it every 2 or 3 years. Otherwise, just let it stay in place and enjoy its easy-care nature.

The primary maintenance most grasses need is a yearly trim. To keep cool-season grasses tidy, combing out any dead foliage with your fingers is usually enough. Warm-season grasses need a hard trim (to a few inches above the ground) in late winter to early spring, before new growth gets going. Hand pruners work fine for smaller grasses; hedge shears are a better bet for big clumps. Wearing gloves is a good idea, too, because some grasses have sharp-edged blades. To save yourself a lot of work, wrap some twine around the foliage of large clumps before you cut. That will leave you with one tidy pile to dispose of, instead of a mess of stems and leaves to rake up and haul away.

Best Grasses for Perennial Borders

Here's a sampling of hardy grasses that we enjoy in our Zone 6 gardens. Remember to double-check with local plant experts before trying these or other grasses in your own gardens, though, to make sure they are adapted to your climate and not likely to be invasive.

Calamagrostis x *acutiflora* (feather reed grass): 'Karl Foerster', 'Overdam' **2**

Carex buchananii (leatherleaf sedge)

C. elata 'Aurea' (Bowles' golden sedge)

C. morrowii (Japanese sedge): 'Ice Dance', 'Silver Sceptre'

C. plantaginea (plantain-leaved sedge)

C. siderosticha (sedge): 'Island Brocade', 'Lemon Zest'

Festuca glauca (blue fescue): 'Boulder Blue', 'Elijah Blue'

Hakonechloa macra (Hakone grass): 'Albo-striata', 'All Gold', 'Aureola'

Luzula (woodrush): *L. nivea*, *L. sylvatica* 'Aurea'

Miscanthus (miscanthus): 'Purpurascens'; *M. sinensis* 'Cosmopolitan', 'Ferner Osten' **1**, 'Little Nicky', 'Morning Light', 'Strictus'

Muhlenbergia capillaris (pink muhly grass)

Panicum (switch grasses): *P. amarum* 'Dewey Blue'; *P. virgatum* 'Dallas Blues', 'Heavy Metal', 'Northwind', 'Shenandoah'

Pennisetum (fountain grasses): *P. alopecuroides* 'Hameln', 'Little Bunny'; *P. orientale* 'Karley Rose'

Schizachyrium scoparium (little bluestem): 'Prairie Embers', 'The Blues'

Sorghastrum nutans (Indian grass): 'Indian Steel', 'Sioux Blue'

Sporobolus heterolepis (prairie dropseed)

Shrubs for Structure and More

WITH SO MUCH OVERLAP between the height ranges of perennials and shrubs, it's a simple matter to make room for both kinds of plants in your designs. Sometimes gardeners relegate shrubs to the back of the border or use them only as background or hedges, but we like to integrate them with perennials throughout the garden. Besides adding year-round height and structure, shrubs can provide colorful foliage; attractive flowers; showy fruits, seeds, and bark; and sometimes evergreen interest too. Not many perennials can claim the same.

Shrubs as Design Elements.

When you're designing a whole area, rather than just one garden, you'll find that shrubs are valuable in their own right. Taller shrubs, for example, are great for adding height in small yards (where a tree may not be practical), as well as for defining spaces and framing views. Like buildings, walls, fences, arbors, and other vertical structures, shrubs provide mass to counterbalance "voids" (flat areas such as lawn, low plantings, and water). A landscape with a balance of masses and voids — or in other words, high spots and low areas — is far more pleasing to the eye than are extremes of one or the other.

Choosing Shrubs That Earn Their Keep.

If you simply want to add a few shrubs to your perennial plantings, there's really no need to worry about masses and voids. The important thing is for you to get the hardest-working shrub that fits your needs and growing conditions. By that we mean a shrub with as many benefits as possible: fantastic fall color and colorful winter bark, for instance, or evergreen foliage plus pretty flowers and showy berries. This is particularly important in small gardens, where space is limited and every plant has to pay its way. That rules out short-blooming, single-season classics like forsythias and weigela, unless you seek out cultivars that also have showy foliage for summer and fall interest — such as 'Kumson' forsythia (*Forsythia koreana*)

TRUE INTEGRATION. Spireas are integral to this garden design, shown here with 'Autumn Joy' sedum. Note how the miniature mounds of the sedum's flowerheads echo the overall shape of the shrubs.

The brilliantly colored berries of this winterberry (*Ilex verticillata* 'Maryland Beauty') are a welcome addition to the late-fall and early-winter garden.

and Wine and Roses weigela (*Weigela florida* 'Alexandra').

What if you're stuck with an existing shrub that has minimal seasonal interest? Consider using it as a living trellis for a clematis, climbing rose, or annual vine. Stephanie did just this in her own garden by planting a 'Niobe' clematis next to a very ugly arborvitae (*Thuja occidentalis*). The clematis has twined its way all the way around the shrub, and its bright red flowers look fantastic against the deep green foliage.

A word of caution: Just as with perennials and grasses, some shrubs have earned a place on gardeners' least-wanted lists due to their tendency to seed into wild areas and crowd out native plants. In our southeastern Pennsylvania area, gardeners think twice about using traditional favorites like colored-leaved Japanese barberry (*Berberis thunbergii*) and butterfly bush (*Buddleia davidii*). The potential threat varies by region, so we encourage you to contact your local Cooperative Extension Agent or Master Gardener program to find out which shrubs you should avoid.

Stephanie Says

Cut Them Down to Size

OF ALL THE WAYS TO WORK WOODY PLANTS into beds and borders, one of my favorites is as "cutback shrubs." These special shrubs are sturdy enough to withstand heavy pruning each year, a technique known as coppicing or stooling (or as I like to call it, whack-and-hack). This hard pruning encourages fast-growing stems with larger-than-usual leaves (a bonus for shrubs with colorful or variegated foliage, or those with exceptional fall color). As a bonus, it controls the size of a plant, making it easy to enjoy the height of a shrub without giving up half your garden to it.

Many people trim their cutback shrubs close to the ground each year or every other year. But if your shrubs are behind a fence, like mine are, trim them back just halfway so they'll be visible again by early summer. Remember to give newly planted cutback shrubs a few years to get established before you start pruning them like this; otherwise, you can weaken them. For suggestions of plants on which to try this handy technique, see Best Shrubs for Perennial Borders on pages 52–53.

Best Shrubs
for Perennial Borders

If we went on describing our favorite uses for shrubs in perennial gardens, this book would be twice as long as it is, so we'll leave you with a list of the much loved shrubs in our own gardens, and encourage you to seek out your favorites in local botanical gardens, arboreta, and garden-center display plantings.

DECIDUOUS SHRUBS

Abelia (abelia): 'Edward Goucher'

Aronia arbutifolia (red chokeberry): 'Brilliantissima'

Buddleia davidii (butterfly bush): 'Ellen's Blue', 'Guinevere', 'Lochinch', 'Potter's Purple' (with careful removal of spent flowers to prevent self-sowing)*

Callicarpa dichotoma (beautyberry): 'Issai'

Calycanthus floridus (sweetshrub): 'Athens Gold'

Caryopteris x *clandonensis* (caryopteris): 'Longwood Blue', 'First Choice', 'Worcester Gold'*

Chionanthus virginicus (fringe tree)

Clethra alnifolia (summersweet): 'Hummingbird', 'Ruby Spice', 'Sixteen Candles'

Cornus (red-twig dogwoods): *C. alba* Ivory Halo ('Bailhalo'), *C. sanguinea* 'Midwinter Fire', *C. sericea* 'Cardinal', *C. stolonifera* 'Hedgerows Gold'*

Corylopsis (wintersweets): *C. pauciflora*, *C. spicata*

Cotinus (smoke tree): *C. coggygria* 'Velvet Cloak', hybrid 'Grace'*

Daphne x *burkwoodii* (Burkwood daphne): 'Carol Mackie'

Deutzia crenata var. *nakaiana* (deutzia): 'Nikko'

Eleutherococcus sieboldianus (five-leaf aralia): 'Variegatus'

Fothergilla (fothergillas)

Hamamelis x *intermedia* (witch hazel): 'Arnold's Promise', 'Jelena', 'Primavera'

Hibiscus syriacus (rose of Sharon): Blue Satin ('Marina'), 'Diana', 'Helene', White Chiffon ('Notwoodtwo')

Hydrangea arborescens (hills of snow): 'Annabelle', White Dome ('Dardom')*

H. macrophylla (large-leaved hydrangea): 'Mariesii Variegata', 'Nikko Blue', 'Pia', 'Tokyo Delight'

H. paniculata (peegee hydrangea): 'Limelight', 'Pink Diamond', 'Tardiva'

H. quercifolia (oak-leaved hydrangea): 'Alice', 'Pee Wee', 'Snow Flake'

Hypericum (St. John's wort): *H . androsaemum* 'Albury Purple'; hybrid 'Hidcote'

Ilex verticillata (winterberry): 'Red Sprite', 'Scarlett O'Hara', 'Winter Gold', 'Winter Red' (plus the required male pollinators, such as 'Apollo' and 'Jim Dandy')

Itea virginica (Virginia sweetspire): 'Little Henry', 'Merlot'

Kalmia latifolia (mountain laurel): 'Kaleidoscope', 'Sarah'

Mahonia japonica (leatherleaf mahonia): 'Bealei'

Physocarpus opulifolius (ninebark): 'Dart's Gold', Diablo ('Monlo'), Summer Wine ('Seward')

Rhododendron (deciduous azaleas): *R. arborescens, R. calendulaceum, R. prunifolium, R. viscosum*

Rhus typhina (staghorn sumac): 'Laciniata', 'Tiger Eyes'

Sambucus (elderberries): *S. nigra* 'Aurea', 'Guincho Purple', 'Marginata'; *S. racemosa* 'Sutherland Gold'*

Spiraea (spireas): 'Golden Elf'; *S.* x *bumalda* 'Coccinea'; *S. japonica*, 'Magic Carpet', 'Neon Flash'; *S. thunbergii* Mellow Yellow ('Ogon')

Symphoricarpos (snowberries)

Syringa (lilacs): Tinkerbelle ('Bailbelle'), *S.* x *laciniata, S. meyeri* 'Palabin', *S. pubescens* subsp. *patula* 'Miss Kim'

Vaccinium (blueberry): 'Ornablue'

Viburnum (viburnums): *V. carlesii* 'Compactum'; *V. dentatum* Blue Muffin ('Christom'); *V. dilatatum* 'Michael Dodge'; *V. nudum* 'Winterthur'; *V. plicatum* f. *tomentosum* 'Mariesii', 'Shasta'; *V. sargentii* 'Onondaga'; *V. trilobum* 'Aureum', 'Wentworth'

Vitex agnus-castus (chastetree)*

Weigela florida (weigela): 'French Lace', Midnight Wine ('Elvera'), 'Rubidor', Wine and Roses ('Alexandra')

EVERGREEN SHRUBS

Chamaecyparis obtusa (false cypress): 'Kosteri', 'Nana Gracilis'

Cryptomeria japonica (Japanese cryptomeria): 'Black Dragon'

Ilex crenata (Japanese holly): 'Sky Pencil'

Picea pungens (blue spruce): 'Montgomery'

Pinus cembra (Swiss stone pine): 'Blue Mound'

Rhamnus frangula (alder buckthorn): 'Asplenifolia', Fine Line ('Ron Williams')

Thuja occidentalis (arborvitae): 'Rheingold'

---

*Good candidate for treatment as cutback shrub (see Cut Them Down to Size on page 51).

Ravishing Roses. One of the most venerable shrub companions for perennials is roses. Paired with classic partners like delphiniums and lavender, the exquisite flowers and fragrance of heirloom and species roses are the crowning glory of the traditional late-spring or early-summer border, and many gardeners have been tempted to re-create these plantings in their own yard. Unfortunately, most of these old-fashioned favorites bloom only once, drop their bottom foliage in summer (leaving ugly, bare stems), and are prone to a number of disfiguring fungal diseases. That makes them fair choices for a garden you'll see only in late spring and early summer, but poor candidates for plantings that need to look great all through the growing season.

Fortunately, it's getting easier to find excellent garden roses that work as hard as all of your other plants. These newer roses bloom from early summer to fall, and many are relatively resistant to diseases such as black spot and mildew. Bushy "shrub roses," such as 'Carefree Sunshine', 'Carefree Wonder', Knock Out, and 'Nearly Wild', work just as well as other shrubs near the middle or back of the border, and they make fine background plants as well. There are also low-growing roses that are spectacular as ground covers (we like the 'Meidiland' series roses, for example). Climbers, such as the ever-popular 'New Dawn', can be used on arbors, fences, trellises, pergolas, pillars, and tuteurs (freestanding supports) to add height to a garden.

All-season bloom is a good enough reason to use any rose that strikes your fancy, but there are several other features that may earn a rose a place in your garden. Wingthorn rose (*R. sericea* subsp. *omeiensis* f. *pteracantha*), for instance, is prized for its stems, with large, bright red thorns that glow when backlit by the winter sun. Red-leaved rose *(Rosa glauca)* produces single pink flowers for only a few weeks in late spring or early summer, but you'll enjoy the purple-flushed, blue-gray foliage through the entire growing season, as well as the showy, orange-red fruits all winter. *R. moyesii* 'Geranium' is another rose that produces great-looking fruits, called hips, for winter color. Stephanie has reported that big hips are back in style, but unfortunately that applies only to roses, not people.

Pair roses with shrubs, annuals, and perennials that have great-looking foliage, and your garden will look glorious even when the roses are past their peak.

For those of you who think roses are too fussy to grow with other plants, well, that's simply not so. In fact, they'll do just fine under the same conditions that many perennials appreciate: full sun and moist, fertile soil. And when you pay special attention to selecting roses with good disease resistance, spraying fungicides is basically not an issue. (Just remember that different areas of the country have different disease problems, so ask your local gardening experts which roses are the best choice for your region.) Accept the occasional spotted leaf or beetle-chewed bloom, and give yourself permission to enjoy these beautiful plants for everything they have to offer.

Shrub and Rose Wrap-Up. When you're using any kind of shrub in a design, be sure to allow each one plenty of space to mature. If you crowd taller perennials up close to them, the roots will compete for nutrients and water, and most of the time the shrub will win this battle. If you don't want to leave a large unplanted space around a shrub in a new border, consider planting annuals there for the first few years. Low-growing, shade-tolerant ground covers are another way to fill this space. Under mature shrubs, try small spring bulbs for early color, then cover the soil with a 2- to 3-inch-deep layer of chopped leaves or bark mulch to keep down weeds.

MIXING IT UP.
Catmints *(Nepeta)* and roses are classic garden partners, while ornamental grasses are an out-of-the-ordinary choice. This daring design brings off the unusual grouping with style.

From Dream to Reality

4

Once you've chosen your site and considered all of your plant options, you can put pencil to paper and get this garden on its way. For many of us, it's the most intimidating part of the whole planning process, but it doesn't have to be. Although it's important to get your new planting off to the best possible start, you don't have to feel stuck with the results. Creating a garden is an ongoing process, not a one-time event, so you'll have plenty of opportunities to fine-tune your design over the years. Still, it makes sense to get as close as possible to your vision on the first try, so let's discuss the nitty-gritty of creating a garden plan.

Bed and Border Basics

FIRST, DECIDE ON THE OUTLINE of the planting area. If you hang around other gardeners for any length of time, you'll hear their gardens described as either borders or beds. In this book, we generally use the term *border* for a garden placed against a wall, fence, hedge, or building, and we use *bed* for any garden not associated with any particular structure. Another way to think of the difference is that a border is seen mostly from one side, whereas a bed can be viewed from several different points. (An *island bed,* in fact, is visible from all sides, because it's surrounded by lawn.) Others may refer to all rectangular-shaped plantings as borders and to all other shapes as beds. Frankly, it doesn't matter in the least what you call your garden, as long as it pleases you and meets your needs.

The Shape of Things to Come.

In many cases, the site itself will give you clues as to the best shape. Rectangular gardens are a natural for long, narrow spaces, such as against the front of your house, along a fence, and edging a path or driveway. Don't feel you need to square off the ends of the planting. If a tree or shrub is in the path of your rectangle, incorporate it into the design. When you come to the end of a wall, use a gentle curve to swing the border around the corner so it doesn't end abruptly.

In open areas, free-form shapes generally look more natural; just remember to keep the outline fairly simple. If you go in and out with curves too many times, it looks like either a misshapen camel or a singularly bad case of seasickness. Sharp angles and fussy scallops can also be a nightmare for the poor soul who has to mow and edge around them. A gently curved, kidney-bean shape is a classic choice for an island bed. If you have existing trees in your yard, avoid the common mistake of creating small "ring-around-the-collar" gardens circling each one. The intention is usually good: to prevent damage to the trees from lawn-care tools. But the result is a lot more trimming work around each of these mini-gardens, and trust us — perennials don't take any more kindly to string trimmers than trees do. You and your plants will be much better off if you create larger beds that link several trees, then fill them with easy-care perennials or ground covers.

Sizing Up Your Garden.

There is no magic formula for determining the best size for a garden. Some experts claim that a border always has to be at least 5 (or 6, or 8) feet wide. That's great if your site can accommodate that size, but it may not be practical (or in proportion) for smaller spaces. Others suggest that a planting be no wider than twice the length of your arm, so you can easily reach in from the sides and don't have to step on the soil. The reasoning is fine, but the reality is that you could end up with a very narrow garden if you can't reach very far. Another theory is to make your beds twice as wide as your tallest perennial. By this logic, if you plant a large grass or perennial that is 8 feet tall, your border should be 16 feet wide. This sounds okay, but if you don't have the space to do it, you'll be reduced to using *very* short plants.

Instead of following a specific rule, simply try to keep your garden in proportion to its surroundings. If there is some sort of structure nearby, making the border slightly wider than half the structure's height usually looks pleasing. (Against an 8-foot-tall hedge, for example, try to make the border about 5 feet wide.) To estimate the ideal length, figure out where you'll most often see the garden from, then cut the distance between that point and the garden in half. If your garden will be 20 feet away from your patio, for instance, consider making it about 10 feet long.

For those of you who are daunted by the thought of all this math, do what we do: Use string or rope to draw the outline of the garden right on the site, and make adjustments as needed until you're satisfied with the result. You could even take this one step further and "plant" your garden using pots to simulate perennials, trash cans for shrubs, and long stepladders or very large boxes for trees. If you use your imagination, you can get a pretty good idea of how all of the proportions are working together. (Just make sure the neighbors are at work or on vacation when you do this, or you'll get some very strange looks!)

Putting Your Ideas on Paper

A PICTURE-PERFECT PLAN.
Even small gardens benefit from a carefully thought-out plan.

I T IS ENTIRELY POSSIBLE to create a new garden without drawing a design on paper. But before you decide to skip this step and jump right into setting out plants, ask yourself this question: If I don't have a plan, how will I know how many plants can fit in the space I've chosen? Unless you can look at a site and automatically calculate with complete accuracy the types and quantities of plants you need, you're going to end up buying fewer or more perennials than are necessary. That means extra trips to the garden center and delays waiting for additional mail-order shipments or money spent on plants you have no room for. Having even a rough plan in hand doesn't guarantee that you won't end up with a few shortages or surpluses, but there's much less of a chance of making serious buying mistakes.

It's a Sketch, Not a Masterpiece.
We'll be honest — neither of us can draw worth a darn. So when we create designs for our own gardens, no one ever sees those plot plans but us. All you have to do is generate a rough sketch that's reasonably legible so you can read your own notes when it's time to plant.

Our favorite design tools are quite simple: a couple of sharp pencils, a *large* eraser, a ruler, and — most importantly — a tablet of graph paper with ¼-inch squares. For most gardens, figure that the side of one square on the paper equals 1 foot in the garden. (If the garden is small, let each square equal 6 inches instead, so you'll have more room to sketch in the plants.) Tape on an extra page or two of graph paper if you need more space for large plantings. Collect all your notes, your wish lists, and the ideas you've been accumulating from books, magazines, and garden visits.

Pull out some recent books and mail-order nursery catalogs, too — the more pictures, the better — for looking up heights and colors. Find a well-lit area with a comfy chair and a table or desk on which to spread out all of your things. Now it's time to start your design.

First, draw in any existing features that will be next to or part of your design, such as walkways, a fence, a deck, and a building. Then draw the outline of your new garden. Remember to keep the outline as simple as possible; avoid tight curves and scallops, which will make mowing and trimming difficult. You may want to draw an arrow indicating north somewhere on the paper, too, to remind you of sun and shade patterns caused by nearby structures. If you're designing a border, add two horizontal lines across the outline to divide the area into thirds from front to back. This little trick will come in handy when you start arranging plants by height (more on this later).

Finally, it's time to start placing your perennials, using the lists of plant possibilities you came up with after reading chapter 2 (Selecting Your Perennials, starting on page 15). How you indicate the specific plants on your plan is up to you. Perhaps you'd like to make circles to indicate the approximate size of each plant. Or you could outline squares to represent individual plants. Some people sketch in the basic shape of the plant. We like to use x's that are the approximate width of the plant and then draw free-form around them to represent a grouping.

Nan's Notebook

Behind the Scenes

WHEN YOU'RE DESIGNING a garden against some sort of structure, be sure to leave a strip at least 1 foot wide — and ideally 18 to 24 inches wide — between the structure and the back of the border for an access path. It may look like wasted space at planting time, but you'll thank yourself for the path when you want to reach the back edge of the garden for staking or trimming, or if you need to do some maintenance on the structure. In my front border, the space was only 5 feet wide to begin with, so covering the back 18 inches with gravel instead of plants made the garden itself much smaller than I'd have liked. By midsummer, though, the path was hardly visible, because the back-of-the-border plants used that space to stretch out a bit, and everything then looked proportional. As a bonus, the gravel path caught the rain from the edge of the roof (as my house doesn't have gutters), so the plants didn't get battered by the runoff or splashed with soil.

If your house has wide roof overhangs (with or without gutters), keep in mind that they often create a "rain shadow": a strip of ground against the house that stays dry even when the outer edge of the border gets ample rainfall. If possible, make your access path as wide as this strip; otherwise, consider drought-tolerant plants for the back of the border, so they won't suffer from the drier soil.

Drifting Along. In the quest to include as many different plants as possible, many beginners make the mistake of using single clumps of each one in their design. But in most cases, single clumps of many different plants are much less attractive than larger groupings of fewer plants. In small spaces, a "one-of-each" garden will look cluttered; in large areas, the space turns into the supreme jumble. When you study pictures of beautiful gardens in books and magazines, you'll often find that it's the masses, or drifts, of plants that give the design its visual impact.

Creating drifts simply means grouping identical plants — usually three or more — in one spot. The ideal size of each drift depends on many factors: the size of the garden, the size of the plants, their season of bloom, the contribution their foliage makes to the design, and their overall health and maintenance needs. We like to build designs around generous drifts of what many gardeners call the "workhorses": perennials that bloom for several months, that have great foliage, that don't need lots of fussy maintenance, and that aren't seriously bothered by pests or diseases. Then we fill in with smaller groupings of perennials that may lack one or two of these traits but are still too pretty to leave out.

In general, the larger the area you have to fill, the bigger your drifts should be. Take into account that bulky perennials, such as goat's beard (*Aruncus dioicus*) and 'Lemon Queen' perennial sunflower (*Helianthus*), need relatively smaller drifts than do more compact plants. As a general rule of thumb, the smallest perennials (those up to about 2 feet tall) look best in groups of at least five; medium-sized perennials (those 2 to 4 feet tall) merit a drift of three or five plants. Small trees and shrubs, as well as tall perennials (4 feet plus) with architectural structure or bold foliage, can have enough impact to look fine in "drifts of one." Tall perennials with fine foliage and airy flowers usually work best in drifts of three. You'll often hear that drifts must contain odd numbers of plants (3, 5, 7, and so on) to look pleasing. That's often true; however, it's an issue mostly when you're dealing with perennials that grow in distinct clumps, such as yuccas. In many cases, the plants will grow together, and no one will be able to tell exactly how many plants you used. So if you have a spot that really lends itself to two or four or six plants, don't stress over trying to fit in an extra one or taking one out.

Keeping Perennials *Out* of Line

Unless you're sure you want to use a row of a specific perennial as a background or as a front edging, avoid placing your plants in straight lines. A staggered, or checkerboard, placement within each drift makes for a much more natural-looking grouping. If you have five plants in a drift, for example, you can plant either two or three in the front and the rest behind them. Every once in a while, break this pattern and do four in front and one in back, so all your drifts don't look identical. Feel free to play with the directions of your drifts, too. (Start a drift in the front and then swing it toward the middle, for instance.) The more you tweak your drifts into different patterns, the more visual interest your design will have.

Get the Drift

Not sure how many plants to put in a drift? The smaller they are, the more you need in order to make a visual impact. With medium-sized plants, you can use fewer clumps. With large, bushy plants, just a couple can do the job.

SMALL	MEDIUM	LARGE

WAVES OF COLOR. Like a dramatic seascape, this lovely fall garden gets its visual punch from the series of large, massed plantings. From front to back: Catmint *(Nepeta),* salvia, 'Fireworks' goldenrod (*Solidago rugosa* 'Fireworks'), Russian sage *(Perovskia),* coreopsis, and asters.

DON'T FENCE ME IN. By allowing the tall rudbeckia in the background to break over the top of the fence, the gardener avoids a hemmed-in look.

Hitting the Right Heights.

When you start filling in the outline of your plan, draw in the shrubs and largest drifts of perennials first; then fill in around them with smaller groupings. In general, it's best to keep the shorter plants in the front, medium-sized plants in the middle, and the big guys toward the back. But like all other design rules, this one is made to be broken. Bringing a few taller plants forward gives the garden more visual appeal and can serve a practical function too, such as covering up a shorter companion that's done flowering. For more tips on effective ways to play with plant heights in your design, turn back to All Shapes and Sizes on page 26.

So how do you decide just how tall the plants should be? Often, the difference between a professional-looking plan and one that looks amateurish is the attention the designer has paid to selecting perennials that are in scale with each other and with their surroundings.

When you're designing a perennial garden in front of a house wall, fence, or hedge, that feature sets the stage for the border. We generally like to include at least one or two plants that are slightly taller than their background (a 7-foot-tall perennial in front of a 6-foot hedge, for example), so it doesn't look like the garden is rigidly enclosed. That obviously isn't practical with perennials against a typical house wall, however. In that case, consider adding a tree or shrub to the design, or perhaps a vine-covered trellis on the wall, then step down to a wide border of perennials in front.

UP AGAINST IT. Wisteria, trained overhead at porch-roof level, forms a transition between the low- to medium-height bulbs and perennials in the garden and the house itself.

If there's no structure to play off, consider the overall site. In a large island bed set in a broad expanse of flat lawn, perennials that reach to 10 feet, 12 feet, or even taller would look perfectly in scale. In a bed that's tucked into a corner somewhere, or in a garden that surrounds a bench, smaller plants (roughly 4 feet tall and shorter) provide more comfortable proportions and keep you from feeling overwhelmed.

Within the garden itself, the height of the tallest plants will determine the relative heights of their bedmates. A good rule of thumb is that each plant should be about three quarters of the height of the plant behind it. If you have a 6-foot-tall perennial in back, for instance, step down to a 4-foot plant in front of it, then down to a 3-foot perennial, and so on. As we mentioned in Sizing Things Up (page 26), don't follow this rule strictly: Use it as a guideline, but go ahead and mix up the heights somewhat to avoid a stair-step effect.

The distance from which you'll see the garden will help determine the size of the smallest plants you should use. In borders along a pathway or by a bench, your front-of-the-border plants may be just 6 inches tall; in a planting seen from a distance, the shortest plants may be 18 inches high or even taller.

Striking a Balance

As you are merrily sketching drifts onto your design, remember to distribute the plant heights and masses fairly evenly from side to side. If you use several large plants in one part and many smaller plants in another, the result will look lopsided. In an island bed where the parts are different sizes, using larger and coarser-leaved plants in the smaller side will help visually balance it with the bigger side 1. In a border, you might use a tree at one end and a grouping of three shrubs near the other to produce the same effect 2. This is called *asymmetrical balance*.

You can also achieve balance by repeating the same group of plants several times in a design to produce *symmetry* 3. If you do this with everything you plant, though, the garden may have a blocky, paint-by-numbers look. A better way to achieve balance is to repeat similar plant shapes, flower forms, or colors, but with different plants 4.

No matter which approach you use, keep in mind that variety adds excitement to your garden and repetition provides unity. Having a balance of these factors is the real secret to creating a fantastic perennial design.

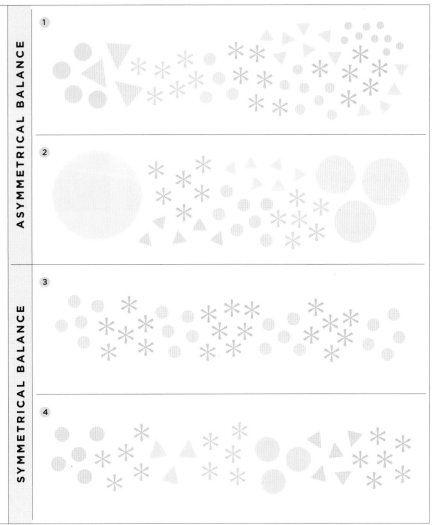

ASYMMETRICAL BALANCE

SYMMETRICAL BALANCE

COLOR ECHOES.
Both flowers and foliage carry out the deep red and purple color scheme. From left: caladiums, redbud (*Cercis canadensis* 'Forest Pansy'), dahlias, barberry *(Berberis)*, and caryopteris.

Don't Forget Color! Once you have the largest plants placed and are starting to fill in around them, it's time to think about how you want to distribute the flower and foliage colors. In a garden with a monochromatic color theme, that pretty much takes care of itself, although even in that case it's important to remember to include some "neutrals" to break up things a bit (see Keeping the Peace, page 23). If you've selected a theme of two or three particular colors, it's best to try to distribute them evenly throughout the planting in order to avoid creating a blotchy effect.

Where color isn't the primary focus of your plant selections, you have two options. One is to keep the brighter and hotter colors near the middle and the softer pastel and neutral colors near the edges — a technique championed by Gertrude Jekyll, the most famous British perennial garden designer of the Victorian age. This approach keeps your eye drawn toward the center of the garden and prevents it from drifting off to the areas beyond it. More-modern designers generally prefer to use a dominant color for each season and repeat it in several locations throughout the planting. This encourages your eye to move from spot to spot over the entire garden area. Both of these approaches have merit, so choose whichever works for you. As long as you don't put the brightest colors at the ends of your border, which will lead your eye right out of the garden, the results should be satisfying.

Unlike an artist painting with oils on a canvas, you are painting a picture with plants, which change from day to day, week to week, and month to month. That means you need to think about how the colors are distributed throughout the garden in each season, not just at one time (unless it's meant to be seen only at a specific time of year, such as a summer garden at a beach house).

To do this, take several pieces of tracing paper and use one for each of the main seasons. Where we live, we generally define March through May bloom as spring; June to mid-August as summer; late August through October as fall; and November to February as winter. "Spring" as well as "fall" may come earlier or later, depending on what part of the country you live in. Lay each piece of tracing paper over your design, trace the drifts that will flower in that season, then add a dot of pen or crayon to indicate the color of each grouping. (If you'd like to color in the whole drift, you can. But we generally advise against it, because it leaves out the neutralizing effect of the green foliage, and you may start thinking you see color clashes that won't actually occur in real life.)

Perennials with colorful foliage all season can go on a separate piece of paper. When you're done, review each overlay to make sure you have plenty of color in each season, that the colors look good together, and that they are evenly distributed. This is also a good time to look for spots where you can add bulbs for spring color, as it will be a simple matter to tuck them in around later-flowering perennials.

Checking Your Work. Once you've filled all the spaces and are satisfied with the distribution of heights and colors, it's smart to check a few more details before you decide you're done. Make sure, for instance, that you don't have too many of the same bloom forms together, such as two daisy-flowered perennials or two spiky-flowered plants right next to each other. Also watch out for leaf shapes and textures that are too similar, such as irises beside grasses or ferns next to lacy-leaved perennials. Double-check that there's a good mix of plant forms as well, so you haven't placed two creepers or two very upright perennials alongside each other.

When you're satisfied with your design, make a shopping list with the names of the plants you've used and how many of each you need. If you're shopping locally, take along your plan as well as your list, in case some of your plants are not available and you need to figure out appropriate alternatives.

Give Them Their Space

While you're figuring out where to place plants in your design, you need to have some idea of how wide they will get, so you can figure out how much space to give them. This is especially important with shrubs and large-growing perennials, which are often quite small when you buy them. If you don't allow them enough room at the start, they might get crowded out in the first year or two by faster-growing companions, or else do the crowding themselves a few years later as they mature.

Within a drift, space the plants far enough that they can mature comfortably, but not so far that they'll become lost in a sea of mulch or weeds. The general rule is to space plants at half their mature spread. For example, if a plant grows to be 2 feet wide, space the clumps roughly 1 foot apart. If you're on a limited budget, set them slightly farther apart and use annuals as temporary fillers; after a few years, the perennials will have filled in and you can omit the annuals.

Now that we've told you what you *should* do, we'll admit using what Stephanie refers to as the "cram-and-jam" method. We like to see the complete design materialize as soon as possible, so we space our plants rather closer than we should. The price we pay for the instant results is that we have to buy more plants at the start, and then must move or divide crowded clumps after the first year or two. (Properly spaced plantings generally don't need this until the third year, at least.) So if this approach appeals to you, at least we've warned you about the extra work involved!

A note of caution here from two of your fellow gardeners who have made lots of mistakes at this point: Be very careful about the substitutions you make during your shopping spree! After you've carefully researched the particular species and cultivars you want, swapping them with other selections simply based on price or availability can spell disaster for your design. There are certainly times when making substitutions can be fine: for instance, using a hosta of the same size but with a slightly different variegation pattern. But buying lupines or delphiniums because they look nicer now than the asters you're supposed to be getting will change the entire effect of the finished garden — and usually not for the better.

A Plan that Grows. Attempting your very first design can be intimidating, but seeing your mental picture turn into a real garden is nothing short of exhilarating. When inspiration simply fails to strike, or when you're just not sure that your skills are up to tackling a particularly large or important area of your yard, you can still use all of the design techniques we've talked about to communicate your wishes to a professional designer. The more specific you are about your likes, your dislikes, and your overall wishes for the garden, the better the chance the designer will create a great plan for your site. Remember, though, that no matter who designs the garden, there will be plenty of opportunities for you to fine-tune it each year as the plants grow or die out and you find new ones to try. An on-paper design represents one moment in time, but a real-world garden changes continually — and true gardeners wouldn't have it any other way.

Designing "On the Fly"

IF YOU'RE STILL NOT CONVINCED that you want to put pencil to paper, you may decide to jump into planning your garden right on the spot. Nine times out of ten, though, this is a recipe for disaster — particularly if you are new to perennial gardening. Planting without some kind of design can lead to wasting hundreds of dollars, being disappointed with the results, and having to fix mistakes that could have been easily avoided if you'd had a plan.

Consider Yourself Warned. The worst idea is to decide one fine spring day that you really want a new garden *now,* so you make the rounds of your local garden centers and come home with a carload of plants. Without having a realistic idea of how big these plants will get, it's likely that you'll have either many more than you need or not enough to fill the space you have available. You'll probably end up with a seasonally lopsided garden, too, because you'll have chosen all of the great-looking early bloomers but few or none to provide color later in the year. The garden centers will love you — at least for a while — because you'll spend lots of money and probably keep coming back to buy more fillers and replacements for poor first choices. But you may end up hating your garden and giving it up altogether, which would be the saddest loss of all.

PAINT YOUR WAGON. Isn't this what cars like this were designed for?

If You Still Want to Try. To be fair, there are some cases where designing on the site works. If you take this route, it's important to have a good mental encyclopedia of plants: knowledge of their colors, bloom times, mature sizes, and preferred growing conditions. That's the only way you can be reasonably sure that the combinations you create will achieve the effect you're aiming for. It also helps to have an extensive stash of plants on hand. Once you've gardened for a while, you'll find it's easy to acquire plants you don't have real plans for: impulse buys from a garden center, perennials you propagate yourself, gifts from gardening friends, and odds and ends you pick up at plant swaps. You've probably collected them because you know they will thrive on your site, because you like their flower or foliage colors, or because you simply had a burning desire to try them. If this sounds like a description of your perennial mania, design-ing "on the fly" can be a perfectly valid way for you to set up a perennial garden.

Whichever approach you choose, you might decide to set out all your plants *before* you prepare the planting site, so you can walk over the area and rearrange the pots as needed without worrying about compacting already loosened soil. Then you can make a rough sketch of where each plant is supposed to be, move all the pots to the side, and get the soil ready for planting. Alternatively, prepare the site first, so you can plant the pots as soon as you're satisfied with the arrangement. In this case, try to reach in only from the sides, or lay boards over the soil to step on; this will spread out your weight and minimize soil compaction. In a very wide garden, consider creating a permanent mulch or stepping-stone access path before placing the plants. This will make both current planting and future maintenance a whole lot easier.

JIGSAW-PUZZLE METHOD. Start with the largest plants, such as bugbane *(Cimicifuga)* 1 and astilbe 2, then add the small ones, such as epimedium 3 and tiarella 4, and, finally, slip in mid-sized plants, such as hosta 5 and hellebore 6.

There are two basic approaches to this kind of design: the jigsaw-puzzle and the building-block methods. Gardeners following the first method begin with the biggest plants, followed by the smallest, then fill in the middle of the garden with a variety of heights and colors to link the front and back (page 70).

Taking the building-block approach, gardeners create groupings of three or four different plants that look good together, then link these groupings by repeating and contrasting colors and textures as they move along the border. Here's how this works:

✱ Let's say you review your cache of collected plants and see a good-looking dark-leaved weigela. You decide to use this shrub and place it near the back at one end of the border.

✱ To repeat the purple color near the front of the border, you select a dark-leaved heuchera and place it near the edge of the planting.

✱ Now you want some variety, so you pick out a few pots of 'Zagreb' coreopsis (*Coreopsis verticillata*). Its fine foliage and golden blooms will contrast nicely with the first two plants, and the dark centers of its flowers will echo the purple leaves.

✱ As a final touch, you select a clump of 'Prairie Sunset' oxeye (*Heliopsis helianthoides*) to join the weigela at the back. Its golden flowers repeat the color of the coreopsis, and its purple stems pick up the purple from the weigela and the heuchera.

✱ To create the next combination, you look carefully at how the first one is working, and perhaps decide you need to add an ornamental grass for a different foliage texture, and then maybe a medium-height purple-leaved plant to bring that color into the middle of the border. You use those two plants for the basis of an adjoining combination, and so on down the border.

BUILDING BLOCK APPROACH. Taking a modular approach, you can develop your garden in sections. At the left, weigela ① and a purple-leafed heuchera ② are joined by coreopsis ③ and heliopsis ④ for the first block. The next block begins with a grass ⑤ and more purple foliage with *Lysimachia ciliata* ⑥.

It's All in the Details

5

W HAT MAKES THE DIFFERENCE between a nice-looking garden and one that's spectacular? It's not the rarity of the plants or the number of fancy, expensive structures. Rather, as the saying goes, it's "the infinite capacity for taking pains." The more attention you pay to the details, the more exciting and satisfying your garden will be. To that end, we have lots of ideas to help you add the perfect finishing touches to your perennial plantings.

Creating
Eye-Catching Combinations

WHEN YOU STUDY PICTURES in gardening books and magazines, you'll notice that they often focus on combinations of just a few plants and not on the gardens as a whole. Just about every garden includes at least one or two of these photo-worthy vignettes, even if they happen just by serendipity. But when a detail-oriented gardener puts his or her mind to creating picture after picture with plant combinations, well, that's when you get a truly breathtaking garden.

Keep Your Eyes Open. As you drew the design for your new perennial garden, you put a lot of care into choosing your plants and arranging them into attractive groupings. But it's tough to come up with amazing combinations on paper, because it takes a keen eye to observe all the features that can make for simpatico garden partners. That's why we've put this information in this chapter on the details and finishing touches: You can always be on the lookout for ways to improve even your best designs every year.

Inspiration for creating striking combinations is all around you. Besides the obvious resources of books and magazines, take notes when you go on garden tours or visit garden centers with good display areas. Another trick is to take snippets of plants you already have and play with different arrangements of flowers and foliage until you come up with pairings you find pleasing. You may discover that by moving around just two or three plants, you can turn a ho-hum bed or border into something really special. Also, watch out for those inevitable nature-made combinations that happen when one plant seeds itself next to, sprawls onto, or weaves into just the right companion. These unplanned but perfect pairings can inspire other groupings that you otherwise wouldn't have thought of.

One word of warning: If you decide to re-create a combination you've seen in a photograph, keep in mind that you can't expect to get the exact results in your own garden. Even if the plants are perfectly suited to your climate and garden conditions, and even if you are able to get the pictured plants, you won't ever get to see your grouping in exactly the same lighting or under the same weather conditions. When Nan was a beginning gardener, for instance, she saw a picture of a fall perennial garden bordered with strawberry plants, where the strawberry foliage had turned amazing shades of red, yellow, and green that perfectly complemented the late-flowering perennials. She attempted to reproduce the effect in her own garden but, sadly, the foliage never turned those colors for her — and she had dozens of unwanted strawberry runners to pull out each summer, too.

Photographs are garden moments frozen in time. A gifted photographer knows how to wait for just the right light conditions, and how to take advantage of angles not always available to the casual garden visitor, like from above. You've probably heard the old saying that pictures never lie, but keep in mind that they may not tell the whole story either. You never get to see the coaxing, primping, and prodding the gardener may have had to do to make the plants look so perfect, or how that same combination will look a week, a month, or a year later. So if you see a photograph you find inspiring, try to figure out what exactly appeals to you about it, then use it as a jumping-off point for building your own picture-perfect combos.

A Balancing Act.

What's the secret to a knock-your-socks-off combination? In most cases, it's a balance of the same two factors that make for a great overall garden design: contrast and unity. If the plants you put together have too many obvious features in common — the same flower form or color, for example, or similar growth habits — the grouping will lack visual excitement. Even if there are also contrasts in more subtle features, such as leaf shape and texture, that's generally not enough to break up the overall similarities. But if every plant is distinctly different from its partners, the grouping lacks

unity and will look like a bunch of randomly placed plants growing together. The knack is learning to find the balance between contrast and unity that feels most comfortable to you.

Flowers Are Just the Beginning.

Blossoms are by far the most obvious feature to base combinations on. But unless you are working with perennials that all have extended bloom periods, you run the risk of missing your carefully planned combo in years when the weather or another factor prevents the bloom times from coinciding. When you use the entire range of plant features — from leaves and stems to fruits and seedheads — the likelihood of creating dependable combinations is far greater. Of course, that doesn't mean the grouping will look exactly the same each year; good combinations tend to evolve, just as the entire garden does.

FOLIAGE FOR EFFECTS.

The bluish *Sedum maximum* contrasts perfectly with the red-purple foliage of the red orach (*Atriplex hortensis* var. *rubra*), both further enhanced by the strong accent of the variegated iris (*Iris pallida* 'Variegata').

Two Takes on Creating Combinations

As with so many other aspects of gardening, the only true measure of a successful combination is how it pleases you — not your spouse, or your neighbor, or members of the local garden club. Stephanie always likes to say that if you put two gardeners together, they'll have ten opinions. The two of us often agree on whether a particular pairing "works"; however, we have very different approaches to coming up with combinations in our own gardens.

STEPHANIE tends to build her combinations around harmonious colors and contrasting flower forms. One of her favorite combinations at the moment is a purple salvia (*Salvia nemorosa* 'Caradonna') ① paired with the Shasta daisy 'Becky' (*Leucanthemum* x *super-bum*) ② and red valerian (*Centranthus ruber* var. *roseus*) ③. The salvia is sturdy and upright with spiky, deep purple flowers; dark stems; and rough-looking, deep green foliage. The taller Shasta daisy has bright white petals, a yellow button center, and a flat flower form over toothed, bright green leaves. The somewhat sprawling red valerian bears tiny, rosy pink flowers, which are grouped into clusters but still impart an airy quality against the plant's narrow, medium-green leaves. This simple combo is effective because the colors are compatible and the leaves blend well together, while the difference in flower and plant forms provides just enough contrast to keep things exciting. And because all three of these plants are in flower for a good part of the summer, this classic combo makes a dependable, long-lasting accent that visitors are sure to admire.

NAN is a self-confessed sucker for colorful foliage, so most of her best-loved combinations feature dramatic contrasts of leaf colors and textures. Some of her favorites are the scalloped, deep-purple leaves of 'Purple Petticoats' heuchera against the tiny, yellow-green leaves of golden oregano (*Origanum vulgare* 'Aureum') ④; the bright yellow leaves of golden feverfew (*Tanacetum parthenium* 'Aureum') rising out of the blue-green foliage of yellow corydalis (*Corydalis lutea*) ⑤; and the broad, bright silver leaves of lamb's ears (*Stachys byzantina*) against the lacy, deep brown foliage of bronze fennel (*Foeniculum vulgare* 'Purpureum'). These kinds of strong contrasts aren't to everyone's taste, of course, but for better or worse, they are definitely eye-catching. And because they are based on foliage, Nan knows she can count on them to look good all through the growing season, and year after year as well.

Planning for Paths and Walkways

Part of the pleasure of a garden is being able to get up close and personal with the plants themselves. Adding a path or walkway leading to, around, or even right through your garden is a wonderful way to put plants within easy reach for touching, smelling, and just plain admiring. A well-planned path, such as a rustic pine-needle path through a woodland garden or quirky stepping stones through a casual cottage garden, contributes to the mood, style, and theme of the planting. Paths serve a practical function, too: They provide safe, clean footing for garden visitors, and they allow easy access for wheelbarrows and other tools come cleanup time. So instead of asking why you should add a path to your design, the better question might be: Why not?

Path-Planning Basics. The size of a path or walkway can vary widely, depending on where it is and how you'll use it. Generally, a main walkway — such as the one from the parking area to your front door — should be at least 4 feet wide. That allows two people to walk side by side without either one feeling crowded. Lesser-used paths are fine at about 3 feet wide; an access path behind a border or through a bed can be as narrow as 12 to 18 inches. Whenever possible, consider making your path 6 to 12 inches wider than these guidelines; we promise you won't be sorry. Plants have a way of leaning or sprawling onto paths, which adds a lot of charm but also cuts down on available walking space. If your path is already narrow, you'll spend a lot of time whacking back the plants.

The course of the path is another issue to consider. Straight paths have a formal appearance and allow people to move quickly to their destination. Curving paths are more informal, and they encourage visitors to slow down and enjoy their surroundings. When those curves swing around a feature that blocks the view, such as a tree, a shrub, or a bed of tall perennials, they add a sense of mystery and excitement to the journey. This trick is especially useful in a wide-open front yard or in a very small area, where you don't want guests to be able to see the whole garden at one glance and then hurry on by.

DOWN THE GARDEN PATH.
This generously wide path, edged on both sides by massed plantings, promises a delightful experience at every turn.

Material Concerns.

One of the most important decisions you must make about your path is what it will be made of. The material you choose depends on your budget, on your site, and on your overall design.

Grass paths are a classic choice for many first gardens, mainly because the grass is already there — no investment or initial work is required. They feel good under your feet, they complement both formal and informal gardens, and they look nice, too: It's hard to beat bright green grass as a setting for colorful flowers. But all of this beauty comes at a price, in the form of continual mowing and edging to keep them neat and to prevent the grass from creeping into the garden. Unless you seldom use them, grass paths can quickly develop bare spots, eventually turning into muddy tracks that are slippery and ugly. Some gardeners try to get around this by placing stepping stones in the grass. Again, the effect can be pretty, but the maintenance involved in having to trim around each of the stones can be a nightmare.

When you need a surface that's sturdier than grass but still fairly inexpensive, gravel could be a good option for you. It comes in a variety of sizes and colors, so you may be able to coordinate the path color with buildings, fences, or other objects in the garden. Gravel also makes a nice scrunching sound when you walk on it (high heels will sink in, though). Because water passes right through it, gravel tends to stay dry in wet weather, although it may get washed away on sloping sites or shift around in low spots where water collects. Gravel also seems irresistible to children, who like to toss the stones into the garden and at each other, so you may want to think twice about using gravel where youngsters will have access to it.

Flagstone, like any other natural stone, weathers well, has interesting variations in color, and lasts for a long time. On the downside, it's expensive. For a less pricey option, look into man-made pavers, many of which are difficult to distinguish from natural stone. Both flagstone and faux stone pavers can work well with any garden style. Brick is another option. New brick lends itself to formal settings; old brick works well in both formal and informal settings.

All of these paving materials need careful site preparation and take some skill to lay properly, so you may decide to have them professionally installed, which will add to the expense. But once they are down, these attractive and sturdy surfaces will withstand many years of heavy wear — including snow shoveling in winter — with minimal upkeep.

Many urban and suburban homes have concrete paths. These are long-lasting and relatively low maintenance but are not very visually appealing. If your budget allows, perhaps you could replace them with something more attractive to complement your garden. When that's not an option, allow edging plants to sprawl or creep into the walkway a bit — this will soften the distinct edges and make the hard surface much less obvious.

For more advice on choosing and installing a wide variety of paths and walkways, see Recommended Reading in the Appendix.

Happy Trails for Shade.
In shady sites, grass grows poorly, and gravel paths will collect a lot of debris from overhanging trees. Fortunately, pine needles or chipped and shredded bark make good substitutes where you'd like a natural-looking path in an informal setting. Because these materials break down over time, you'll need to top them off with fresh needles or bark every year or two. Overall, though, these kinds of paths don't take a lot of work to install or maintain, and they are fairly inexpensive as well.

Stepping Up.
Unless your property is completely flat, you'll also need to think about steps when you're planning garden paths. Outdoor steps are usually much broader and shallower than indoor steps, to provide sturdy footing and to encourage visitors to linger. Allowing the tread (the horizontal part of a step) to hang over the riser (the vertical part) an inch or so casts a small shadow and more sharply delineates the edge, which makes for safer strolling.

Unless you have planned for super-wide steps, think twice about trying to re-create those grand garden stairways replete with small specimen plants and alpines tucked into the crevices. Where plants and stairs meet, the need for safe, solid footing always comes first. As with paths and walkways, allowing plants to sprawl onto your steps a little bit is a nice way to integrate the hard surface with your garden — but don't overdo it.

COMFORT CONSIDERATIONS. Flagstones are well spaced for a comfortable pace through this informal garden. Note the discreetly placed garden light, which ensures safe passage on an evening stroll.

Garden Lighting

DOUBLE YOUR PLEASURE. Gardens can be enjoyed well into the evening when flowers are tastefully illuminated.

W HEN YOU'RE IN THE MIDST of planning your first few gardens, worrying about fine details like lighting simply isn't a practical use of your energy. But once your plant knowledge has broadened and you've gained some confidence in your design abilities, you'll realize that light has a significant effect on how you enjoy your plantings.

Lighting Up the Night.

Nighttime presents special opportunities for creating exciting effects with light. Carefully placed fixtures can illuminate certain plants and garden structures for evening enjoyment — a big plus if you're away from home most of the day and can enjoy your garden only after dark. Of course, lighting can also serve a practical purpose: to brighten walkways and steps for safe and pleasant nighttime strolling.

For the most pleasing effect, look for fixtures that both complement your garden and provide sufficient lighting. In Stephanie's front garden, for example, she chose metal fixtures shaped like mayapple (*Podophyllum*) plants; they provide ample lighting at night and double as small garden accents during the day. Avoid the common mistake of using small, upturned lights placed every 2 or 3 inches lining the sides of a path. You want a pleasing, welcoming path for your visitors — not a landing-strip.

Bright Ideas for Garden Lighting.

Lighting can be retrofitted into an existing perennial garden, but this is a costlier and more troublesome option than planning it at the initial design stage — or at least before you plant. It's best to have the soil prepared for planting *before* the lights are installed, to minimize the risk of digging into the wiring. You'll also want to carefully mark the location of the wires on your design so you can avoid them during later planting or digging.

It is possible to install garden lighting yourself, but we highly recommend you consult an electrician or company that specializes in garden lighting. They can show you books with many interesting fixtures to choose from, and they can look at your property and offer suggestions as to where additional lighting might be placed. You should also check with your local building inspector to see if there are regulations you must comply with before adding electrical fixtures and outlets to your garden. It's far less trouble to do everything right from the beginning than have to remove an unsafe or illegal installation later.

Sunshine and Shadow. Natural lighting affects how the eye perceives color, line, and texture. Any plant viewed against the light stands out dramatically from its background. Backlighting can also create memorable color effects, as sunlight shining through thin leaves turns ordinary greens to brilliant emeralds, yellows to glowing golds, and reds to radiant rubies. To take advantage

A TOUCH OF STAGECRAFT. Take advantage of light effects on plants with foliage that glows as sunlight passes through it. Here, 'Gold Sword' yucca (*Yucca filamentosa*) with Japanese blood grass (*Imperata cylindrica* 'Rubra').

of these spectacular light effects, try to site your garden where it will be backlit by the rising or setting sun. Be sure to include some tall grasses in your designs; these plants are unrivaled for producing amazing interactions with low light angles.

Another way to emphasize light in the garden is with water. Still water draws down the colors of the sky to ground level, where they complement reflections of plants or artfully placed objects and create a tranquil setting. Fountains and running water, on the other hand, break the reflection into an impressionistic painting, as well as adding soothing burbles or splashes to suit your garden's mood.

If water is not part of your design, you can use small mirrors placed in strategic locations to take advantage of your light source. Placing a mirror on a small garden wall amplifies available light, brightening the whole area and making the garden look more spacious. Stephanie once visited a small garden with a gate that looked like a window. It was actually a mirror that reflected the back of the garden, making the whole area look nearly twice as large as it was. Keep in mind that mirrors can look like open spaces to birds, which may fly into the mirrors by mistake. This seems to be less of a problem when the mirror is mostly filled with reflections of plants, rather than open sky.

LIGHT REFRESHMENT. Even small areas of water pick up the sparkle and glow of sun and sky.

Growing Up: Fences, Walls, and Trellises

W HEN YOU FEEL your perennial plantings need added height or structure, fences, walls, hedges, and trellises are all great options to incorporate into your design. These vertical features are also classic choices for defining boundaries, either along property lines or within the property itself to define spaces and create smaller "garden rooms." In addition, you'll find that you can use them to complement the style of the garden, add color accents, provide year-round interest, and shelter both you and your plants.

SCALING THE HEIGHTS. Pyramidal trellises covered with honeysuckle (Lonicera) add old-fashioned romance along with dramatic height to this large-scale garden, but the same element can be used in small gardens just as effectively.

Please Fence Me In. Of all the available materials for garden fencing, wood is probably the most popular. There's a wood fence to enhance just about any garden style, from split rail for a naturalistic planting, to picket for a country cottage garden, to elegant board-on-board (also called shadowbox) for a contemporary look. This versatile material also offers a wide range of finishing options. You can stain it to preserve the warm wood tones, paint it any color to complement or contrast with your home or plants, or simply let it weather to a neutral gray for a rustic look. Because paints and stains require regular applications to keep their color, it's vital to leave access room between the fence and the plants for routine fence maintenance.

"Solid" wood fences, such as those with closely spaced boards or pickets, provide privacy and a more formal backdrop than do "open" types (like split rail). They also offer more protection from wind in exposed sites. Reflected light and heat from white or light-colored fences can benefit plants in cool areas but could damage them in hot climates. Solid-wood fences also block air circulation, which means that the plants within may be more prone to disease problems.

Wrought iron is another classic choice for garden fencing. It lasts for ages, but you need either to paint it every few years or to let it turn rusty. Wrought-iron fences come in both simple and complex patterns that cast attractive shadows over your garden, especially in winter. Their openness doesn't provide much privacy, but it does allow for good air circulation around your plants, which is an asset. Wrought-iron fences can complement a wide variety of garden styles.

Stephanie Says

Over the Garden Gate

WHEN YOU ENCLOSE A GARDEN WITH FENCES, walls, or hedges, you also need to plan for access — often in the form of gates. Gates that contrast with their setting serve as an accent or focal point; those that blend in with their surroundings are much more subtle entrances and exits. See-through gates invite visitors to come in, which makes them ideal for front entrances or transitions between two garden areas. Solid gates, especially those too tall to see over, have a private or even somewhat forbidding quality; this makes them useful for creating "secret" gardens or concealing utility areas (where you keep your trash cans or your compost bins, for example).

Don't think you have to have a fence, wall, or hedge to have a gate. A small gate that is freestanding with just two posts creates the illusion that you are entering a completely different part of the garden and that there is definitely more to view. I have a simple gate set up like this as a transition between my front garden and the lawn and meadow areas beyond. It's fun to see how visitors are drawn to open the gate and step through, even though they could easily walk right around it. ✳

Walls and Hedges. Another way to divide garden spaces is with walls. Tall walls can either enclose a space or act as a division between two different spaces. Low walls serve the utilitarian purpose of retaining earth around planting beds or in areas where there is a change in grade level. Stone walls — either mortared together or dry-stacked — are a handsome choice where natural stone is plentiful. Other alternatives are brick, concrete retaining wall blocks, and stucco. Low walls (up to about 2 feet in height) are within the abilities of most do-it-yourself gardeners, especially when they're made from dry-stacked (unmortared) stone or commercial retaining wall blocks. Higher walls are best left to professionals, for safety as well as aesthetic reasons.

The "organic" way to eliminate fences and walls is to use hedges. These living walls lend themselves much more readily to curves than do rigid building materials, and you can keep them any height you want. Clipped hedges require the most maintenance but make an elegant background for formal gardens. Unclipped hedges are well suited to more casual settings (such as naturalistic gardens). They can provide flowers and fragrance, and they offer great shelter for wildlife as well. Hedges are typically much less expensive to install than are fences or walls, but you'll have to wait for the plants to fill in. Hedges will also compete with your perennials for water and nutrients, so you'll want to leave 2 feet or more between the garden and any hedge.

SHOWCASING STONE. A natural, dry-stacked stone retaining wall provides planting pockets for a variety of rock garden plants.

This pergola adds
height to the garden
and support for
plants, while at the
same time it offers an
open but shady
retreat for relaxing or
entertaining.

Trellises and Arbors.
Trellises have
their own special role to play in the garden,
particularly in small spaces. They add height
and vertical interest, so they help to draw
your eye upward, and they make excellent
supports for climbing plants. If you attach a
trellis to a wall or fence, use hinges at the
base so you can gently tip the trellis outward
when you need to maintain the wall behind
it. Trellises with closely spaced horizontal
bars work best for vines that climb by tendrils
or twining leaf stalks, such as clematis. Vines
with twining stems, like honeysuckles
(*Lonicera*), work better on structures with
strong vertical parts for them to wrap themselves around. You'll also want to match the

strength of the trellis to the vigor of the vine:
A fast-growing, woody-stemmed wisteria
needs a much sturdier support than does a
delicate hybrid clematis.

Arbors and arches can also be used to
support plants, act as entrances and exits
to different areas of the garden, and give the
illusion of increased depth in a smaller space.
They also provide an enchanting space to sit,
relax, and read in a shady place. An arbor set
away from your house can serve as a focal
point when it is covered attractively with
vines, and it can form a small seating area to
establish a mood of seclusion or intimacy.
A pergola can screen and divide areas on a
grander scale.

Ornaments: All in the Eye of the Beholder

From the time the first gardens came into existence, gardeners began adding practical features as well as their own personal touches. Early gardens included sundials for time-telling, structures for storing items and housing animals, and water for drinking, laundry, or bathing. Over time, these practical features have been transformed into more artistic creations. Today, gardens are most likely to have ornaments that reflect the gardener's taste or enhance the style and mood of the planting.

Choosing Art for Your Garden.

When it comes to choosing garden ornaments, the possibilities are endless. Statuary and sculptures, both large and small, range from inexpensive "found" objects, to readily available garden-center pieces, to elaborate large bronzes that cost thousands of dollars. Some gardeners utilize old farm implements, pieces of driftwood, and antique objects found at garage sales, flea markets, or antique emporiums.

You may select something that is both practical and attractive, such as a bench, pot, or urn, or something purely decorative. An ornament that is particularly special or meaningful to you can make a wonderful garden accent, to highlight an important area or simply make you smile as you walk by it every day. Or you might fling caution to the wind and go for something bizarre or quirky, like a garden gnome, a gargoyle, a cement alligator, or a gaggle of gazing balls. Garden signs can also be good for getting a chuckle out of visitors. Some of our favorites are "Bambi Sleeps Here", "Gardeners Know the Best Dirt", "Plant Thieves Will Be Composted", "Weeds for Sale — Pick Your Own", and "Visit Our Resident Woodchuck". No one can ever say gardeners lack a sense of playfulness and humor!

A TOUCH OF NOSTALGIA.
An antique water pump doesn't necessarily have to be in working order to play an important role in the garden.

REFLECTED
GLORY.

Consider colorful
ornaments that offer
a chance to capture
and disperse
reflections (at left), or
those with a touch of
whimsy, like this
handsome chicken
that is reflected in the
nearby faux window
fabricated from a
mirror (below).

Placing Garden Ornaments.

The worst way to use any garden accent is
to plunk it down in the first open space you
find. Generally, it has to serve some kind of
design purpose or otherwise make sense in
its surroundings to work effectively. A single
distinctive piece can stand alone as a focal
point or be part of an overall composition
with other objects, such as a bench next to a
water feature. You can also place it to hide
a bad view. Large ornaments with simple
lines typically look best against a pattern of
deciduous foliage; very detailed statues are
better displayed in front of a solid evergreen
background. Our favorite use of ornaments
is to have them nestled among the flowers
and foliage, where they seem to rise out of
the garden.

Of course, there are times when you might
decide to place an ornament in a totally unre-
lated setting, such as a flock of pink flamingos looking over a formal-looking bed of

ground covers or a classical Greek statue
smothered in a riot of cottage-garden flowers.
When all is said and done, the real test of
whether a particular ornament "works" is
how *you* feel about it. Until we hear of a gardener getting arrested by the Lawn Police for
flagrant disregard for good taste, that's our
advice, and we're sticking to it.

W E'VE COME A LONG WAY through the last few chapters: From setting your basic goals and putting down those ideas on paper to interpreting them with plants and embellishing them with the perfect finishing touches. So what else is there to talk about? Well, we've barely scratched the surface of particular kinds of gardens — to fit a particular site, to explore a certain color scheme, to celebrate a specific season, to evoke a distinct mood. Each kind of garden is a study unto itself, based on both practical and aesthetic considerations. So in the next part of the book, we'll investigate 20 different "theme" gardens, with exciting pictures and plans to get you inspired and down-and-dirty details to help you make your favorites a reality in your own yard. Ready to get growing?

part two

Putting Perennials to Work

Problem-Solving with Perennials

PERENNIALS ARE MORE than just pretty flowers; they can be perfectly practical, too. Sun or shade, wet soil or dry: You name the site, and you're sure to find perennials that can thrive there. Matching plants to the growing conditions you have to offer, rather than trying to change your site to fit the plants, is the surest way to create a perennial planting that will thrive with minimal fuss.

Solutions for Soggy Sites

YOU KNOW WHAT WE'RE talking about here: those low spots in your yard where the soil stays squishy long after a rain, and those boggy areas along pond edges and streambanks. Left to their own devices, wet sites tend to be maintenance headaches, as it's difficult to get a mower into them, and tall, weedy perennials and grasses tend to take off like gangbusters with all that moisture to draw from. Why not put that trouble spot to work for you and fill it with beautiful flowers instead?

Reflected serenely in a small dammed-up area, these irises and ferns thrive with wet feet.

Consider the Possibilities

Just as with any other challenging site, you have various options for coping with wet areas. In this case you can:

✴ Stop the water from getting (or settling) there in the first place;

✴ Build raised beds to improve the drainage of the root zone; or

✴ Choose plants that enjoy growing in the existing conditions.

Changing the way water flows on your property is a permanent solution but it's usually a costly one, involving heavy equipment and lots of labor to change the grade, break up compacted subsoil, or install drainage pipes. For most of us, building raised beds is a more practical option. There's still a cost factor, of course: for the topsoil you need to bring in (enough for at least a 6-inch-deep layer), for the material you need to build a "frame" to hold the soil in place (such as timbers, rocks, or bricks), and for the labor to construct the beds (if you don't have the time to do it yourself). The result, though, will be a handsome landscape feature that provides ideal growing conditions for a wide range of beautiful perennials.

But before you go to all that effort, please consider making the most of what you already have. Evenly moist soil provides perfect conditions for some stunning moisture-loving perennials that dry-soil gardeners would give their green thumb to grow. Put your money into plants instead of backhoes and trucked-in topsoil, and you can have a gorgeous garden filled with foliage and flowers even when the rest of your yard is gasping for rain.

Don't Dig in — Just Yet, Anyway

When it comes to getting a wet-site garden off to a good start, timing is everything. For an average-soil site, spring and fall are when to dig and plant, because rainfall is more dependable then. But if your soil is normally on the soggy side, you really don't need any more moisture than you already have. In this case, midsummer to early fall — when the summer sun has had a chance to dry out things a bit — may be the ideal time to get your plants in the ground. That way, you won't have to fight with sticky clay, and you'll do the least damage to the soil's natural structure. You'll probably want to water once or twice after planting to get your new garden off to a good start, but by the following spring, the plants will have a good enough root system to support themselves.

One other tip: Hold off on applying heavy mulches to wet-soil gardens; they'll just keep things even wetter, possibly promoting root rot and definitely encouraging slugs. But also keep in mind that weeds will seed into wet soil like crazy if you leave it uncovered. To get around this problem, try Stephanie's "fudge factor": Set your perennials a few inches closer than you usually would, so they'll fill in quickly and cover up any bare soil before weeds can get going.

Who Ya Gonna Call? Clay Busters!

Soil that's dependably moist all through the growing season is one thing, but what if your site is soggy in spring and bone-dry during the summer? You have the same three options that other wet-site gardeners do, even down to choosing plants that are naturally adapted to alternating wet and dry conditions. Dubbed "clay busters" by Neil Diboll, of Prairie Nursery in Westfield, Wisconsin, these tough-as-nails perennials are a perfect solution for heavy soils that cause daintier plants to turn up their toes and die. Here's a sampling of some top-notch clay busters that have proved themselves in Neil's test plantings:

Aster laevis (smooth aster)
A. novae-angliae (New England aster)
Baptisia australis (blue false indigo)
B. lactea (white false indigo)
Coreopsis lanceolata (lance-leaved coreopsis)
Dodecatheon media (shooting star)
Echinacea pallida and *E. purpurea* (purple coneflowers)
Eryngium yuccifolium (rattlesnake master)
Helianthus helianthoides (oxeye daisy)
Lychnis pycnostachya (prairie blazingstar)
Monarda fistulosa (bergamot)
Panicum virgatum (switch grass)
Parthenium integrifolium (wild quinine)
Penstemon digitalis (foxglove penstemon)
Ratibida pinnata (yellow coneflower)
Rudbeckia hirta and *R. subtomentosa* (black-eyed Susans)
Silphium laciniatum (compass plant)
Solidago rigida (stiff goldenrod)
Sorghastrum nutans (Indian grass)
Veronicastrum virginicum (Culver's root)

Let's Get
Our Feet Wet

Have a full-sun site that tends to be soggy all through the growing season? This island bed planting could be the perfect solution to your problem. It's packed with lush leaves and bright blooms to turn that trouble spot into an eye-catching accent from spring through fall.

Ample moisture supports vigorous growth from large-flowered plants, like the 'Gateway' Joe-Pye weed (*Eupatorium maculatum*) and 'Kopper King' hibiscus: Shrub-sized perennials that are large enough hold their own when planted in "drifts of one." To balance these bold beauties, we've surrounded them with drifts of ferny and grasslike foliage and narrow, spiky blooms for exciting contrast. But this garden is about more than aesthetics. It's also a haven for butterflies and beneficial insects!

PLANT LIST

1	*Astilbe* 'Deutschland'	3 plants
2	*A.* 'Diamont'	3 plants
3	*Camassia quamash* 'Orion'	6 bulbs
4	*Carex elata* 'Aurea'	6 plants
5	*Chelone lyonii* 'Hot Lips'	4 plants
6	*Eupatorium maculatum* 'Gateway'	1 plant
7	*Hibiscus* 'Kopper King'	2 plants
8	interplanted with *Primula veris*	10 plants
9	*Iris pseudacorus* 'Variegata'	6 plants
10	*Lobelia siphilitica* 'Blue Select'	6 plants
11	*Lysimachia punctata* 'Alexander'	3 plants
12	*Physostegia virginiana* 'Miss Manners'	3 plants
13	*Veronicastrum virginicum*	3 plants

PLANTING PLAN

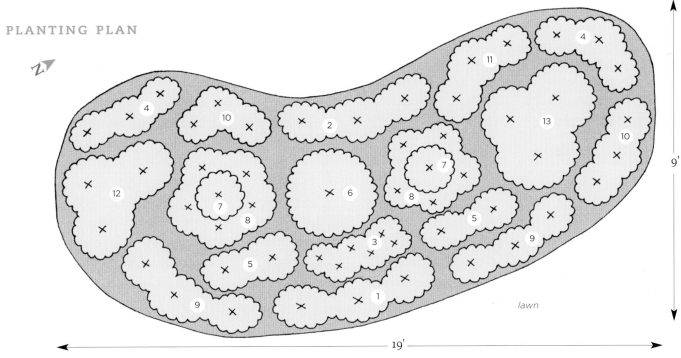

lawn

9'

19'

DESIGNER'S CHECKLIST

☐ **Think big.** Ample moisture encourages lush growth, so wet-soil perennials usually grow significantly taller than their drier cousins. That means the scale for a soggy-soil garden tends to be on the large side, so plan accordingly when you draw your design: Allow for large beds where tall plants won't look out of place.

☐ **Go for the bold.** Rose mallows *(Hibiscus)*, as used here, ligularias, and many other large-leaved perennials love sites with ample moisture, so be sure to make the most of them.

☐ **Toss in some fine foliage,** like that of astilbes, as well as slender, grassy leaves, such as those of sedges *(Carex)* and irises, for a terrific textural contrast with the bold-leaved plants.

☐ **Consider color.** Basing any design on two or three colors that you think look good together makes it a lot easier to focus your plant choices, but don't think you have to follow the same scheme throughout the growing season. This design is mostly blue and yellow in spring, white and yellow in early to midsummer, and blue, pink, and white in fall. Changing colors with the seasons is a great way to get extra zip out of even a small bed or border.

☐ **Try the layered look.** Unless you're planning a garden for a spectacular single-season display, include perennials that bloom at different times to spread out the show. In this design, for example, we suggest planting spring-blooming cowslip primroses around the base of the mallows (and they could go under the Joe-Pye weed, too). For even more early interest, scatter some seeds of water forget-me-not *(Myosotis scorpoides)* into the bed as well. Once these low-growers are done, their taller, summer-blooming partners will take over the show, followed by the biggest (and usually latest-blooming) species for late summer and fall.

Marvelous Moisture Lovers for Sun

Astilbe
(Astilbes)

Typically considered shade plants, astilbes can tolerate ample sunshine if their roots never dry out. Dense clumps of deeply dissected, rich green leaves look great season long; showy flower plumes attractive long after blooms fade. 'Deutschland' (to 2 feet tall and 1 foot wide) and 'Diamont' (30 to 40 inches tall and about 2 feet wide) are both pure white and flower from early to midsummer. ZONES 4–8.

ALTERNATIVES: Any white astilbe cultivar of similar height.

Camassia quamash 'Orion'
(Camassia)

Unlike most other bulbs, this beauty thrives in damp-soil sites, producing low clumps of grasslike foliage and upright, 12- to 18-inch stems with spikes of deep purple-blue flowers in late spring. Plant bulbs 6 inches apart. ZONES 4–8.

ALTERNATIVES: Another camassia species or cultivar, such as 'Blue Melody' (with cream-edged foliage) or C. leichtlinii.

Carex elata 'Aurea'
(Bowles' golden sedge)

Upright to arching, bright yellow blades thinly edged with green form graceful clumps about 18 to 24 inches tall and about 18 inches across in late spring and early summer. ZONES 5–8.

ALTERNATIVES: Tradescantia 'Sweet Kate'.

Chelone lyonii 'Hot Lips'
('Hot Lips' pink turtlehead)

Upright, reddish stems from 2 to 4 feet tall are topped with clusters of rosy pink blossoms from late summer to early fall; foliage has a reddish cast in spring but turns deep green for the summer. Clumps are 24 to 30 inches wide. ZONES 3–9.

ALTERNATIVES: Another turtlehead species or cultivar, 'Marshall's Delight' bee balm (Monarda 'Marshall's Delight'), or swamp milkweed (Asclepias incarnata).

Eupatorium maculatum 'Gateway'
('Gateway' Joe-Pye weed)

Perfect for the middle of an island bed or the back of a border, this 5- to 6-foot-tall, 2- to 3-foot-wide perennial produces upright, purplish red stems clad in whorled leaves featuring clusters of mauve-pink flowers from midsummer to early fall. ZONES 4–8.

ALTERNATIVES: Another Joe-Pye selection, such as lavender-pink 'Carin' or deeper purple 'Atropurpureum'.

Hibiscus 'Kopper King'
('Kopper King' mallow)

Shrubby clumps of lobed, burgundy-red leaves are accented with huge, light pink, red-eyed flowers from mid- or late summer to early fall; clumps are 3 to 4 feet tall and 3 feet wide. ZONES 4–9.

ALTERNATIVES: Another mallow hybrid or H. moscheutos cultivar of same height range with pinkish or white flowers, such as lavender-pink 'Fantasia' or white 'Everest White'.

Iris pseudacorus 'Variegata'
(Variegated yellow flag)

Showy, 1- to 2-foot-wide, gradually expanding clumps of upright green leaves are showily striped with yellow in spring; they turn mostly green by summer. Bright yellow flowers bloom atop 3- to 5-foot stems in late spring to early summer. ZONES 3–9.

ALTERNATIVES: Variegated sweet flag (Acorus calamus 'Variegatus').

Lobelia siphilitica 'Blue Select'
('Blue Select' blue lobelia, a.k.a. 'Blue Selection')

From late summer into fall, the upright, 3-foot stems produce spikes of blue flowers over bright green leaves in clumps 1 to 2 feet across. ZONES 3–8.

ALTERNATIVES: The straight species (L. siphilitica).

Lysimachia punctata 'Alexander'
('Alexander' yellow loosestrife)

Upright clumps of creamy white-and-green leaves showcase starry yellow flowers from early to mid- or late summer; about 2 feet tall, and can quickly spread to a similar width. ZONES 4–8.

ALTERNATIVES: The straight species (L. punctata).

Physostegia virginiana 'Miss Manners'
('Miss Manners' obedient plant)

Much less of a spreader than the species, this cultivar truly lives up to its name. Upright clumps to 30 inches tall but only 1 foot wide produce spikes of bright white flowers throughout summer into early fall. ZONES 4–8.

ALTERNATIVES: White-flowered blue lobelia (L. siphilitica 'Alba') or white turtlehead (Chelone glabra).

Primula veris
(Cowslip primrose)

Rosettes of bright green leaves sport clusters of nodding, bright yellow blossoms through spring; clumps are 6 to 8 inches tall and wide. ZONES 4–8.

ALTERNATIVES: Common primrose (P. vulgaris).

Veronicastrum virginicum
(Culver's root)

Narrow, upright clumps produce slender spikes of white blossoms from mid- to late summer over whorls of narrow, deep green leaves; 4 to 6 feet tall and 2 feet across. ZONES 3–8.

ALTERNATIVES: 'Ice Ballet' swamp milkweed (Asclepias incarnata 'Ice Ballet').

Made for the Shade

W HEREVER THERE ARE TREES and shrubs, there is (or eventually will be) shade. For some people, the gradual transition from a sunny yard to a shady one is a welcome change; for others, it's a gardening nightmare. If you're not sure what to do with an increasingly shady yard, or if you've bought a home with an already mature landscape, you have two options: Call a tree service and say good-bye to your shade for good or make the best of what you have and discover the many joys of shade gardening.

Getting a Handle on Shade

There are as many ways to describe shade as there are gardeners who have it. Dense shade, partial shade, light shade, filtered shade: What does it all mean? Well, the most basic definitions relate to the number of hours of direct sun a particular site receives.

❋ Full sun: At least 8 hours of full sun a day

❋ Partial shade (or partial sun): Four to 8 hours of direct sun a day

❋ Full shade: Less than 4 hours of sun a day

Carefully chosen and laid out foliage in a variety of colors and textures combine dramatically in this welcoming shady entrance.

That's a fair place to start, but these general guidelines leave a lot to be desired. For instance, perennials that supposedly need full sun may do well in a site with only 6 hours of afternoon sun; full-shade plants may do fine with 5 hours of morning sun (technically partial shade in both cases). Sun intensity also plays a part in the equation: Perennials that thrive in all-day sun in Vermont or Oregon will fry to a crisp with more than a few hours of strong southern sunshine. Then there's the issue of what is causing the shade. A building or solid fence casts heavier shade than does a piece of lattice or a tiny-leaved tree that allows lots of sunlight to filter through. And as if all this weren't enough, sun and shade amounts on a single site can change dramatically over the course of the growing season, as the sun changes position, as well as over a period of years, as trees and shrubs become larger and leafier.

So what's a gardener to do? The standard recommendation is to carefully observe your planned garden site over the course of one growing season, making notes all the while of where the sun strikes and how many hours of light the site gets over the course of each day. And that's excellent advice, if you're willing to follow it — but honestly, how many of us have the discipline to do that? Fortunately, it's entirely possible to create a pleasing shade garden without taking endless sun and shade readings. The key is to base your design on adaptable perennials that can tolerate a wide variety of light conditions, then experiment with a few new plants each year to see how they perform in your particular site. And if something you'd really like to grow doesn't succeed at first, don't be afraid

EVER WONDER WHY SHADY GARDENS typically aren't as flower-filled as sunny ones? It's simple: Making flowers takes lots of energy, which plants get from sunlight. The less sun that's available, the less energy the plants have and the fewer flowers they produce. That doesn't mean you won't have flowers at all, of course; it's just that most of them won't be as big and abundant as you'd find in sun-filled sites — at least during the summer and fall. (Gardens under deciduous trees can be absolutely spectacular in spring, when many woodland wildflowers take advantage of the ample light available before the trees leaf out and block the sun.)

Focus on Foliage

In exchange, shady beds provide ample opportunity to create intricate interplays of foliage textures and colors: an exciting challenge for any adventurous perennial gardener. And when it comes to my favorite foliage colors for shade, silvers and golds are really where it's at! In a sunny site, golden foliage can simply look sick unless you make a special effort to integrate it into your borders (by repeating it often, for instance, or using it in masses). But in a darker area, even a single yellow-leaved plant will look like a pool of sunshine lighting up the gloom.

So what's the bottom line? Take a good look at the leaves of any plant you're considering and ask yourself if you'd buy it even if it never flowered. If you love the leaves enough to say "Who cares?" about the flowers, you'll never be disappointed in the way your garden looks, and the blooms that do show up will be a bonus. ✳

to try again . . . and again. As the light levels on your site change over the years, you might find just the right spot where that special treasure can thrive. This sort of fine-tuning is what really brings your on-paper design to life, allowing you to grow and change along with your garden.

With golden Hakone grass (*Hakonechloa macra* 'Aureola'), Japanese painted fern (*Athyrium niponicum* var. *pictum*), and dwarf astilbes, there's no lack of color in this shady garden.

Dealing with Spaces under Trees and Shrubs

When you're trying to garden under trees and shrubs, you'll quickly notice that different plants cast different types of shade. Those with large leaves, for example, such as many maples (*Acer*), tend to cast heavier shade than do little-leaved trees like birches (*Betula*). The dappled shade cast by the latter group gives you the widest range of planting options.

If you're starting a new landscape from scratch, do your research before you plant any tree to find out what kind of shade it casts.

Better yet, visit an arboretum to see for yourself how large your potential addition can get and what kinds of plants grow well underneath. Choosing trees that cast only light shade will give you the widest range of gardening options for the future.

What if you're stuck with someone else's choices in an established landscape? Judicious thinning by qualified tree-care professionals can dramatically brighten up a heavily shaded lot, and will improve the health of your trees as well. This is not a permanent solution, however, as the canopy will eventually fill in again. Consider removing any crowded or poorly placed trees, or you can focus your shade-busting efforts closer to ground level. Shrubs are a lot easier to reach than trees for routine pruning, and most look better with some regular thinning anyway. Some are even tough enough to spring back from drastic renovation — in other words, being cut back nearly to the ground — if they start taking up too much valuable gardening space. Chastetrees *(Vitex),* elderberries *(Sambucus),* forsythias, and weigelas are just a few good candidates for this tough-love treatment.

Evergreens are a special challenge, because the soil tends to be dry beneath them, and they cast very dense shade. In most cases, you're best off not even attempting to garden right under them; just rake out the buildup of needles every few years, and toss in some compost or other organic mulch to help keep the soil in good shape. If a tree has branches all the way to the ground, do *not* limb it up. (That's garden-speak for cutting off the lower branches.) Enjoy its natural beauty as a back-drop for your perennials, instead of spoiling its shape to create a garden bed where peren-nials probably won't thrive anyway.

If you've inherited an evergreen that has already been limbed up, you have some options:

✳ Spread bark mulch underneath, then add some chairs to create a shady sitting area.

✳ Dress up the area underneath with contain-ers of shade-tolerant perennials and annuals. Be sure to water them regularly.

✳ If the tree is just plain ugly or has outlived its usefulness, consider removing it. You don't wear clothes from 40 or 50 years ago, and your yard shouldn't either.

Nan's Notebook

I AGREE WITH STEPHANIE 100 percent about the importance of foliage in creating great shade gardens, with one warning: Watch out how you use perennials with leaves, like maroon, black, and brown. I'm a big fan of these colors, especially for creating contrasts with silvers and golds, but if you use them in masses (three or more in one spot, depending on the size of the plants), you risk creating a "black-hole" effect. From a distance, these dark colors blend right into the soil or mulch, and it may look as though you left big gaps among your lighter-colored perennials. This is less of a concern if you're using dark foliage where it will be seen close up: right next to a path or bench, for example. ✳

Look to the Leaves

A Shady Sitting Area

WHAT COULD BE MORE WELCOMING on a hot summer day than a shady backyard sitting area surrounded by crisp white blooms and cool silvery foliage? This simple but elegant grouping features a variety of low-growing perennials, ferns, and ground covers to provide easy-care beauty from mid- or late spring well into fall. It's designed as an island bed, but you could easily modify the layout to surround a shaded low deck or patio; because none of the plants (except the trees, of course) is more than 2 feet tall, nothing will block the view of your yard beyond.

In any setting, relying on masses of low-growing perennials and groundcovers is a great way to enjoy season-long color, while keeping maintenance to an absolute minimum: very little weeding, watering, mulching, and fertilizing — and *no* staking!

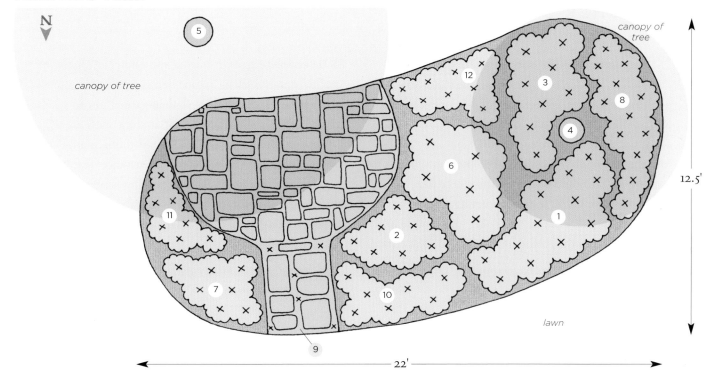

N

canopy of tree

canopy of tree

12.5'

lawn

22'

PLANT LIST

1	*Aruncus aethusifolius*	12 plants
2	*Astilbe* 'Ellie'	7 plants
3	*Athyrium niponicum* var. *pictum*	8 plants
4	*Cornus* x *rutgersensis* Stellar Pink	1 plant
5	*Gleditsia triacanthos* f. *inermis*	1 plant
6	*Hosta* 'Patriot'	5 plants
7	*Lamiastrum galeobdolon* 'Herman's Pride'	7 plants
8	*Lamium maculatum* 'Purple Dragon'	12 plants
9	*Mazus reptans*	6 plants
10	*Pulmonaria* 'Silver Streamers'	7 plants
11	*Tiarella* 'Dark Star'	7 plants
12	T. 'Oakleaf'	8 plants

DESIGNER'S CHECKLIST

☐ **Bring light into the darkness.** For both flowers and foliage, the same rule applies: The darker the area you're working with, the lighter the colors you need. Red astilbes, for example, look fine in the light shade out toward the tips of tree branches, but they'll fade into the gloom as you get closer to the trunk; here, white, pale pink, and peach are the colors that will catch your eye. If you're contemplating a color but aren't sure it will work for your site, take a piece of cloth or fabric in that color and see how it looks there.

☐ **Be consistent with hardscape choices.** Whenever you incorporate paths, patios, steps, and other hardscape features into your perennial garden, try to stick to just a few similar materials: flat stone with gravel, brick with cement pavers, and wood-timber paths with wooden decking. (This design, for instance, features a flagstone patio with flagstone stepping-stones.) Matching materials as closely as possible gives your project a well-planned, professional look that's always visually appealing.

☐ **Try textural contrasts.** Sure, color is an obvious factor to consider when putting together perennials, but it's not the only one: Contrasting textures are another good jumping-off point for exciting combinations, especially in shady sites. The lacy leaves and brushy flower spikes of some foamflowers (*Tiarella*), for example, are perfect partners for broad, flat hosta foliage; so are the feathery fronds of ferns.

☐ **Think foliage first, flowers second.** We simply can't say this enough: The key to any successful perennial design is using lots of plants with great-looking foliage. Leaves need less maintenance than flowers, look good for most (if not all) of the growing season, and are a dependable source of color in sites that are too shady for an abundance of bloom.

☐ **Make the most of spring sunshine.** Take a tip from Mother Nature and get your flower fix in the spring, when sunshine is abundant under deciduous trees. Tuck in lots of crocus, scillas, and other early bulbs, and enjoy loads of color just when you need it most. They'll go dormant about the same time the trees leaf out, and they won't care how much shade the site gets in summer and fall. As a bonus, the expanding leaves of the perennials will quickly cover up the yellowing foliage as the bulbs die back.

Aruncus aethusifolius
(Dwarf goat's beard)

Looking much like a dwarf astilbe, this little charmer grows in clumps of deeply dissected, dark green foliage 6 to 8 inches tall and 10 inches across. Creamy white flower spikes 12 to 14 inches tall appear in early summer, and the seedheads remain attractive through the rest of the summer (or you can remove them). ZONES 4–8.
ALTERNATIVES: Snowdrop anemone (*Anemone sylvestris*) or any foamflower (*Tiarella*).

Athyrium niponicum var. *pictum*

Astilbe 'Ellie'
('Ellie' astilbe)

Blooming in midsummer, this excellent selection has much denser flower clusters than those of most other white astilbes, with lacy, deep green leaves that spread to 18 inches; it's 24 to 30 inches tall in bloom. ZONES 4–8.
ALTERNATIVES: Any other white astilbe in the same size range, such as 'Bridal Veil' or 'Deutschland'.

Athyrium niponicum var. pictum
(Japanese painted fern)

Low-spreading mounds of silvery gray fronds on arching, maroon stems look good from late spring to frost; they grow 18 inches tall and 2 feet across. ZONES 4–9.
ALTERNATIVES: Any cultivar of this species, such as 'Silver Falls' or 'Ursula's Red', or the more upright hybrid 'Ghost'.

Hosta 'Patriot'
('Patriot' hosta)

This hosta sports broad green leaves with wide, pure white margins; clumps are 1 foot tall and 3 feet wide. Lavender flowers bloom atop stalks to 18 inches tall in early- to midsummer. ZONES 3–9.
ALTERNATIVES: Any white-variegated hosta of a similar size, such as 'Minute Man' or 'Remember Me'.

Lamiastrum galeobdolon 'Herman's Pride'
('Herman's Pride' lamiastrum, a.k.a. *Lamium galeobdolon* 'Herman's Pride')

Dense, 12- to 18-inch-wide clumps of upright, 10- to 12-inch stems are clad in bright silver, green-veined leaves. Bright yellow flowers bloom in late spring. ZONES 3–9.
ALTERNATIVES: Any silver-leaved lamium or pulmonaria.

Tiarella cordifolia

Lamium maculatum 'Purple Dragon'
('Purple Dragon' lamium)

Clusters of large, bright purplish pink blooms form in spring over 12- to 18-inch-wide carpets of silver-and-green leaves; height is 6 inches. ZONES 3–8.
ALTERNATIVES: 'Beacon Silver', 'White Nancy', or any other silver-leaved cultivar.

Mazus reptans
(Creeping mazus)

A ground-hugging, 2-inch-tall, fast-spreading creeper with small, purplish blue blooms in spring, mazus is great between stepping-stones because it can tolerate some foot traffic. ZONES 3–9.
ALTERNATIVES: Creeping Jenny (*Lysimachia nummularia*).

Pulmonaria 'Silver Streamers'
('Silver Streamers' pulmonaria)

Clumps of long, silvery leaves that are about 10 inches tall and 12 to 18 inches across, with clusters of pink buds and blue blooms atop 1-foot-tall stems in early- to mid-spring. ZONES 3–8.
ALTERNATIVES: Any other cultivar with silver-splashed foliage.

Tiarella
(foamflower)

These top-notch shade perennials with foliage in a wide range of shapes, often with maroon or deep purple markings, produce brushy flower spikes to 1 foot tall through spring. Many have attractive reddish leaf tints from fall into winter. **'Dark Star'** boasts star-shaped, dark-centered leaves and pinkish white flowers; T. **'Oakleaf'** has broad, bright green, three-lobed leaves and white blooms. Both form spreading clumps 6 inches tall and (eventually) 2 feet wide. ZONES 4–9.
ALTERNATIVES: Any cultivar of your choice.

Soaked in Sunshine

AMPLE SUNSHINE means ample opportunity for fantastic, flower-filled perennial gardens. But if you're just starting out — or if you're looking to add yet another garden to your existing collection — the wide range of options you have with a sunny site can make it difficult to decide where to begin. We've got some thoughts on that very topic we'd like to share with you, as well as a few pointers for making sure your perennials aren't getting more sun than they need.

Start with the Soil

No matter where you garden — sun or shade, wet or dry, North or South — giving your perennials healthy, root-friendly soil will make the difference between a ho-hum planting and a knock-your-socks-off garden. You can create the most meticulously planned design anyone's ever seen, but if you don't take the time to improve the soil before you plant, you're virtually guaranteed to be dis-

appointed in the results. On the other hand, even a not-so-hot design will turn into a decent-looking garden if the plants are happy where you put them. It all comes down to the soil, and it's up to you to provide the site preparation that will be best for your plants.

It's a simple fact that construction of most homes starts with a piece of earth-moving equipment scraping the topsoil off to one side of the site. If you're lucky, the builder puts back all that soil onto your site, but you can't assume that's the case; in a new development, especially, you may be lucky to get back just a few inches of topsoil spread over the construction-compacted subsoil. That can be enough to get a decent lawn established, but deeper-rooted plants (like most perennials) simply aren't going to thrive there without a little help.

And don't assume your soil's fine just because your house has been around for a while, either. Unless you've already put in a few gardens and know firsthand what's under the surface, you too could have inadequate topsoil, compacted subsoil, or even long-buried construction debris to deal with.

So what's the answer? Actually, you have two basic two options: Either dig down or build up. Digging the soil deeply (down at least a foot), then spreading a 3-inch layer of compost on top and working it in, can go a long way toward loosening up compaction, improving drainage, and building soil fertility as well. Building raised beds — "frames" of rocks or timbers with a deep layer of compost-enriched topsoil — provides similar benefits without all of the heavy-duty digging. Both approaches provide loose, rich soil that

Stephanie Says

WHEN IT COMES TO FOUNDATION PLANTINGS, think outside the box — and the cube and the "green meatball", too. After all, there's no law that says you have to surround your home with boring evergreen shrubs tightly clipped into eccentric shapes. There are lots of other options, including compact deciduous shrubs that can offer beautiful blooms, lovely foliage, showy fruits, or fantastic fall color. I have included a few of my favorites in this design, but they are just the beginning. Combine colorful shrubs of your choice with your favorite perennials, and you'll create a foundation planting that will complement your home instead of just cover it up. ✳

encourages good root growth, and that leads to naturally healthy, vigorous perennials.

Too Much of a Good Thing?

Once you've taken care of the below-ground parts of your plants, they'll be in good shape to take advantage of the sunshine the site has to offer. Depending on where you live, though, all that sun may be more than they can handle. Those of you in the South know that many plants commonly described as needing full sun — like campions *(Lychnis)* and many irises — actually do best in light shade in your climate. Pale yellow and white, thin-petaled flowers can also be damaged by strong sunshine where deeper colors of the same perennial perform just fine.

Even in more temperate areas, not all sun-loving perennials are created equal. Many bee balms *(Monarda)* and bellflowers *(Campanula)*, for example, thrive in full sun as long as the soil stays evenly moist throughout the growing season; if dry spells are common in the summer, these plants do better with at least a bit of shade.

Some signs of too much sun are a brownish cast to the leaves, crispy leaf edges, scorched or washed-out blooms, and frequent wilting, as well as overall poor growth. If you notice these symptoms on already planted perennials, try moving them to a site with light all-day shade or morning sun and afternoon shade. Water them well and they should recover. To avoid problems before planting, do your research carefully as you prepare the plant list for your design, and situate sun-sensitive perennials on the north or east side of taller companions to give them a bit of shade during the hottest part of the day.

If you're blessed with a sunny spot, you'll be able to carpet the area with a wide variety of colorful perennials and shrubs.

^A Sun-Splashed Front-Yard Garden

WHO SAYS A FRONT YARD has to be plain green lawn? Even a small property can sparkle with spectacular color from spring through fall, thanks to this classic double-border design. It's filled with an assortment of long-flowering perennials that thrive in a sunny, well-drained site with a minimum of care (just a few minutes of removing the spent blossoms every few days to keep the borders looking tidy). As a bonus, many of these perennials make great cut flowers, so you can easily snip a few on your way into the house to brighten your dinner table.

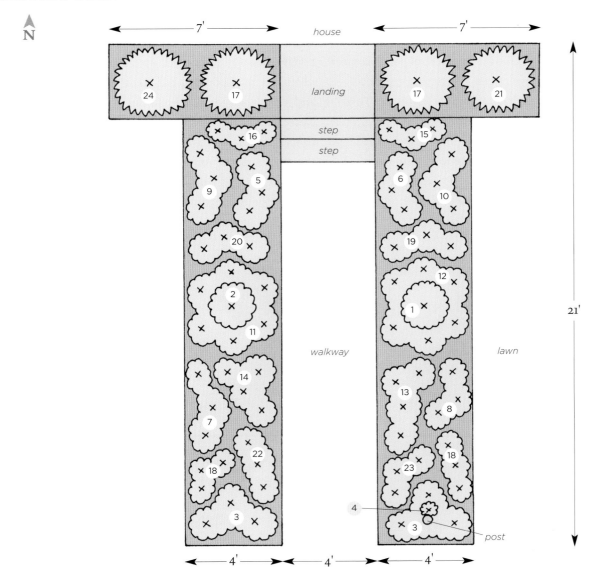

PLANT LIST

1	*Caryopteris* x *clandonensis* 'Dark Knight'	1 plant
2	*C.* x *clandonensis* 'Longwood Blue'	1 plant
3	*Ceratostigma plumbaginoides*	6 plants
4	*Clematis* 'Henryi'	1 plant
5	*Coreopsis verticillata* 'Moonbeam'	3 plants
6	*C. verticillata* 'Zagreb'	3 plants
7	*Echinacea purpurea* 'Kim's Knee High'	3 plants
8	*E. purpurea* 'Ruby Star'	3 plants
9	*Geranium* 'Brookside'	3 plants
10	*G.* 'Rozanne'	3 plants
11	*Hemerocallis* 'Double Cutie'	6 plants
12	*H.* 'Happy Returns'	6 plants
13	*Heuchera* 'Harmonic Convergence'	4 plants
14	*H.* 'Montrose Ruby'	4 plants
15	*Leucanthemum* x *superbum* 'Little Princess'	3 plants
16	*L.* x *superbum* 'Snowcap'	3 plants
17	*Rosa* 'The Fairy'	2 plants
18	*Rudbeckia fulgida* var. *sullivantii* 'Goldsturm'	6 plants
19	*Salvia nemorosa* 'East Friesland'	3 plants
20	*Salvia* x *sylvestris* 'May Night'	3 plants
21	*Syringa pubescens* subsp. *patula* 'Miss Kim'	1 plant
22	*Veronica spicata* 'Blue Fox'	3 plants
23	*V. spicata* 'Icicles'	3 plants
24	*Viburnum carlesii* 'Compactum'	1 plant

DESIGNER'S CHECKLIST

☐ **Take color cues from existing features.** To tie a perennial planting visually into the rest of your property, include some flowers and foliage that repeat colors in your house, fencing, or outdoor furniture. This is an especially good idea for a front-yard planting, where most people will view it from the street with your home as a backdrop. For example, echo white window trim with Shasta daisies, as in this design, or you could complement a white picket fence with white-variegated ornamental grasses.

☐ **Don't bite off more than you can chew.** It's easy to get led astray by gorgeous pictures of huge, flower-filled perennial borders, but don't get carried away and make your perennial planting too big to care for easily, especially if it's your first garden. You may want to try just one side of this plan to start with, then add the other side the following season. It's always possible to expand a small garden, but it's another matter to cut down once you've put time, effort, and money into one that's bigger than you can handle.

☐ **Narrow borders make for easier maintenance.** It's true that borders at least 6 feet wide give you plenty of space to play with different heights and combinations, but they can be difficult to maintain. (If you've ever found yourself balancing precariously on one foot while trying to snip out a dead bloom in the center of a big border, you know what we mean.) Each of the 4-foot-wide borders in this plan is edged by the entry path on one side and lawn on the other, so it's a snap to reach in from either direction to deadhead or cut back any perennial that needs it.

☐ **Keep paths and walkways clear.** It's fine to allow front-of-the-border plants to spill onto a path a bit, but don't force your family to fight their way to the front door. Plants that creep or flop more than a few inches onto a walkway can make for unpredictable footing, soak your clothes when you brush by them after a rain, and bring you closer to bees, wasps, and other insects than you want to be. Instead, stick with compact cultivars or naturally low-growing plants closest to main access routes, and be prepared to snip wayward leaves and shoots as necessary.

Caryopteris x clandonensis
(Caryopteris)

Bushy clumps grow to 3 feet tall and 2 to 3 feet across, with elongated, gray-green leaves and clusters of purple-blue flowers in late summer and early fall. May need a bit of afternoon shade in hot climates. Technically, this is a shrub, but caryopteris is usually sold with and grown as a perennial. **'Dark Knight'** has very dark blue blooms; **'Longwood Blue'** is more purplish blue. ZONES 5–9.

ALTERNATIVES: Any other caryopteris cultivar, such as 'First Choice', or English lavender (*Lavandula angustifolia*).

Caryopteris x *clandonensis*
'Longwood Blue'

Ceratostigma plumbaginoides
(Plumbago, a.k.a. leadwort)

Clusters of true-blue blooms from late summer to mid-fall seem to float atop 8- to 10-inch-tall stems, with rich green leaves that turn shades of maroon in fall. Low, mounding plants spread 12 to 18 inches across. Plants leaf out late in spring, so interplant with crocus for early color. ZONES 5–9.

ALTERNATIVES: 'Blue Clips' Carpathian harebell (*Campanula carpatica* 'Blue Clips') or hardy ice plant (*Delosperma cooperi*).

Geranium

Coreopsis verticillata
(Thread-leaved coreopsis)

Dense mounds of narrow green leaves practically smothered in flat-faced, yellow to gold blooms in early to midsummer; will repeat bloom well into fall if deadheaded. Height and spread range from 1 to 3 feet. **'Moonbeam'** is usually 18 to 24 inches tall and wide, with butter-yellow blooms; **'Zagreb'** is about the same size but has golden yellow flowers. ZONES 3–9.

ALTERNATIVES: Another coreopsis of similar size, such as golden *C. grandiflora* 'Sunray'.

Echinacea purpurea
(Purple coneflower)

Sturdy, upright stems sport dark green leaves and are topped with bronze-centered, daisy-form flowers with rosy pink petals through the summer. Clumps are usually 2 to 4 feet tall and 18 to 24 inches across. **'Kim's Knee High'** is a compact selection (18 to 24 inches tall and wide). **'Ruby Star'** has more-horizontal and richer-colored petals on 36- to 40-inch stems. ZONES 3–8.

ALTERNATIVES: Any other cultivar, such as 'Bright Star' or compact white 'Kim's Mop Head'.

Geranium
(Hardy geraniums)

These mound-forming perennials come in a wide range of sizes, leaf shapes, and bloom colors.

'Brookside' has lacy leaves and bright blue flowers on clumps 18 inches tall and 24 inches wide; trim lightly after the first flush of bloom to encourage repeat flowering into fall. ZONES 5–8.

'Rozanne' is more purplish blue and blooms from early summer into fall; 12 to 18 inches tall and 18 to 24 inches across. ZONES 4–8.

ALTERNATIVES: Another geranium cultivar, such as *G. clarkei* 'Kashmir Purple', or a balloon flower (*Platycodon grandiflorus*) cultivar, such as 'Double Blue' or 'Hakone Blue'.

Echinacea purpurea

Hemerocallis
(Dwarf daylilies)

It's hard to imagine a sunny garden without at least a few daylilies. Their strappy foliage looks excellent for most of the growing season, and when you choose repeat-blooming cultivars, you can enjoy flowers from midsummer well into fall. **'Double Cutie'** has greenish yellow, double blooms over several months; 12 to 15 inches tall and 18 inches wide. **'Happy Returns'** is a bright lemon yellow selection with particularly good repeat bloom; 12 to 18 inches tall and 18 inches wide. ZONES 5–9.

ALTERNATIVES: Another dwarf daylily in the same height range, such as 'Eenie Weenie' or 'Stella d'Oro'.

Hemerocallis 'Stella d'Oro'

Heuchera
(Heucheras)

These clump-forming perennials have lovely lobed leaves in many shades of purple, brown, and green, often attractively mottled with silver. Airy clusters of small white or pink flowers appear atop wiry stems (usually 18 to 24 inches tall) in late spring and early summer. **'Harmonic Convergence'** has purple-brown leaves heavily shaded with silver; **'Montrose Ruby'** has deep reddish purple foliage with silver mottling. Foliage clumps of both are 1 foot tall and 18 inches across. ZONES 4–9.

ALTERNATIVES: Any other purple-hued heuchera.

Leucanthemum x superbum
(Shasta daisy)

White-petaled, golden-centered daisies are borne on upright stems. The foliage is a nice deep green; height ranges from 1 to 3 feet tall and plants grow 18 to 24 inches across. Most flowers appear in early to midsummer, but deadheading can encourage repeat bloom into fall. **'Little Princess'** has 2- to 3-inch-wide flowers on plants to 12 inches tall and 18 inches across; **'Snowcap'** is similar but a few inches taller (to about 15 inches). ZONES 4–8.

ALTERNATIVES: 'Silver Princess' or 'Snow Lady'.

Rudbeckia fulgida var. sullivantii 'Goldsturm'
('Goldsturm' orange coneflower)

Twelve- to 18-inch-wide clumps of deep green foliage support upright, 24- to 30-inch stems of golden yellow, brown-centered daisies from midsummer to early fall. ZONES 3–9.

ALTERNATIVES: *R. fulgida* var. *fulgida* is similar but more compact (18 to 24 inches tall) and blooms into October.

Salvia
(Perennial salvia)

Spiky, purple-blue blooms appear from early to midsummer, often with repeat bloom if you deadhead regularly; height and spread range from 18 to 36 inches. **S.** *nemorosa* **'East Friesland'** has deep purple-blue blooms, and **S. x** *sylvestris* **'May Night'** is very deep blue; both are 18 inches tall and wide. ZONES 4–8.

ALTERNATIVES: 'Blue Queen' or 'Caradonna'.

Veronica spicata
(Spike speedwell)

Another useful spiky-flowered perennial, this one is clad in blue, pink, or white flowers from late spring to midsummer (or later) on upright plants anywhere from 1 to 3 feet tall and 18 to 24 inches across. **'Blue Fox'** has light purplish blue spikes and **'Icicles'** is white; both are about 18 to 22 inches tall and wide. ZONES 3–8.

ALTERNATIVES: Another spike speedwell selection, such as 'Blue Spires', or the variety *alba* (for white flowers).

Rudbeckia

Dry-Soil Sites

ONE-DRY SOIL does make gardening a challenge, but with careful plant selection and good site preparation, plus a little design know-how, you can turn a parched problem area into an impressive landscape accent.

Use These Clues

If summer dry spells occur regularly in your area, or your soil is so sandy that any rain you get drains through before it helps your plants, it's best to stick with perennials that are naturally adapted to these dry conditions — unless you enjoy spending your summers with a garden hose attached to your hand!

✳ Look at the leaves. Your perennials' foliage color and texture is a good clue as to their water needs. Those with very narrow leaves (like grasses) and those with succulent leaves (like sedums) are designed to minimize water loss through their foliage. Gray or silvery foliage (like that of artemisias and lavenders) is another good clue to look for.

✳ Get to the root of the matter. Other clues to drought tolerance are out of sight. Perennials with fine, close-to-the-surface roots, such as hardy ice plants (*Delosperma*) and rock roses (*Helianthemum*), can soak up even the lightest rainfall before the soil dries out. Perennials like daylilies (*Hemerocallis*) and torch lilies (*Kniphofia*) depend on thickened, moisture-storing roots to get them through dry spells. The roots of others, such as butterfly weed (*Asclepias tuberosa*) and false indigos (*Baptisia*) go deep to seek summer moisture.

✳ Do a background check. Perennials native to dry climates are a natural choice for parched-soil sites. Thymes, oreganos, lavenders, and other herbs that thrive on Mediterranean hillsides, for instance, adapt readily to fast-draining soil in other regions, too. And plants native to dry parts of your own region are adapted to your temperatures as well as to your normal rainfall patterns.

Coping with Slopes

Sloping sites make the dry-soil issue more of a challenge. Even where rainfall is dependable, soil on a slope may stay parched, with most water running off before it soaks in (often carrying precious topsoil with it). A low wall (6 to 12 inches high) across the slope is a great solution to the problem, slowing down the flow of water, as well as preventing erosion. A well-built wall also serves as an access path, giving you secure footing for weeding and other maintenance tasks.

Many colorful rock garden plants thrive in sunny, gravelly spots, like those of their native origin.

Making the Grade

THIS SIMPLE BUT EFFECTIVE DESIGN is planned for a sunny slope, but the basic idea could work with any dry area where you need a band or two of color — in the strip between a street and the sidewalk, for example. These tough-as-nails perennials will provide plenty of color and texture from late spring through most of the fall, primarily in pinks, white, and blues for summer and sunny golds and tawny grasses in fall. For an extra burst of bright blooms, feel free to tuck in lots of crocuses, species tulips, and other small bulbs to add color from late winter through spring.

N

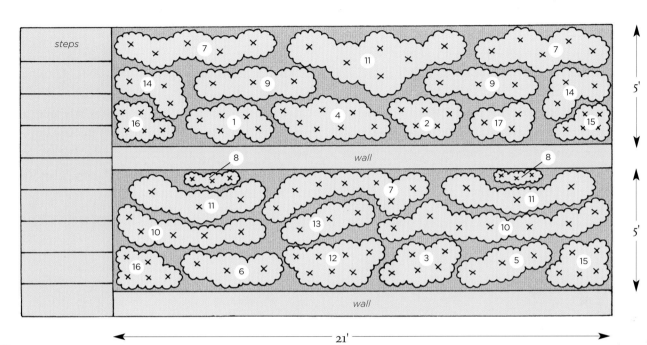

5'

5'

steps

wall

wall

21'

PLANT LIST

1	*Allium senescens* var. *glaucum*	5 plants
2	*A. thunbergii* 'Ozawa'	5 plants
3	*Armeria maritima* 'Rubrifolia'	5 plants
4	*Dianthus* 'Mountain Mist'	7 plants
5	*Gypsophila repens* 'Alba'	3 plants
6	*G. repens* 'Rosea'	3 plants
7	*Helianthus* 'Low Down'	17 plants
8	*Lilium* 'Pink Pixie'	6 bulbs
9	*Nepeta* x *faassenii* 'Blue Wonder'	6 plants
10	*N. racemosa* 'Little Titch'	12 plants
11	*Pennisetum alopecuroides* 'Hameln'	12 plants
12	*Salvia nemorosa* 'Marcus'	7 plants
13	*Sedum* 'Ruby Glow'	3 plants
14	*S.* 'Vera Jameson'	6 plants
15	*Thymus serpyllum* 'Pink Chintz'	10 plants
16	*T. serpyllum* 'Snowdrift'	10 plants
17	*Veronica spicata* 'Goodness Grows'	3 plants

DESIGNER'S CHECKLIST

☐ **Size up your options.** Drought-tolerant perennials are able to make the most of limited resources, although they typically aren't as tall and lush as those growing in evenly moist soil. But if you need tall plants, check out the many beautiful prairie plants that are naturally tolerant of dry sites. They tend to take a few years longer than other perennials to look their best, but once they have established a good root system, these hardy plants will thrive for years with only minimal maintenance, creating a dependable display of summer and fall color right at eye level.

☐ **Keep it short on slopes.** When you're choosing plants for a sloping site, stick with species and cultivars that are about 2 feet tall or shorter; any taller and they'll tend to flop onto each other. If the site slopes away from you, keep the shortest plants near the top; if it slopes toward you, use the taller ones at the top and place the short ones at the base.

☐ **Give grasses a try.** Many ornamental grasses are ideally suited for dry sites, and they come in an array of heights, habits, and colors to fit into almost any design. Keep in mind, though, that not everyone appreciates the natural beauty of these plants. If you're gardening in a highly visible site, such as a front yard garden, and you're worried about people thinking your grasses look weedy, consider using perennials with grasslike foliage instead, such as daylilies and torch lilies. Or go ahead and grow grasses anyway; chances are, your glorious-looking grasses will start a new trend in your neighborhood!

☐ **Show your softer side.** In any garden that includes hardscaping — steps, paths, walls, and similar structures — trailing and sprawling plants such as thymes and creeping baby's breath (*Gypsophila repens*) are invaluable for softening the "sharp" edges. You don't have to obliterate the edges, of course, unless you're going for a very casual, cottage-garden look; in a more formal setting, just a few plants leaning into a path or over a wall will break up an otherwise sterile expanse of paving.

Allium

(Ornamental onions)

These bulbous or rhizomatous perennials come in a range of heights and colors, generally with grasslike leaves and clustered blooms atop leafless stems. **A. senescens** var. **glaucum** (curly chives) grows in swirled, 6-inch-tall clumps of twisted blue-green leaves accented with pompons of lavender-pink flowers on 6- to 12-inch stems from mid- or late summer into fall; plants are 8 to 10 inches across. **A. thunbergii 'Ozawa'** is about 1 foot tall in bloom, with rosy pink flowers from mid- to late fall; clumps are 8 inches across. ZONES 4–8.

ALTERNATIVES: A. cyaneum, with blue flowers in early summer; or pink, summer-blooming 'Forescate' chives (A. schoenoprasum 'Forescate'), but deadhead the latter to prevent self-sowing.

Armeria maritima 'Rubrifolia'

(Red-leaved sea thrift)

Sea thrift forms tight, 4- to 6-inch-tall buns of slender, grasslike leaves that are reddish purple from fall through spring and red-tinted green in summer. Rose-pink flowers cluster atop 8-inch stems from late spring to early summer; spreads to 6 to 12 inches across. ZONES 4–8.

ALTERNATIVES: Another sea thrift species or cultivar.

Dianthus 'Mountain Mist'

('Mountain Mist' dianthus)

Dense, 6- to 8-inch-tall clumps of bright silvery blue, slender leaves look good all year, with fringed, pink, lightly fragrant flowers blooming on 1-foot stems in mid- to late spring, sometimes with repeat bloom later in the season. Spreads to about 1 foot across. Excellent heat and humidity tolerance. ZONES 3–8.

ALTERNATIVES: Another dianthus species or cultivar of a similar size, such as cheddar pink (D. gratianopolitanus).

Allium senescens var. *glaucum*

Gypsophila repens

(Creeping baby's breath)

Four- to 6-inch-tall mounds of gray-green foliage are covered with clouds of tiny white or pink blooms from early summer to fall. **'Alba'** is white; **'Rosea'** is pink. ZONES 3–9.

ALTERNATIVES: Snow-in-summer (Cerastium tomentosum).

Helianthus 'Low Down'

('Low Down' swamp sunflower)

Compact, upright clumps of narrow, green leaves are covered with bright yellow, dark-centered daisies in mid-fall; to 1 foot tall and about 18 inches across. ZONES 6–9.

ALTERNATIVES: A low-growing coreopsis, such as Coreopsis grandiflora 'Baby Sun' or 'Early Sunrise'.

Lilium 'Pink Pixie'

('Pink Pixie' Asiatic lily)

Upright, 12- to 18-inch stems support yellow-centered, pink-and-white blooms in midsummer. Plant bulbs 6 inches deep and 6 to 8 inches apart in fall. ZONES 4–8.

ALTERNATIVES: Another compact lily, like 'Blushing Elf' or 'Denia', or pink rain lily (Zephyranthes grandiflora) in Zones 7–9.

Nan's Notebook

Planting Pointers for Dry Sites

WHEN IT COMES TIME TO TURN A DRY-SITE DESIGN INTO REALITY, I've always had the best luck when I've timed the planting for early spring or (even better) early to mid-fall, when rain tends to be more abundant. And if time and materials are abundant as well, I try to add plenty of organic matter to the soil before planting. A 2- to 3-inch layer of compost worked into the top 6 to 8 inches of soil is my goal, although I often don't have quite that much energy or organic matter available. On a sloping site, extensive digging or tilling isn't practical, so I simply work a few handfuls of compost into each planting hole and hope for the best.

I think the most important step is to be absolutely sure each root-ball is thoroughly soaked before you put it in the ground. I fill a large bucket with water, then plunge each pot into it (so the root-ball is submerged) until no more bubbles rise to the surface. That way, I know the growing mix is saturated, and the roots will have plenty of water to draw from — for the first few days, anyway. I still water the whole site thoroughly after planting, of course, and then mulch generously, to keep the site as moist as possible while my plants are establishing new roots. ✳

Nepeta

(Catmints)

These sun-loving, drought-tolerant perennials typically bloom in shades of purple to blue in summer.

N. x *faassenii* **'Blue Wonder'** has grayish green foliage in mounds 15 inches tall and wide, with purplish blue flowers from late spring through summer. ZONES 4–8.

N. racemosa **'Little Titch'** grows in dense, 8-inch-tall, 15-inch-wide carpets of gray-green foliage, with blue flowers at the stem tips from late spring or early summer to early fall. ZONES 5–8.

ALTERNATIVES: Another compact catmint or lavender.

Nepeta

Pennisetum alopecuroides 'Hameln'

('Hameln' fountain grass)

Mounds of slender, arching, rich green foliage grow to 18 to 24 inches tall and wide, with brushy, greenish to grayish tan spikes up to 3 feet tall from late summer through fall. ZONES 6–9.

ALTERNATIVES: Oriental fountain grass (*P. orientale*) or prairie dropseed (*Sporobolus heterolepis*).

Salvia nemorosa 'Marcus'

('Marcus' salvia)

Growing only 8 inches tall and about as wide, this compact cutie bears short spikes of purple-blue blossoms from early to midsummer (even longer if deadheaded) over bright green leaves. ZONES 3–8.

ALTERNATIVES: 'Goodness Grows' spike speedwell (*Veronica spicata* 'Goodness Grows') or Siberian dragon's head (*Dracocephalum ruyschianum*).

Sedum

(Sedums)

These classic drought-tolerant perennials come in an array of sizes, shapes, and colors, so you're sure to find several that are perfect for any sunny, dry site. **'Ruby Glow'** grows to 1 foot tall and 12 to 15 inches across, with upright, reddish stems that bear purplish gray leaves and clusters of pinkish red flowers from midsummer to early fall. **'Vera Jameson'** has purple stems clad in purple- or pink-blushed green leaves featuring clusters of rosy pink flowers from late summer into fall; 8 to 12 inches tall and about 18 inches across. ZONES 4–8.

ALTERNATIVES: Another compact sedum species or hybrid, such as 'Purple Emperor' or October daphne (*S. sieboldii*).

Thymus serpyllum

(Creeping thyme)

Creeping thyme forms a low carpet of trailing stems with tiny green leaves and small clusters of flowers in early to midsummer; 4 to 8 inches tall and 1 foot wide. **'Pink Chintz'** has light pink flowers; **'Snowdrift'** is white. ZONES 4–8.

ALTERNATIVES: Any other thyme.

Veronica spicata 'Goodness Grows'

('Goodness Grows' spike speedwell)

Low-spreading clumps of bright green leaves send up slender spikes of rich blue flowers from late spring through summer; about 1 foot tall and 12 to 18 inches across. ZONES 3–8.

ALTERNATIVES: 'Marcus' salvia (*Salvia nemorosa* 'Marcus') or Siberian dragon's head (*Dracocephalum ruyschianum*).

Stephanie Says

MY DESIGN RULE FOR ANY DIFFICULT SITE is a simple one: *No plants on life-support systems!* There's simply no sense in fighting with your perennials to make them grow where they're just not happy. And in the case of dry sites, why

Soak It to 'Em

waste precious water on plants that will look lousy no matter how often you turn on the sprinkler?

I agree with Nan, though, that it's critical to keep the soil moist right after planting, because even drought-tolerant plants need some time to get their root systems established.

Fortunately, soaker hoses are a good compromise. Lay them on top of the soil right after planting and then mulch over them, and you won't even see them. Use the hoses as needed through the first full growing season to gently soak the soil, then remove them and use them to start new gardens elsewhere. Don't think you'll do established dry-soil perennials a favor by providing them with an extra drink now and then; they'll just be prone to rot. *

Small-Garden Strategies

ONCE YOU'VE BEEN BITTEN by the gardening bug, it seems like there's never enough room to grow all the perennials you want to. And when your yard's on the small size to begin with, it just makes matters that much more desperate. Although we can't magically make your property as large as you'd like, we can give you some tips for making the most of the space you have to work with.

The Show Must Go On

Where gardening space is limited, there's no room for slackers; every plant has to earn its place. This means that it needs to look good in at least two seasons, and ideally longer.

Use climbing plants and garden ornaments to get all the gardening space you can out of a small area.

An extended flowering season is great, but attractive foliage is even more important, as that's what you'll be looking at for all the time that plant is *not* in bloom. You can achieve extra interest by choosing perennials with showy fall leaf color, evergreen foliage, attractive seedheads, and interesting stems. For more hints on choosing plants with multi-season interest, check out Perennial Gardens for All Seasons, starting on page 160.

Limiting yourself to only hardworking plants will go a long way to whittling down your list of possible perennials, but if you're a real gardening nut, you probably still have more candidates than could ever fit in your space. Luckily, you can break one of the most often quoted design rules: "Don't plant just one of anything; always groups of three or more." Go ahead and put in single plants, if you want to; just remember to repeat the colors and textures with similar plants so you don't end up with a spotty hodgepodge. If you really like purple foliage, for example, grow five different dark-leaved heucheras instead of five plants of the same cultivar, or else one heuchera and four other purple-leaved perennials.

Think Twice about Turf

To have lawn or not to have lawn? That's a question only you can answer. If you have kids or dogs, it's really nice to have at least a small patch of grass for them to play on, and it won't take all that much time to maintain. But if you really want as much gardening space as possible, and you don't want to bother with even minimal mowing and edging, consider replacing that grass with larger beds linked by mulch or gravel paths.

Your
Secret
Garden

THIS TINY TOWNHOUSE BACKYARD may be small on space, but it's definitely big on charm. It's packed with colorful foliage to provide dependable beauty as the various perennials come into and go out of bloom, and accented with a few choice shrubs and trees for light shade, rich fragrance, fall color, bright berries, and showy winter stems. We've added a hidden seating area and a little water feature to create a private space — a perfect getaway for relaxing after a rough day at the office.

Besides helping to screen out some background noise, the splashing water in the fountain provides another benefit: It attracts songbirds to this little backyard haven.

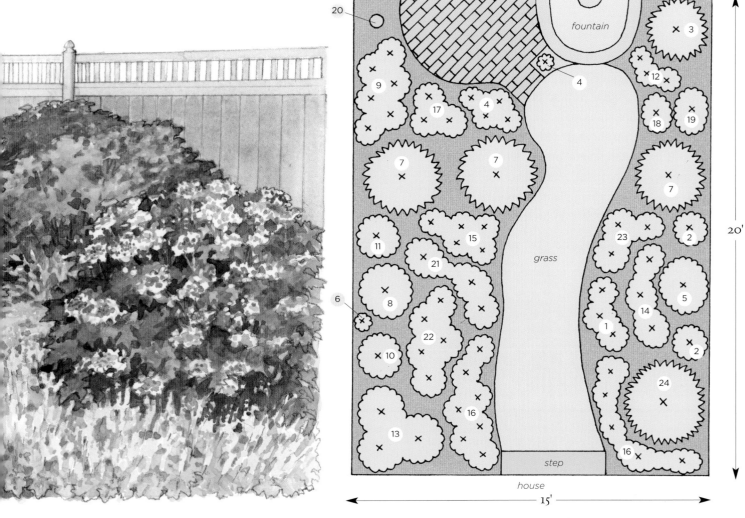

PLANT LIST

1	*Alchemilla mollis*	3 plants
2	*Calamagrostis x acutiflora* 'Avalanche'	2 plants
3	*Calycanthus floridus* 'Athens'	1 plant
4	*Carex buchananii*	5 plants
5	*Cimicifuga* 'Hillside Black Beauty'	1 plant
6	*Clematis tangutica* My Angel	1 plant
7	*Cornus sanguinea* 'Midwinter Fire'	3 plants
8	*Dicentra spectabilis* 'Goldheart'	1 plant
9	*Dryopteris erythrosora*	6 plants
10	*Geranium* 'Nimbus'	1 plant
11	*G.* 'Philippe Vapelle'	1 plant
12	*Hakonechloa macra* 'Aureola'	3 plants
13	*Helleborus foetidus*	3 plants
14	*Hemerocallis* 'Pardon Me'	3 plants
15	*Heuchera* 'Chocolate Ruffles'	5 plants
16	*x Heucherella* 'Sunspot'	12 plants
17	*Hosta* 'Blue Cadet'	3 plants
18	*H. montana* 'Aureomarginata'	1 plant
19	*Kirengeshoma palmata*	1 plant
20	*Magnolia virginiana*	1 plant
21	*Phlox paniculata* 'Becky Towe'	3 plants
22	*Tiarella* 'Winterglow'	5 plants
23	*Tricyrtis hirta* 'Alba'	3 plants
24	*Viburnum sargentii* 'Onondaga'	1 plant

DESIGNER'S CHECKLIST

☐ **Think vertically.** In addition to privacy and mystery, tall narrow screening plants bring vertical interest to a small yard. Other ways to provide visual excitement are to plant vines on a fence or a trellis (or let them scramble up shrubs), and to add one or more *tuteurs* (freestanding metal or wooden structures used to support vines or roses). Have a boring wall that needs dressing up? Hang planters on it, or stencil vines and leaves on it, for multi-season appeal.

☐ **Go for the layered look.** When you want to pack as many perennials as possible into a small yard, it's easy to forget about larger plants like trees and shrubs, but these bigger guys may be exactly what your garden needs. Well-chosen "woodies" are some of the very hardest-working plants in a small space, providing multiple levels of branches to draw your eye upward, so you're not focusing just at ground level. Plant perennials of varying heights underneath them, right down to soil-hugging ground covers, and even a tiny garden can have ample visual interest.

☐ **Don't forget fragrance.** Small enclosed spaces are ideal for experiencing fragrant flowers, because scents tend to linger in still air. Don't overdo it, though: Just one or two fragrant plants in bloom at any time will be pleasant without being overpowering. Add a bench or garden chair, and maybe a trickling water feature to provide a soothing sound, and you'll create a perfect spot for relaxing. Whether you're reading or simply taking a break, you're sure to enjoy the scents and serenity.

☐ **Divide and conquer.** Another trick for making a small space look larger is to divide it up, so you don't see the whole area at once. Using shrubs, tall grasses, or a trellis as a screen can provide hidden nooks that encourage visitors to walk around and explore the garden, instead of just glance at it from a distance.

Alchemilla mollis
(Lady's mantle)

This plant forms a mound of scalloped, light green leaves with airy sprays of tiny, yellow-green flowers from late spring to midsummer; 12 to 18 inches tall and about as wide. Cut back plants by about half in midsummer for a flush of new foliage to enjoy for the rest of the growing season. ZONES 3–9.

ALTERNATIVES: Alpine lady's mantle (A. alpina) or 'Herman's Pride' lamiastrum (Lamiastrum galeobdolon 'Herman's Pride').

Alchemilla mollis

Calamagrostis x acutiflora 'Avalanche'
('Avalanche' feather reed grass)

Green leaves sport a white center stripe. Plants grow in narrow, upright clumps to 1 foot wide. The 3- to 4-foot stems are topped with pinkish tan plumes that emerge in midsummer and last well into winter. If the foliage turns brown in mid- to late summer, cut down and discard the top growth (do not compost it); new leaves will quickly appear. ZONES 4–8.

ALTERNATIVES: The cultivar 'Overdam', with white-edged green leaves.

Carex buchananii
(Leather-leaved sedge)

Clumps of upright tufts of slender brown blades grow 18 to 24 inches tall and wide; definitely different and eye-catching! ZONES 6 OR 7–9.

ALTERNATIVES: Bronze sedge (C. comans 'Bronze') or red wood rush (Luzula sylvatica 'Ruby Stiletto').

Cimicifuga 'Hillside Black Beauty'
('Hillside Black Beauty' bugbane)

Bushy clumps of dissected, purple-black leaves are 4 feet tall and 3 feet across, accented with foot-long spikes of fragrant, pinkish white flowers over the foliage from late summer into fall. ZONES 4–8.

ALTERNATIVES: The cultivar 'Black Negligee' or 'Brunette'.

Dicentra spectabilis 'Goldheart'
('Goldheart' bleeding heart)

This bleeding heart has bright yellow spring foliage and arching, 3-foot stems with dangling pink hearts in mid- to late spring; clumps are 2 feet across. Cutting back the stems lightly in early to midsummer encourages new growth. ZONES 4–8.

ALTERNATIVES: 'Worcester Gold' caryopteris (Caryopteris x clandonensis 'Worcester Gold').

Dryopteris erythrosora
(Autumn fern)

Bright copper fronds in spring age to a glossy deep green through the summer, in clumps about 2 feet tall and wide. ZONES 5–9.

ALTERNATIVES: Christmas fern (Polystichum acrostichoides) or Japanese painted fern (Athyrium niponicum var. pictum).

Geranium
(Hardy geraniums)

These mound-forming perennials come in a wide range of sizes, leaf shapes, and bloom colors. 'Nimbus' produces loose clumps about 18 inches tall and 2 feet across, with white-centered purple flowers over starry green leaves from late spring into fall. 'Philippe Vapelle' forms dense mounds of lobed, gray-green leaves with deep purple-blue flowers from early summer to fall; 1 foot tall and 18 inches across. ZONES 5–8.

ALTERNATIVES: 'Brookside', 'Rozanne', or other geranium cultivars.

Hakonechloa macra 'Aureola'
(Golden Hakone grass)

Narrow, arching, yellow-and-green-striped leaves form in slowly expanding clumps 12 to 18 inches tall and eventually about as wide; flowers aren't showy. ZONES 6–9.

ALTERNATIVES: The cultivar 'All Gold' or 'Albo-Striata' or Tradescantia 'Sweet Kate'.

Hakonechloa macra 'Aureola'

Helleborus foetidus
(Bear's foot hellebore)

Bushy clumps of upright stems are clad in deeply cut, leathery, evergreen leaves and topped with clusters of pale green bells from mid- or late winter to mid- or late spring; 18 to 30 inches tall and 18 to 24 inches across. ZONES 4–9.

ALTERNATIVES: Corsican hellebore (*H. argutifolius*) or a hybrid hellebore (*H. x hybridus*).

Helleborus x *hybridus*

Hemerocallis 'Pardon Me'
('Pardon Me' daylily)

Fragrant, pinkish red, yellow-throated, blooms are borne atop 18-inch stems from midsummer well into fall, above clumps of grasslike, bright green foliage. ZONES 4–9.

ALTERNATIVES: Another 18- to 30-inch-tall, repeat-flowering daylily.

Heuchera 'Chocolate Ruffles'
('Chocolate Ruffles' heuchera)

Mounds of purplish green to chocolate-brown leaves with ruffled edges grow to about 1 foot tall and 18 inches across. Airy clusters of tiny white flowers bloom on 18- to 24-inch purple stems in late spring and early summer. ZONES 4–9.

ALTERNATIVES: 'Purple Petticoats' or another purple-leaved heuchera.

x Heucherella 'Sunspot'
('Sunspot' heucherella)

Heuchera-like mounds of lobed, bright yellow foliage feature a red star in the center of each leaf, accented with 18-inch spikes of bright pink flowers in late spring; foliage clumps are 8 to 12 inches tall and 12 to 18 inches across. ZONES 5–9.

ALTERNATIVES: Heuchera 'Amber Waves' or 'Beedham's White' lamium (*Lamium maculatum* 'Beedham's White').

Hosta
(Hostas)

These classic, no-fuss perennials are grown primarily for their foliage, which comes in a variety of shapes, sizes, and colors to fit any shade garden. **'Blue Cadet'** forms blue-green mounds 1 foot tall and wide, with pale purple flowers on 18-inch stems in mid- to late summer. *H. montana* **'Aureomarginata'** has large green leaves irregularly edged with gold and pale lavender flowers in early to mid-summer; to 3 feet tall and wide. ZONES 3–8.

ALTERNATIVES: Any hosta in the same color and height range.

Heuchera **'Purple Petticoats'**

Kirengeshoma palmata
(Yellow waxbells)

Large, shrubby clumps (3 to 4 feet tall and 2 to 3 feet wide) have maplelike green leaves and clusters of nodding yellow bells at the stem tips in late summer and early fall. ZONES 5–8.

ALTERNATIVES: A compact oak-leaved hydrangea (*Hydrangea quercifolia*), such as 'Pee Wee' or yellow-leaved 'Little Honey'.

Phlox paniculata 'Becky Towe'
('Becky Towe' phlox)

Upright stems support clusters of fragrant, salmon-rose flowers in mid- to late summer over green leaves edged in gold (fading to creamy green); the mildew-resistant clumps are 2 feet tall and 18 inches across. ZONES 4–8.

ALTERNATIVES: 'Oehme' palm sedge (*Carex muskingumensis* 'Oehme').

Tiarella 'Winterglow'
('Winterglow' foamflower)

Eight-inch-tall, 1-foot-wide mounds of deep green leaves turn bronzy yellow with reddish speckles in winter. One-foot-tall spikes of white flowers bloom through spring. ZONES 3–8.

ALTERNATIVES: 'Crow Feather' or another foamflower cultivar.

Tricyrtis hirta 'Alba'
(White toad lily)

Arching stems clad in hairy, light green leaves support pure white flowers from late summer to mid-fall; clumps are about 2 feet tall and wide. ZONES 4–9.

ALTERNATIVES: The cultivar 'White Towers' or a yellow-flowered species, such as *T. macrantha*.

Bringing Large Landscapes Down to Size

A LARGE PROPERTY CAN BE a gardener's paradise — and the biggest nightmare as well. The whole process of figuring out where even to begin can be overwhelming, not to mention the daunting prospect of all the time and money involved in developing grand-scale gardens. But there's no need to lose sleep over the situation; just try some of these pointers we've picked up over the years, and you'll soon be on your way to creating order out of chaos.

Exploring Your Options

Selecting plants for a large perennial design comes down to the three Bs: big, bold, and bright. It's important to keep the plants in scale with their setting, so the dainty ground-huggers aren't going to do the job: You need large bushy plants, or at least substantial groupings of smaller perennials, to make an impact. Large leaves and flowers also help to keep the plants in proportion with their surroundings. And because you'll be seeing the planting from some distance, you'll want lots of bright colors so the bed or border doesn't blend into the background.

Now, all this is well and good, but unless you have an unlimited plant-buying budget, just how are you supposed to afford all of the big, bold, and bright perennials you need for a new planting? Here are a few ideas:

* Investigate options for buying at wholesale nurseries in your area; you could save a bundle that way.

* Stick with older, tried-and-true cultivars; they'll be far less expensive than the latest introductions.

* Purchase one or a few pots of each perennial you want, then grow them in a "nursery bed" — a special bed set aside just for young plants — for a year or two, until they are big enough to divide and move to your new garden.

* Grow them from seed. When you're looking at a garden from a distance, the small variations in height and color that are possible with seed-grown perennials won't matter at all. It will probably take 2 or 3 years for the seedlings to reach garden size, but in the long run, you can easily produce hundreds of dollars' worth of perennials from just $30 or so of seed.

Large areas require a bold approach, with masses of big bushy plants.

Bigger *IS* Better!

THIS OVER-THE-TOP ISLAND BED is just the thing you need to wow your neighbors and inspire envy in the hearts of your local garden club members. Filled with statuesque perennials arranged in large drifts, the full-sun site will explode with color from midsummer on, just when most other gardens are fizzling out from the summer heat.

PLANTING PLAN

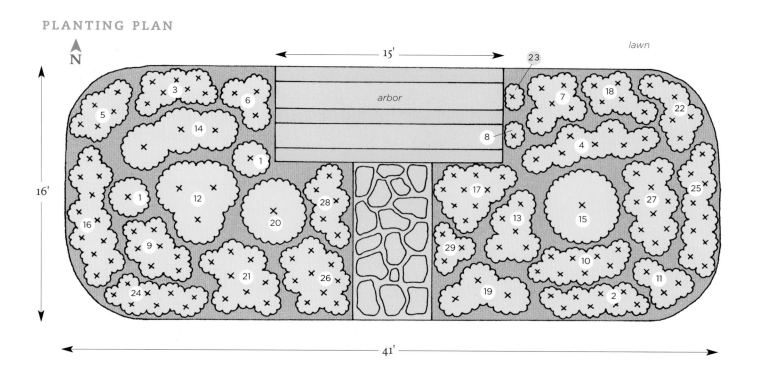

PLANT LIST

1	*Acanthus spinosus*	2 plants		16	*Oenothera fruticosa* 'Summer Solstice'	11 plants
2	*Achillea* 'Anthea'	8 plants		17	*Origanum laevigatum* 'Hopleys'	9 plants
3	*A.* 'Moonshine'	7 plants		18	*Pennisetum orientale* 'Karley Rose'	5 plants
4	*Agastache* 'Blue Fortune'	7 plants		19	*Perovskia atriplicifolia*	3 plants
5	*A.* 'Red Fortune'	5 plants		20	*Persicaria polymorpha*	1 plant
6	*Aster oblongifolius* 'October Skies'	3 plants		21	*Phlox paniculata* 'Little Boy'	8 plants
7	*Chrysanthemum* 'Sheffield Pink'	5 plants		22	*P. paniculata* 'Shortwood'	5 plants
8	*Clematis* 'Polish Spirit'	1 plant		23	*Rosa* 'New Dawn'	1 plant
9	*Echinacea purpurea* 'Magnus'	7 plants		24	*Sedum* 'Autumn Fire'	8 plants
10	*E. purpurea* 'Ruby Star'	8 plants		25	*S.* 'Matrona'	9 plants
11	*Eupatorium coelestinum* 'Cory'	3 plants		26	*Solidago* 'Crown of Rays'	9 plants
12	*Helianthus* 'Lemon Queen'	3 plants		27	*S. rugosa* 'Fireworks'	9 plants
13	*Heliopsis helianthoides* 'Prairie Sunset'	5 plants		28	*Stokesia laevis* 'Klaus Jelitto'	5 plants
14	*Miscanthus sinensis* 'Ferner Osten'	3 plants		29	*S. laevis* 'Silver Moon'	3 plants
15	*M. sinensis* 'Variegatus'	1 plant				

DESIGNER'S CHECKLIST

☐ **Plan access paths.** When you're planning borders that are much wider than 6 feet, it's critical to plan ahead for some kind of access. It doesn't have to be a formal walkway wide enough for two people to stroll along, unless that's what you want; a simple stepping-stone path will let you sneak in for grooming, pruning, and other maintenance tasks without trampling your plants or compacting the soil.

☐ **Start with a structure, if possible.** Designing your new garden around an arbor, terrace, shed, tree, or water feature makes the whole planning process a lot easier. The structure will help give your bed or border the right scale and provide a jumping-off point for a color theme; plus, it will take up space, so you won't need quite as many plants to make an impact.

☐ **Forget the ankle-biters for edges.** If you're accustomed to gardening on an average-size lot (about a half acre), you'll need to think on an entirely different scale when it comes to designing for a large space. Front-of-the-border plants in a typical garden are usually in the 4- to 12-inch-tall range, grading up to 4- to 5-foot-tall plants in the back. But in a large border, the biggest plants can be 6, 8, or even 10 feet tall, so your edging plants need to be taller, too, to stay in scale; the 18- to 36-inch-tall range is about right.

☐ **Go bananas with bulbs.** Tall-growing perennials tend to be late bloomers (from midsummer on), but that doesn't mean you have to wait for flowers. Go ahead and tuck in all kinds of spring-blooming bulbs: crocus, squills (*Scilla*), species tulips, ornamental onions (*Allium*), and whatever else strikes your fancy. As the perennials grow up, the bulb foliage will disappear — and you'll have a steady show of color from March through October.

☐ **Take it step-by-step.** As you create your design, think about ways you could break it into sections, so you don't have to install the whole project at once. This plan, for instance, could be implemented over a period of 2 or 3 years: pergola and path first, then one side of the bed, and then the other side. Or you could work from the inside out, placing the biggest plants first, then gradually expanding the bed outward as time and money permit.

Bold Beauties for Sun

Acanthus spinosus

(Spiny bear's breeches)

Spiny, deeply cut, dark green leaves grow in 3-foot-tall and -wide clumps, with upright stems bearing 5-foot-tall spikes of purple bracts and white flowers from late spring or early summer to midsummer. ZONES 5–9.

ALTERNATIVES: Another species of bear's breeches or ornamental rhubarb (Rheum palmatum).

Achillea

(Yarrows)

Flat-topped clusters of bright or pastel blooms are produced all through the summer over clumps of fernlike leaves. Both 'Anthea' and 'Moonshine' have pale yellow blooms and gray-green leaves; however, 'Anthea' seems to have better heat and humidity tolerance. Both grow 18 to 24 inches tall and 12 to 18 inches wide. ZONES 2–9.

ALTERNATIVES: Another yarrow.

Agastache

(Agastaches)

Dense, bushy clumps of upright stems are clad in licorice-scented leaves and topped with brushy flower spikes from early summer into fall. 'Blue Fortune' has purple-blue blooms; 'Red Fortune' has rosy pink spikes. Both are about 3 feet tall and 2 feet wide. ZONES 6–9.

ALTERNATIVES: Anise hyssop (Agastache foeniculum) or long-leaved speedwell (Veronica longifolia).

Aster oblongifolius 'October Skies'

('October Skies' aster)

Mounded, 2-foot-tall and -wide clumps are smothered in deep blue, daisylike blooms in early to mid-fall. ZONES 5–9.

ALTERNATIVES: 'Fanny's Aster', 'Raydon's Favorite', or another aster species or hybrid.

Chrysanthemum 'Sheffield Pink'

('Sheffield Pink' chrysanthemum, a.k.a. 'Hillside Sheffield Pink', 'Sheffield', Dendranthema 'Sheffield')

This plant forms loose, somewhat sprawling mounds of rich green leaves, 2 to 3 feet tall and wide, and sports large, peachy pink, daisylike flowers from early to late fall. ZONES 4–9.

ALTERNATIVES: 'Cambodian Queen', 'Mei-Kyo', or another cultivar.

Echinacea purpurea

(Purple coneflower)

Sturdy, upright stems are clad in dark green leaves and feature bronze-centered, daisy-form flowers with rosy pink petals through summer; clumps are usually 2 to 4 feet tall and 18 to 24 inches across. 'Magnus' has very large flowers; 'Ruby Star' has particularly rich-colored petals. ZONES 3–8.

ALTERNATIVES: Another cultivar, such as 'Bright Star' or 'Ruby Giant'.

Practical Matters

Before committing to a large-scale perennial design, think about the long-term issues too, such as where you're going to put it, how you're going to prepare the site, and how you're going to handle the maintenance. You don't want to put lots of time and money into a garden that's going to end up in the way of a future swimming pool or new driveway, so it's smart to think about preparing a master plan for your whole property before you start plunking down gardens hither and yon. If you don't feel comfortable roughing out a 5- to 10-year plan by yourself, it's certainly fine to hire a landscape designer. You may not follow the finished plan exactly, but the process of assessing what you have to start with and discussing what you'd like to have in the future can be invaluable for avoiding major mistakes in placing and shaping individual beds and borders.

Unless you're a glutton for punishment, relying on hand power to prepare a large planting site can be a big mistake. At the very least, consider renting a sod stripper to remove the existing grass and a heavy-duty tiller to prepare the soil. A motorized wagon or even a small front-end loader can be an enormous help for moving and spreading organic matter and mulch. If all this still seems like too much labor, consider hiring a landscape service to do the site preparation for you.

And one last point: Think about what you're going to do with all the debris you'll end up with at garden-cleanup time. We're not just talking about a small compost pile here, because the stems of some big perennials can get as thick and hard as tree saplings. Instead of simply dumping all this slow-to-decay material in a big pile, you may want to rent or even buy a chipper/shredder to reduce the debris to a more manageable state. The chopped material will take up much less space and will compost quickly — and it'll make great mulch, too.

Eupatorium coelestinum 'Cory'

('Cory' hardy ageratum)

Fluffy clusters of lavender-blue blooms sit atop 2- to 3-foot-tall, deep red stems in late summer and early fall. This ageratum spreads by rhizomes to form large patches, so divide every other year to keep it under control. ZONES 5–9.

ALTERNATIVES: The straight species (*E. coelestinum*).

Helianthus 'Lemon Queen'

('Lemon Queen' perennial sunflower)

Six- to 8-foot-tall, upright stems are clad in rough green leaves and topped with lemon yellow blooms from mid- or late summer into fall; clumps are 3 feet across. ZONES 4–9.

ALTERNATIVES: 'Sheila's Sunshine' giant sunflower (*H. giganteus* 'Sheila's Sunshine') or another tall perennial sunflower cultivar.

Heliopsis helianthoides 'Prairie Sunset'

('Prairie Sunset' oxeye)

Masses of maroon-centered, bright yellow daisies bloom in mid- to late summer on 4- to 6-foot, deep red stems with dark green leaves; spreads to 3 feet. ZONES 4–8.

ALTERNATIVES: Another oxeye cultivar or swamp sunflower (*Helianthus angustifolius*).

Miscanthus sinensis

(Japanese miscanthus)

Fountainlike, slowly expanding, 3- to 5-foot-wide clumps of arching foliage are accented with whisklike flower plumes in late summer or fall and lasting well into winter. Be warned: Can be invasive by self-sowing in warm climates (roughly Zone 7 and south).
'Ferner Osten' (a.k.a. 'Far East') has green leaves that turn coppery red in fall, with reddish flowers atop 4- to 5-foot-tall stems. ZONES 5–9.
'Variegatus' has green leaves striped with creamy white and blooms late atop 6- to 8-foot-tall stems. ZONES 4–9.

ALTERNATIVES: Another late-flowering cultivar, such as 'Morning Light' or 'Zebrinus', or another tall ornamental grass, such as Indian grass (*Sorghastrum nutans*) or switch grass (*Panicum virgatum*).

Oenothera fruticosa 'Summer Solstice'

('Summer Solstice' sundrops)

Slow-spreading clumps of upright stems sport cupped, bright yellow flowers over red-tinged leaves from early summer to early fall; 18 to 24 inches tall and wide. ZONES 3–9.

ALTERNATIVES: The cultivar 'Fireworks'.

Origanum laevigatum 'Hopleys'

('Hopleys' oregano, a.k.a. 'Hopley's Purple')

Clusters of rosy pink flowers set among reddish purple bracts bloom from early summer into fall over aromatic, dark green leaves; clumps are 2 to 3 feet tall and 18 inches across. ZONES 6–9.

ALTERNATIVES: The cultivar 'Herrenhausen' or red valerian (*Centranthus ruber*).

Pennisetum orientale 'Karley Rose'

('Karley Rose' Oriental fountain grass)

Upright, 18-inch-wide clumps of narrow, rich green leaves are accented with brushy, purplish pink spikes atop 3-foot stems from early or midsummer into fall. ZONES 5– OR 6–9.

ALTERNATIVES: Another fountain grass species or cultivar.

Perovskia atriplicifolia

(Russian sage)

Shrubby clumps of gray-white stems are clad in deeply cut, silvery green leaves and tipped with purple-blue flowers from late summer into fall; 3 to 4 feet tall and about 3 feet across. ZONES 6–9.

ALTERNATIVES: Any cultivar of Russian sage or caryopteris (*Caryopteris* x *clandonensis*).

Persicaria polymorpha

(White fleeceflower, a.k.a. *Polygonum polymorphum*)

Dense clumps of medium green leaves on stout stems are topped with large white plumes from early to late summer; 4 to 6 feet tall and 3 to 4 feet wide. ZONES 4–9.

ALTERNATIVES: 'Crimson Beauty' Mexican bamboo (*Polygonum cuspidatum* 'Crimson Beauty') or the shrub summersweet (*Clethra alnifolia*).

Phlox paniculata

(Garden phlox)

Large clusters of fragrant flowers from mid- or late summer into fall rise atop upright stems with narrow green leaves. **'Little Boy'** has purple flowers with a lighter eye; 12 to 18 inches tall and about 1 foot across. **'Shortwood'** has bright pink blooms with a darker eye; 4 feet tall and 2 feet across. Both are mildew-resistant. ZONES 4–8.

ALTERNATIVES: Another mildew-resistant cultivar, such as white 'David' or the soft pink 'Tracy's Treasure'.

Perovskia atriplicifolia and *Solidago rugosa* 'Fireworks'

Sedum
(Sedums)

Clustered flowers bloom in mid- to late summer atop upright stems over succulent leaves. **'Autumn Fire'** grows 2 to 3 feet tall and 18 to 24 inches across, with blue-green leaves and pinkish red flowers that turn bronze in fall. **'Matrona'** has purple stems with purple-tinged green leaves and clusters of pink flowers from late summer into fall; 24 to 30 inches tall and 18 to 24 inches across. ZONES 3–9.
ALTERNATIVES: 'Autumn Joy', 'Brilliant', 'Purple Emperor', or another upright cultivar.

Sedum

Solidago
(Goldenrods)

Sprays or plumes of golden, late-summer and fall blooms form atop upright or arching stems with narrow green leaves. The hybrid **'Crown of Rays'** has dense, horizontally branched flower clusters; 18 to 24 inches tall and 18 inches across. **S. *rugosa* 'Fireworks'** has bright yellow flowers in long, arching sprays; 30 to 40 inches tall and 24 to 30 inches across. ZONES 3–8.
ALTERNATIVES: Another goldenrod species or hybrid.

Stokesia laevis
(Stokes' aster)

Clumps of deep green leaves and upright stems are topped from midsummer into fall with large flowers that look like shaggy daisies; clumps are 18 to 24 inches tall and 12 to 18 inches across. **'Klaus Jelitto'** has lavender-blue blooms; **'Silver Moon'** has white flowers. ZONES 5–9.
ALTERNATIVES: Another cultivar, such as 'Honeysong Purple' or 'Skyrocket'.

Nan's Notebook

WHEN I MOVED to my current property a few years ago, it was just an open, 5-acre hayfield: pasture grasses, weeds, and no trees. I had lots of plants from my previous garden, however, so my first order of business (even before building the house) was to construct a 40- by 10-foot raised bed to act as a temporary home for them. I used rocks scrounged from the land itself to build the frame, then filled it in with a few truckloads of a commercial topsoil/compost mix and stuck in the plants. I also threw in seeds of self-sowing annuals, such as red orach (*Atriplex hortensis* var. *rubra*) to fill in any empty spaces. It certainly wasn't planned by any design rules, but it was colorful and cheerful nonetheless, and the plants thrived in the rich soil.

Build a Holding Bed

Each spring and fall, I move out some of the perennials to fill borders I've built elsewhere on the property, and I stick in other seedlings and divisions acquired from friends and plant swaps. In another year or two, I hope to have moved out all of the perennials, and then I'll use the remaining rocks and soil as the base for a new (permanent) raised bed in another spot and return that area to mown grass or meadow. But in the meantime, I'll keep enjoying the benefits of having my own nursery of big, garden-sized clumps of perennials that are free for the digging. *

7 Creative Color Effects

FOR MANY OF US, the whole point of gardening is to create a beautiful setting for our home, and choosing just the right colors is a key part of the process. From vibrant reds to soothing blues, colors influence our moods, set a scene for relaxing or entertaining, and add elegance or drama to the landscape. Whether you're planning a perennial garden based on color or you're just looking for tips on incorporating color concepts into your other garden designs, we have lots of ideas to share with you.

Color-Theme Gardens

No MATTER HOW MUCH GARDENING experience you have, creating a color-theme garden will probably be one of the easiest designs you'll ever do. In its purest form, it's simply a matter of choosing one, two, or maybe three colors that you like, then selecting plants with flowers, foliage, or other features in those colors. Picking a few favorite colors is also helpful for narrowing down your plant options when you're working with a broad overall concept, such as a formal garden, a naturalistic garden, or a spring garden.

Consider Your Options

Choosing colors for your perennial garden can be as simple or as difficult as selecting the colors for the inside of your home. If you already have definite preferences, that's great; they can work just as well in your garden as they do in your bedroom or kitchen. Not sure what you want? Take color cues from existing features in your yard or on your home — the front door, the trim around your windows, and your boundary fence, for example — and then use them to guide your plant choices. Or look for pictures of plantings that appeal to you, and go on local garden tours to see what strikes your fancy.

Unless you're fully committed to a particular color theme, it's wise to start with a small bed or border and observe it over a full season. Once you've decided how you feel about it, you can expand the theme to other beds, add another color to change the effect, or take out all the plants and start over from scratch.

Many shades of purple and violet, along with cool blue-greens, are echoed by the container as well.

Be Open to Extreme Possibilities

Remember: An important key to creating a successful garden is combining the colors that *you* find appealing. Sure, you can play it safe and go with a traditional combination like pink, blue, and silver, or a classic all-white border; the result will look attractive to lots of people. But if it doesn't thrill *you*, you're wasting your time. The same goes for an unusual or trendy color combination, such as maroon and chartreuse or pink and yellow. It may be featured in all of this year's gardening magazines, but if it doesn't really reflect your own tastes, chances are you'll be ripping it out after just a season or two, and all your work will be for naught.

You may be relieved to know that it's possible to create beautiful color gardens without ever referring to a color wheel, looking up the definition of *analagous color scheme,* or memorizing the differences among a hue, a tint, and a shade. Go ahead and combine whatever flower and foliage colors you find most pleasing, and see what you think of the result. If you're not thrilled with how things look, it's an easy matter to fix them: Simply replace some of the plants, or else move them around to try out different effects. (In fact, some of the best design work is done, not on paper, but in the garden itself.) We promise that the horticultural police will not arrest you for pairing pink with orange or lavender with red. There are no right and wrong decisions when it comes to combining colors: just likes and dislikes.

Nan's Notebook

SURE, THERE ARE PLENTY OF ANYTHING-BUT-GREEN-LEAVED PERENNIALS to fill a color garden, but why stop there? Annuals, tender perennials, bulbs, and shrubs can also provide outstanding foliage to complete your favorite color scheme. These alternatives are especially useful when you're seeking good purple foliage because, unfortunately, two of the showiest purple-leaved perennials — *Euphorbia dulcis* 'Chameleon' and *Lysimachia ciliata* 'Purpurea' — can also become major garden pests under some conditions (the former by self-sowing and the latter by creeping roots). So unless you want to stick with heucheras and sedums for front-of-the-border and mid-border color, check out some of these dusky beauties: purple basils (such as 'Dark Opal' and 'Purple Ruffles'), dark-leaved dahlias (like 'Bishop of Llandaff' and 'Ellen Huston'),

compact weigela cultivars (Midnight Wine and Wine and Roses), and even red-leaved lettuces (my favorite is 'Merlot', but there are many others). For more height, there are plenty of dark-leaved shrubs to fit the bill, including Black Beauty elderberry (*Sambucus* 'Gerda'), Diabolo ninebark (*Physocarpus opulifolius* 'Monlo'), and a variety of purple smokebushes (including 'Royal Purple' and 'Velvet Cloak').

When you start looking for good purple-leaved shrubs, you'll quickly find that some of the best are cultivars of Japanese barberry (*Berberis thunbergii*). Be warned, though: This plant is considered a serious invasive in parts of the United States (particularly in the Northeast states) and Canada, due to its seeding into natural areas and crowding out native vegetation. Let that knowledge guide you in deciding whether or not to use its cultivars in your own garden.

Dawn
and Darkness

ONCE YOU'VE TRIED YOUR HAND at a color garden or two, chances are you'll start seeing ideas for new combinations everywhere you look. It might be the elegant blue-and-white pattern on your grandmother's prized willowware platter, or the rich jewel tones of a Renaissance painting, or maybe a summer sunrise casting shifting pools of light into the darkness of a densely wooded area. That's the inspiration for this dramatic design for a sunny to lightly shaded area, filled with foliage in shades of sun-bright yellow and moody maroons and purples.

PLANTING PLAN

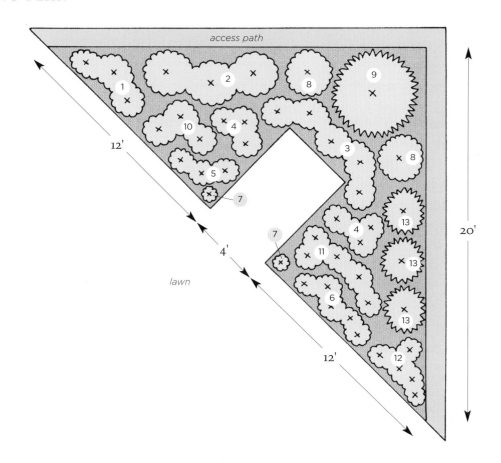

PLANT LIST

1	*Aster lateriflorus* 'Lady in Black'	3 plants
2	*Caryopteris* x *clandonensis* 'Worcester Gold'	3 plants
3	*Euphorbia dulcis* 'Chameleon'	5 plants
4	*Hemerocallis* 'Royal Occasion'	6 plants
5	*Heuchera* 'Amber Waves'	3 plants
6	H. 'Plum Pudding'	5 plants
7	*Imperata cylindrica* 'Rubra'	2 plants
8	*Panicum virgatum* 'Shenandoah'	2 plants
9	*Sambucus racemosa* 'Sutherland Gold'	1 plant
10	*Sedum telephium* subsp. *maximum* 'Atropurpureum'	3 plants
11	*Tanacetum vulgare* 'Isla Gold'	5 plants
12	*Tradescantia* 'Sweet Kate'	5 plants
13	*Weigela florida* Midnight Wine	3 plants

DESIGNER'S CHECKLIST

☐ **Foliage comes first.** Even the longest-flowering perennials are in bloom for only a few months, but you have to look at the leaves all through the growing season, so it makes sense to give serious thought to foliage. Besides giving a continuous clue to your color scheme, anything-but-green foliage offers significant color impact with a fraction of the care that flowers need to look their best.

☐ **Choose blooms carefully.** If you're using a scheme of more than one color, try to include some flowers that contain at least two of your choices. The bicolor blooms of blanket flower *(Gaillardia* x *grandiflora)*, for instance, are a natural choice for a red-and-yellow border, as they contain both colors. Daylilies *(Hemerocallis)* with contrasting "zones" or throats are also particularly good for tying together a multicolor scheme (or for inspiring one).

☐ **Up the ante with exciting contrasts.** Pairing light and dark flowers and foliage is one surefire way to create a dramatic design — but don't forget about texture as well. As you plan color-based combinations, look for opportunities to play ferny leaves off broad, flat foliage, or rounded leaves off lacy ones.

☐ **Be adventurous with accents.** Who says color has to stop at the edge of the garden? With a bit of creativity and a can of paint, you can give your color-theme planting extra impact with color-coordinated accessories, such as benches, trellises, pots, posts and fences, and the like.

Aster lateriflorus 'Lady in Black'

('Lady in Black' calico aster)

Dense, 18- to 24-inch-wide clumps of slender, upright, 3-foot stems have narrow, purple-black leaves and feature masses of tiny, pinkish white, daisylike flowers in late summer to early fall. ZONES 5–8.

ALTERNATIVES: The cultivar 'Prince'.

Caryopteris x clandonensis 'Worcester Gold'

('Worcester Gold' caryopteris)

Bushy clumps that are about 3 feet tall and 2 to 3 feet across, with elongated, bright yellow leaves, produce clusters of blue flowers in late summer and early fall. ZONES 5–9.

ALTERNATIVES: 'Gold Mound', 'Lime Mound', or 'Magic Carpet' spirea (all selections of *Spiraea japonica*).

Euphorbia dulcis 'Chameleon'

('Chameleon' euphorbia)

Rounded mounds that are about 1 foot tall and wide, with maroon leaves and stems, are topped with tiny, greenish yellow flowers in late spring to early summer. Will self-sow. ZONES 4–9.

ALTERNATIVES: 'Bishop's Children' dahlia, purple basil, or a dark-leaved pepper (*Capsicum annuum*) such as 'Black Prince' or 'Pretty Purple'.

Hemerocallis 'Royal Occasion'

('Royal Occasion' daylily)

This daylily forms 2-foot-wide mounds of narrow, arching green leaves with leafless, 2- to 3-foot stems bearing 5-inch, deep purple-red, chartreuse-centered blooms in midsummer, with some rebloom later. ZONES 3–9.

ALTERNATIVES: 'Jungle Beauty', 'Romulus', or another cultivar with dark flowers and a chartreuse eye.

Heuchera

(Heuchera)

Mound-forming perennials sport lovely lobed leaves in many shades of purple (brown and green too), often attractively mottled with silver. Airy clusters of small white or pink flowers appear atop wiry stems (18 to 24 inches tall) in late spring and early summer. **'Amber Waves'** has golden yellow leaves; **'Plum Pudding'** has deep purple foliage with silver mottling. Foliage clumps of both are 1 foot tall and 18 inches across. ZONES 4–9.

ALTERNATIVES: Any other golden or purple-hued heuchera.

Heuchera 'Plum Pudding'

Imperata cylindrica 'Rubra'

(Japanese blood grass, a.k.a. 'Red Baron')

Upright, narrow green leaves are tipped with red, turning all cranberry red by fall; clumps are 12 to 18 inches tall and wide, gradually spreading wider. Be aware that the straight species *I. cylindrica* is classified as a noxious weed. So far, this cultivar appears to be safe to grow, but if any all-green shoots appear, remove them immediately. ZONES 5–9.

ALTERNATIVES: The tender perennial dwarf red fountain grass (*Pennisetum setaceum* 'Eaton Canyon').

Panicum virgatum 'Shenandoah'

('Shenandoah' switch grass)

Narrowly upright, 3-foot-tall clumps of slender green leaves with reddish purple tips turn all maroon by fall, when the airy flower clusters appear; clumps are 24 to 30 inches across. ZONES 5–9.

ALTERNATIVES: The cultivar 'Rotstrahlbusch'.

Sedum telephium subsp. maximum 'Atropurpureum'

('Atropurpureum' sedum)

Upright clumps of dark purple stems and leaves are topped with clusters of rosy pink flowers in late summer and early fall; 18 to 24 inches tall and 12 to 18 inches wide. ZONES 5–9.

ALTERNATIVES: The hybrid 'Mohrchen'.

Tanacetum vulgare 'Isla Gold'

('Isla Gold' tansy)

Ferny, bright yellow leaves on 18- to 30-inch stems are topped with golden yellow, buttonlike flowers in summer; spreads to 2 feet by creeping roots, but not as invasive as the straight species. ZONES 4–8.

ALTERNATIVES: Golden feverfew (*Tanacetum parthenium* 'Aureum').

Tradescantia 'Sweet Kate'

('Sweet Kate' tradescantia, a.k.a. 'Blue and Gold')

Grasslike, 1-foot-tall and -wide clumps of slender, bright yellow leaves are accented with flat, rich blue blooms all through summer. ZONES 4–9.

ALTERNATIVES: 'Norton's Gold' oregano (*Origanum* 'Norton's Gold').

Handling Hot Colors

ROUSING REDS, AWESOME ORANGES, and glowing golds: the hues of high summer, and a preview of fall beauty too. These bright, cheerful colors are perhaps not a great choice for a soothing getaway garden where you want to relax and read a book, but they're ideal as an exciting, invigorating backdrop for lively summer fun, such as weekend cookouts, a Fourth of July picnic, and swimming parties.

Lipstick red poppies take center stage in this garden combination.

Hot Enough for Ya?

If you're looking for a garden that can really take the heat, hot colors will do the trick. They won't fade no matter how much sun they get, so you can count on them to look great even on sultry summer afternoons — a big plus if you get to spend time in your garden only on weekends. Admittedly, hot colors may clash with some house colors, such as pinkish brick, so think carefully about where to situate beds and borders. You'll be fine if you site them along a back fence, out along your property line, or in an island bed surrounded by lots of green lawn. Bold, striking colors in a well-designed bed are sure to garner lots of compliments.

Power Flowers

If you're ready to give a hot-color perennial planting a try, you'll want to pay special attention to the hues you choose. Yellows and orange generally look good together, but reds are another matter altogether. They range from blue-tinged red (crimson) to pure red to orange-red (scarlet), with various tints and shades (from moody maroons to rosy pinkish reds) as well, so you need to consider carefully the types of red you're pairing or risk creating some uncomfortable combinations.

Our advice when working with reds is to never rely on catalog descriptions of "red" flowers, and be cautious about trusting photographs as well. It's best to see the plants in bloom for yourself before you choose them — or be prepared to move them if they're not what you expected. Another option is to separate different red flowers with other hot colors, or with lots of green foliage, so your eye won't take in both reds at the same glance.

Orange You Glad?

When you're planning a hot-color garden, it's easy to think of gold and yellow flowers, and there are a fair number of great reds as well. But when it comes to orange, do you draw a blank? Well, here's a list of some excellent sun-loving options, including annuals and bulbs: enough to create an entire orange garden, if that's your heart's desire!

Asclepias tuberosa (butterfly weed): Zones 4–9

Calendula officinalis (calendula): annual

Canna (cannas): 'Orange Punch', 'Phaison' (Tropicana), and 'Wyoming'; usually Zones 8–9

Carthamnus tinctorius (safflower): annual

Chrysanthemum (mums): many selections available; hardiness varies

Cosmos sulphureus (orange cosmos): annual

Crocosmia (crocosmias): many cultivars, including 'Emily McKenzie' and 'Star of the East'; Zones 6–9

Dahlia (dahlias): many to choose from; 'Ellen Huston' (a.k.a. 'Ellen Houston') has dark foliage; usually Zones 8–9

Echinacea (coneflower): Orange Meadowbrite ('Art's Pride'); Zones 3–9

Erysimum x *allionii* (Siberian wallflower): Zones 3–7

Eschscholzia californica (California poppy): annual

Euphorbia griffithii (Griffith's spurge): 'Dixter', 'Firecharm', and 'Fireglow'; Zones 5–9

Fritillaria imperialis (crown imperial): Zones 5–9

Geum (avens): 'Mrs. J. Bradshaw' (a.k.a. 'Fireball'); Zones 5–9

Helenium (sneezeweeds): orange cultivars, like 'Coppelia' and 'Moerheim Beauty'; Zones 4–8

Helianthus annuus (sunflower): 'Soraya' is particularly pretty; annual

Hemerocallis (daylilies): lots of orange-flowered hybrids to choose from; usually Zones 3–9

Impatiens (impatiens) the New Guinea type 'Tango'; frost tender

Kniphofia (torch lilies): several cultivars, including 'Wayside Flame' (a.k.a. 'Pfitzeri'); usually Zones 6–9

Leonotis leonurus (lion's ear): frost tender

Lilium (true lilies): some species and hybrids (especially in the Asiatic group) have orange blooms; hardiness varies

Lychnis x *arkwrightii* (Arkwright's campion): 'Vesuvius', with dark foliage, is especially nice; Zones 5–8

Oenothera versicolor (sundrops): 'Sunset Boulevard'; Zones 5–9

Papaver orientale (Oriental poppy): Zones 4–9

Rosa (roses): 'Fred Loads', 'Livin' Easy', and 'Marmalade Skies'; hardiness varies

Tagetes (marigold): many, including the small-flowered 'Tangerine Gem'; annual

Tithonia rotundifolia (Mexican sunflower): annual

Tropaeolum majus (nasturtium): 'Vesuvius' is especially showy; annual

Tulipa (tulips): many selections; usually Zones 4–7

Viola (pansies and violas): annual or biennial; 'Padparadja' and 'Penny Orange'; Zones 4–8

Zinnia (zinnias): 'Profusion Orange' and *Z. haageana* 'Orange Star' (a.k.a. 'Classic' or *Z. angustifolia*); annual

Hemerocallis fulva

Living on the Edge

TURN UP THE HEAT on summer activities with this striking perennial design. It's planned to flank the corner of a pool, but it could work just as well wrapped around a corner of a ground-level deck or patio. Packed with attractive foliage as well as bright blooms, this bountiful border will fill your days with color from early summer to early fall (even longer with regular deadheading). Leave the garden cleanup until early spring, and you can enjoy the forms of the grasses and seedheads well into winter — that's a lot of long-lasting beauty from one easy-care garden.

PLANT LIST

1	*Achillea* 'Coronation Gold'	3 plants
2	A. 'The Beacon'	3 plants
3	*Aster novae-angliae* 'September Ruby'	3 plants
4	*Coreopsis lanceolata* 'Sunburst'	3 plants
5	*Gaillardia* x *grandiflora* 'Dazzler'	3 plants
6	*Heliopsis helianthoides* var. *scabra* 'Goldgreenheart'	5 plants
7	*Hibiscus moscheutos* 'Lord Baltimore'	1 plant
8	*Imperata cylindrica* 'Rubra'	6 plants
9	*Kniphofia* 'Springtime'	1 plant
10	*Monarda* 'Jacob Cline'	3 plants
11	*Oenothera fruticosa* 'Fireworks'	3 plants
12	*Panicum virgatum* 'Northwind'	3 plants
13	*Phlox paniculata* 'Starfire'	3 plants
14	*Rudbeckia maxima*	3 plants
15	*Sanguisorba menziesii*	2 plants

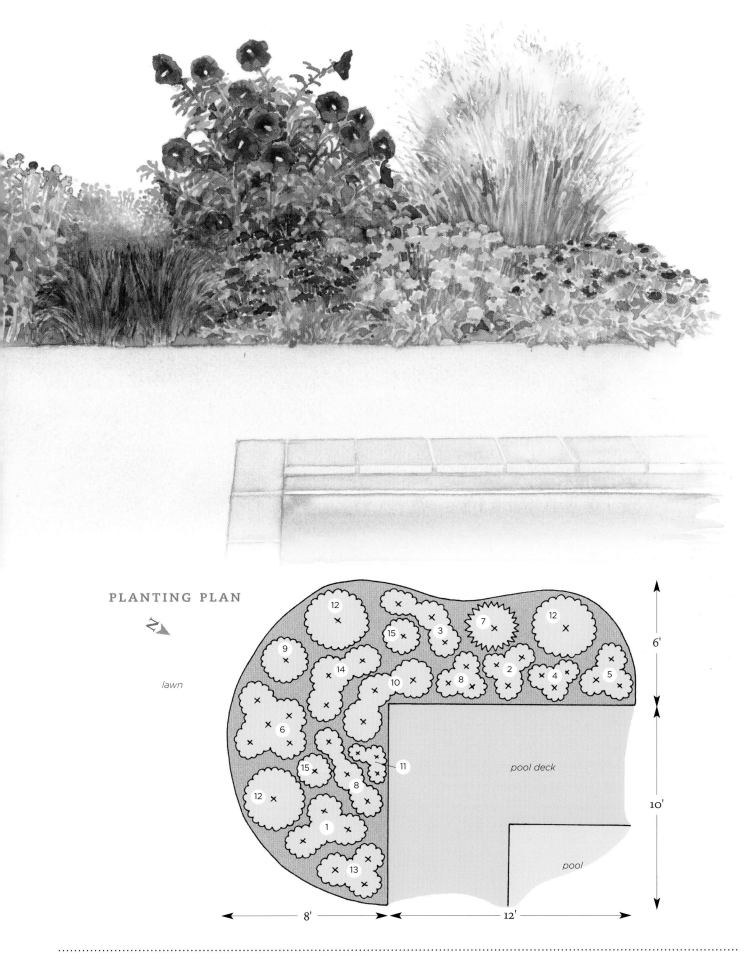

PLANTING PLAN

N

lawn

pool deck

pool

6'

10'

8'

12'

DESIGNER'S CHECKLIST

☐ **Hit the right height.** Tall perennials are a perfect choice for providing vertical interest around a deck or pool where a tree would add unwelcome shade or dropped leaves and fruits. Six to 8 feet tall is about the right scale to give a pleasing vertical effect without making people feel overwhelmed by the plants.

☐ **Green grasses make good partners.** No doubt about it: Ornamental grasses are great companions for hot-colored flowers. Their rich greens provide a cool contrast that makes reds, oranges, and golds really "pop."

☐ **Try tall perennials as a temporary wall.** Tall plants are ideal for providing beautiful summer and fall screening around a pool, deck, or other outdoor entertaining area without the permanence of a hedge or the expense of a privacy fence. To minimize staking chores, look for species and cultivars that are touted as having strong stems, and hold off on irrigation and fertilizers, which can promote fast but weak growth. If your plants still tend to flop, try cutting them back by about half in early summer to get bushier (albeit shorter), self-supporting stems.

☐ **Go wild for wildlife.** Brightly colored blooms tend to attract butterflies and hummingbirds, so a hot-color garden can do double-duty as a habitat planting. That's a bonus around a pool, patio, or deck, where you can sit back and watch the action. A birdbath or other source of fresh clean water will help attract even more critters, and fanciful birdhouses can make fun garden accents.

☐ **Be unrestrained with containers.** Pots and planters filled with annuals, perennials, tropicals, bulbs, herbs, and even grasses are a great way to link a garden to a pool, deck, or patio — especially when you use some of the same colors, or even the same plants, in both groupings.

Top-Notch Hot Colors for Sun

Achillea

(Yarrows)

Flat-topped blooms over deeply cut leaves come in a wide range of bright and pastel colors and last throughout the summer. **'Coronation Gold'** has golden yellow flowers and gray-green leaves; height to 3 feet, spread is 18 inches. ZONES 3–9. **'The Beacon' (a.k.a. 'Fanal')** has red flowers with yellow centers and green foliage; height is 18 to 24 inches with similar spread. ZONES 4–8.

ALTERNATIVES: For 'Coronation Gold', *A. filipendulina* 'Gold Plate'; for 'The Beacon', try 'Red Beauty' or 'Red Velvet'.

Aster novae-angliae 'September Ruby'

('September Ruby' New England aster)

Rich pinkish red, yellow-centered flowers bloom from late summer through early fall atop well-branched, 4-foot stems clad in narrow, bright green leaves; spread is 18 to 24 inches. ZONES 4–8.

ALTERNATIVES: *A. novi-belgii* 'Crimson Brocade'.

Coreopsis lanceolata 'Sunburst'

('Sunburst' coreopsis)

Twenty-four- to 30-inch stems are topped with semi-double, golden yellow flowers from early summer into early fall over lance-shaped green leaves; spread is 18 inches. ZONES 4–9.

ALTERNATIVES: 'Double Sunburst' or *C. verticillata* 'Zagreb'.

Gaillardia x grandiflora 'Dazzler'

('Dazzler' blanket flower)

Orange-red, daisylike flowers with yellow petal tips bloom throughout the summer atop 18- to 24-inch stems over medium green leaves; spread is 12 to 18 inches. ZONES 3–8.

ALTERNATIVES: The shorter cultivar 'Baby Cole' or 'Kobold' (a.k.a. 'Goblin').

Heliopsis helianthoides var. scabra 'Goldgreenheart'

('Goldgreenheart' oxeye)

Three-foot stems are clad in rough, medium green leaves and feature double, bright yellow, daisylike flowers with green-tinged centers from midsummer into fall; spread to about 2 feet. ZONES 2–9.

ALTERNATIVES: The cultivar 'Light of Loddon' or 'Summer Sun'.

Hibiscus moscheutos 'Lord Baltimore'

('Lord Baltimore' rose mallow)

This rose mallow offers gigantic, bright red blooms from mid- or late summer until frost over broad, lobed green leaves on shrubby, 5-foot-tall and 4-foot-wide plants. ZONES 5–9.

ALTERNATIVES: Swamp hibiscus (*H. coccineus*).

Imperata cylindrica 'Rubra'

(Japanese blood grass, a.k.a. 'Red Baron')

Upright, narrow green leaves are tipped with red, turning all burgundy red by fall; clumps are 12 to 18 inches tall and wide, gradually spreading wider. Be aware that the straight species *I. cylindrica* is classified as a noxious weed. So far, this cultivar appears to be safe to grow, but if any all-green shoots appear, remove them immediately. ZONES 5–9.

ALTERNATIVES: The tender perennial dwarf red fountain grass (*Pennisetum setaceum* 'Eaton Canyon').

Out by the Pool

Swimming pools and perennial gardens make perfect partners if you keep a few tips in mind as you plan your design. Here are some basics to get you started:

* It's generally best to keep plants away from the very edge of a pool; otherwise, dropped leaves and petals will clog the pool's filters.

* Pots and planters filled with annuals and tropicals are excellent for adding color impact, but keep them a few feet away from the edge of the pool so they aren't in the way.

* Choose plants with low maintenance in mind. You want to be able to relax around your pool, not feel guilty about staking you forgot to do.

* For safety, don't plant perennials with sharp or thorny leaves, such as yuccas and miscanthus, near the poolside edge of the garden.

* If there's a fence around your pool, plan the garden to flow through it (in other words, so it's on both sides of the fence). That will eliminate tedious trimming along the outside of the barrier.

For more ideas and inspiration, check out *Poolscaping: Gardening and Landscaping around Your Swimming Pool and Spa,* by Catriona Tudor Erler (see Recommended Reading in the Appendix).

Kniphofia 'Springtime'

('Springtime' torch lily)

Tufted clumps of slender, gray-green, evergreen leaves send up 30- to 36-inch stems topped in early or midsummer with dense spikes of tubular blooms that are red in bud and creamy white when fully open; spread to about 2 feet. ZONES 5–9.

ALTERNATIVES:

K. uvaria or any hybrid in a similar height range, such as 'Wayside Flame' (a.k.a. 'Pfitzeri').

Kniphofia

Monarda 'Jacob Cline'

('Jacob Cline' bee balm)

Shaggy-looking clusters of rich red flowers bloom from mid- to late summer atop 4- to 5-foot stems clad in aromatic, mildew-resistant green leaves; spread is 2 to 3 feet. ZONES 3–9.

ALTERNATIVES:

Another red, mildew-resistant hybrid, such as 'Colrain Red' or 'Kardinal'.

Oenothera fruticosa 'Fireworks'

('Fireworks' sundrops)

Slow-spreading clumps of upright stems are clad in red-tinged leaves, with red buds that open into cupped, bright yellow flowers from early summer to early fall; 18 inches tall and wide. ZONES 3–9.

ALTERNATIVES:

The cultivar 'Summer Solstice'.

Panicum virgatum 'Northwind'

('Northwind' switch grass)

'Northwind' forms very upright, 24- to 30-inch-wide clumps of medium-green foliage that turns yellow in fall, plus 5- to 6-foot stems topped with airy, yellowish flower plumes in late summer and lasting into winter. ZONES 4–9.

ALTERNATIVES:

Another cultivar, such as 'Rotstrahlbusch' or 'Shenandoah'.

Phlox paniculata 'Starfire'

('Starfire' phlox)

'Starfire' bears large clusters of fragrant, glowing crimson-red flowers from midsummer to early fall atop 2- to 3-foot stems with green, maroon-tinged leaves; spread is 18 to 24 inches. ZONES 4–8.

ALTERNATIVES:

The cultivar 'Nicky' or 'Tenor'.

Rudbeckia maxima

(Giant coneflower)

Three-foot-wide clumps of blue-gray leaves in late summer and early fall send up 5- to 7-foot stems topped with raised, dark cones surrounded by bright yellow petals. ZONES 5–9.

ALTERNATIVES:

R. 'Herbstsonne'.

Rudbeckia maxima

Sanguisorba menziesii

(Burnet)

Two-foot-wide clumps of toothed green leaves with wiry, 18- to 24-inch stems tipped with maroon to pinkish support interesting bottlebrush-like spikes in early summer. ZONES 4–8.

ALTERNATIVES:

Knautia macedonica.

Working with White

OVER THE YEARS, some gardeners have developed practically a cult around the concept of a white garden. But creating a garden based on whites, silvers, and grays is no more difficult that creating any other kind of perennial garden.

Why White?

White gardens have many advantages besides trendiness. For gardens usually viewed from a distance, bright white blooms are real eye-catchers. The crisp, clean appearance of white flowers and variegated foliage brightens up the gloom of shady spots and makes you feel cool even on a sultry summer day. A white garden is also a fantastic place for evening and nighttime relaxing and entertaining. Reds, blues, and other deep colors seem to disappear at dusk, but whites and silvers really "pop" in even the slightest amount of moonlight. So even if you're not at home during the day, you can still enjoy beautiful flowers and lovely leaves all evening.

White Is White . . . or Not

All whites are not created equal! Besides pure white ('David' phlox), you'll find creamy or yellow-tinged whites ('Joan Senior' daylily), greenish whites (*Hydrangea arborescens* 'Anna-belle'), bluish whites ('Mrs. Robert Brydon' clematis), and pink-tinged whites (heucheras and tiarellas). Many white flowers include blotches or centers of another color. If you want to minimize the differences, separate plants with green, blue, gray, or silvery foliage to make the variations less noticeable. Happily, all whites look pretty much the same at night, so in the evening, the obvious differences during the day become negligible.

One other warning: White flowers are lovely in their glory, but they look terrible as they die. So unless you plan to deadhead twice daily, avoid putting a white garden in a highly visible area, such as near a main entrance or along a heavily used path. Those browning flowers won't be nearly as noticeable at a distance, or at all after dusk.

Catching the late afternoon sun, these white flowers seem to glow within.

Dressed Up in White

IF YOU ENJOY planning gardens by color, chances are you'll want to try your hand at a white garden at some point, and this design may be just the thing to inspire you. It's a classic long border packed with white flowers and silvery foliage for interest from late spring through mid-fall. The ultimate finishing touch would be a path of rich green turf or cool gray flagstone along the front for good looks and foot-friendly strolling.

PLANTING PLAN

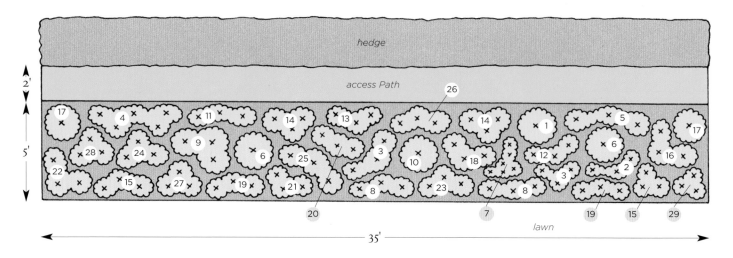

PLANT LIST

#		
1	*Alcea rosea* 'Chater's Double White'	1 plant
2	*Anemone sylvestris*	3 plants
3	*Anthemis* 'Susanna Mitchell'	6 plants
4	*Aster pringlei* 'Monte Cassino'	5 plants
5	*Boltonia asteroides* 'Snowbank'	3 plants
6	*Crambe cordifolia*	2 plants
7	*Crocus speciosus* f. *albus*	6 bulbs
8	*Dianthus* 'Mrs. Sinkins'	6 plants
9	*Echinacea purpurea* 'White Swan'	3 plants
10	*Gypsophila paniculata* 'Bristol Fairy'	1 plant
11	*Iris* 'Immortality'	3 plants
12	*I. pallida* 'Argentea Variegata'	3 plants
13	*I. sibirica* 'Fourfold White'	3 plants
14	*Leucanthemum* x *superbum* 'Becky'	6 plants
15	*L.* x *superbum* 'Snowcap'	6 plants
16	*Lychnis chalcedonica* 'Alba'	3 plants
17	*Miscanthus sinensis* 'Morning Light'	2 plants
18	*Nepeta* x *faassenii* 'Snowflake'	3 plants
19	*Pennisetum alopecuroides* 'Little Bunny'	6 plants
20	*Phlox paniculata* 'David'	3 plants
21	*Potentilla tridentata*	3 plants
22	*Salvia argentea*	3 plants
23	*S.* x *sylvestris* 'Snow Hill'	3 plants
24	*Sedum* 'Frosty Morn'	3 plants
25	*Tradescantia* 'Osprey'	3 plants
26	*Verbascum bombyciferum* 'Arctic Summer'	3 plants
27	*Verbena* 'Snowflurry'	3 plants
28	*Veronica spicata* 'Alba'	3 plants
29	*V. spicata* subsp. *incana*	3 plants

DESIGNER'S CHECKLIST

☐ **Be aware of the backdrop.** If you're planning a garden to go in front of a wall, fence, or hedge, keep in mind that this feature will influence the scale of the whole design. Against a 4-foot-tall backdrop, for instance, the tallest plants should be in the 4- to 6-foot range; against an 8-foot wall, a few 10- or 12-foot plants wouldn't be amiss. Having a few tall plants that peek over the top softens the hard lines of a clipped hedge, wall, or fence and visually ties the border to its background.

☐ **Have stand-ins waiting in the wings.** When you look at a multicolored garden, your eye tends to pause at different sections, so you see the bed or border as a series of vignettes. But in a one-color garden, you see the whole thing at once, so any spaces where flowers are missing will be immediately obvious. Keeping some potted annuals on hand — white cosmos (*Cosmos bipinnatus*) and flowering tobaccos (*Nicotiana*) are particularly good choices — lets you fill these spaces as soon as they appear and keep your garden looking lush all through the growing season.

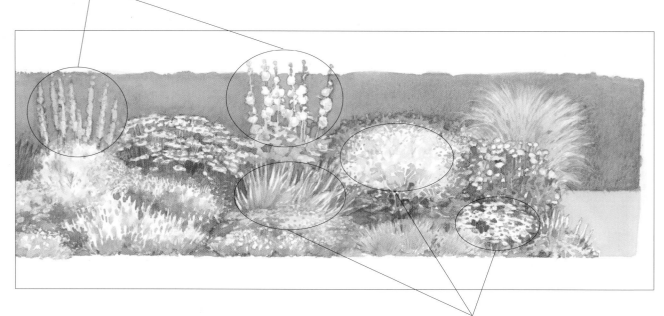

☐ **Don't get hung up on white-and-only-white.** When you really look at plants, it's easy to see that there's no such thing as a true monochromatic (one-color) garden. Even if you choose only pure white flowers, you still have leaves in all shades of green, as well as the different colors of buds and seeds, for example. So if you're worried about your white garden looking a bit dull, go ahead and add a few splashes of maroon, yellow, blue, or another color to liven things up — the whites will look all the better for the contrast.

☐ **Pay attention to shapes.** In a monochromatic garden, the visual excitement that usually comes from different colors comes from the interplay of various flower forms and foliage textures. Thus, as you're planning combinations, it's important to mix up bloom shapes — clouds, spikes, daisies — as well as leaf forms (ferny against flat, narrow against broad, and so on).

Alcea rosea 'Chater's Double White'

('Chater's Double White' hollyhock)
Two-foot-wide mounds of rounded, bright green leaves with spikes of full, ruffled white blooms early to midsummer on 5- to 6-foot-tall stems. Short-lived; replace plants every 2 to 3 years. ZONES 3–8.
ALTERNATIVES: Culver's root (*Veronicastrum virginicum*); white foxglove (*Digitalis purpurea* 'Alba').

Anemone sylvestris

(Snowdrop anemone)
Cupped white flowers with yellow centers over deeply lobed, green leaves bloom mainly in late spring, with scattered rebloom later, followed by fluffy white seedheads; about 1 foot tall and wide. Can spread quickly by creeping roots, divide every other year for control. ZONES 4–9.
ALTERNATIVES: White pasqueflower (*Pulsatilla vulgaris* f. *alba*).

Anthemis 'Susanna Mitchell'

('Susanna Mitchell' anthemis)
This plant has bushy, 12- to 18-inch-tall and -wide clumps of ferny, silvery leaves and creamy white, yellow-centered daisies from early summer into fall. ZONES 3–7.
ALTERNATIVES: 'Little Princess' Shasta daisy (*Leucanthemum* x *superbum* 'Little Princess').

Aster pringlei 'Monte Cassino'

('Monte Cassino' aster)
Three-foot-tall, 1-foot-wide clumps of upright stems are virtually smothered in small, white, yellow-centered, daisylike flowers from late summer through fall. Popular as a cut flower too. ZONES 4–8.
ALTERNATIVES: Calico aster (*A. lateriflorus* 'Horizontalis').

Boltonia asteroides 'Snowbank'

('Snowbank' boltonia)
Upright, 4- to 5-foot-tall stems are clad in narrow, blue-green leaves and topped with white, yellow-centered, daisylike blooms from late summer well into fall; 18- to 30-inch clumps. ZONES 4–9.
ALTERNATIVES: 'Wedding Lace' New England aster (*Aster novae-angliae* 'Wedding Lace').

Crambe cordifolia

(Crambe)
Two-foot-tall, 3-foot-wide mounds of broad, crinkled, deep green leaves send up 4- to 6-foot branched stalks tipped in small, sweetly scented white flowers in early to midsummer. ZONES 5–8.
ALTERNATIVES: Baby's breath (*Gypsophila paniculata*).

Crocus speciosus f. albus

(White fall crocus)
Goblet-shaped, white fall flowers 4 to 6 inches tall; grasslike spring leaves are dormant by midsummer. Plant bulbs 4 inches apart. ZONES 3–8.
ALTERNATIVES: *C. ochroleucus*.

Dianthus 'Mrs. Sinkins'

('Mrs. Sinkins' dianthus)
Richly fragrant, fringed-edge, pure white double blooms in midsummer atop 6- to 10-inch stems over leafy mat. ZONES 5–9.
ALTERNATIVES: Any other white dianthus, such as *D. plumarius* 'Itsaul White'.

Echinacea purpurea 'White Swan'

('White Swan' purple coneflower)
Daisylike blooms with white petals and raised orange-bronze centers in mid- to late summer (some rebloom into fall); deep green leaves on 2- to 3-foot stems; 12- to 18-inch-across clumps. ZONES 3–9.
ALTERNATIVES: The cultivar 'White Lustre'.

Gypsophila paniculata 'Bristol Fairy'

('Bristol Fairy' baby's breath)
Baby's breath forms rounded, airy, 2- to 3-foot-tall and -wide mounds of narrow, blue-green leaves and sports small, double white flowers from early or mid- to late summer. ZONES 3–7.
ALTERNATIVES: Bowman's root (*Gillenia stipulata* or *G. trifoliata*) or gaura (*Gaura lindheimeri*).

Iris

(Irises)
Although short-lived, iris blooms are some of the best whites you'll ever find. 'Immortality' is a hybrid with pure white petals and a light yellow "beard" in early summer and again in late summer or fall over sword-shaped, blue-green leaves; 30 inches tall, 18 inches wide. ZONES 4–9. *I. pallida* 'Argentea Variegata', with white-striped, blue-green leaves, has blue

Stephanie Says

Behind the Border

THERE'S NOTHING LIKE A DARK GREEN BACKGROUND to set off white flowers, so we've set this design against a 6-foot-tall arborvitae (*Thuja*) hedge. Don't have a hedge? A fence or wall will serve just as well. Whatever the backdrop, remember to leave at least 18 inches between it and the back of the border so you can get in for easy maintenance. If you're planting against a hedge, there's another good reason to leave some space behind the border: Hedge roots can suck up water and nutrients like nobody's business! Keeping your perennials out from the hedge a bit will minimize the chance of serious root competition, so both the hedge and the garden will be better off. ✳

flowers in early summer; 2 to 3 feet tall and 18 to 24 inches across. ZONES 5–9. *I. sibirica* **'Fourfold White'** blooms in late spring to early summer, with pure white blooms touched with gold near the center over grasslike green leaves; 3 to 4 feet tall and 2 feet across. ZONES 3–8.

ALTERNATIVES: Another white-flowered iris.

Leucanthemum x superbum

(Shasta daisy)

White-petaled, golden-centered daisies atop upright stems and deep green leaves in early to midsummer; deadhead for repeat bloom into fall. **'Becky'** grows 30 to 36 inches tall and 2 feet wide with large blooms on sturdy stems. **'Snowcap'** has 2- to 3-inch-wide flowers; plants are 15 inches tall, 18 inches wide. ZONES 4–8.

ALTERNATIVES: For 'Becky', use 'Alaska'; for 'Snowcap', another compact cultivar, such as 'Silver Princess' or 'Snow Lady'.

Lychnis chalcedonica 'Alba'

(White Maltese cross)

Upright, 3- to 4-foot-tall stems are topped with clusters of white flowers in early and midsummer; clumps are 1 foot wide. ZONES 4–8.

ALTERNATIVES: White rose campion (*L. coronaria* 'Alba').

Miscanthus sinensis 'Morning Light'

('Morning Light' miscanthus)

Fountainlike clumps of arching, very narrow green leaves edged with white have a silvery appearance from a distance; reddish bronze flower plumes appear in fall and last into winter. Clumps are 4 to 6 feet tall and 3 to 4 feet across. ZONES 5–9.

ALTERNATIVES: A blue-leaved switch grass (*Panicum virgatum*) cultivar, such as 'Cloud Nine' or 'Dallas Blues'.

Nepeta x faassenii 'Snowflake'

('White Wonder' catmint)

Mounds of small, gray-green leaves send up clusters of white flowers from early summer into fall (especially with regular deadheading); 1 foot tall and 18 inches across. ZONES 4–8.

ALTERNATIVES: 'White Cloud' calamint (*Calamintha nepeta* 'White Cloud').

Pennisetum alopecuroides 'Little Bunny'

('Little Bunny' fountain grass)

Twelve- to 18-inch-wide tufts of green leaves are accented with brushy, 12- to 18-inch, silvery green spikes in late summer. ZONES 5–9.

ALTERNATIVES: A cultivar of fescue (*Festuca*), such as 'Elijah Blue' or 'Siskiyou Blue'.

Phlox paniculata 'David'

('David' phlox)

Clusters of fragrant, snowy white blooms appear on 36- to 40-inch stems from midsummer to early fall over rich green, mildew-resistant foliage; clumps are 18 inches across. ZONES 4–9.

ALTERNATIVES: The cultivar 'Mt. Fuji', 'White Admiral', or 'World Peace'.

Potentilla tridentata

(Three-toothed cinquefoil)

Clusters of white flowers blossom throughout summer on 6- to 8-inch-tall, 1-foot-wide evergreen carpets of three-toothed, glossy, deep green leaves that turn red in fall. ZONES 2–8.

ALTERNATIVES: White sea thrift (*Armeria maritima* 'Alba').

Salvia

(Salvias)

Spiky flowers appear in summer over green or grayish leaves.

S. argentea (silver sage) grows in 2-foot-wide rosettes of woolly white leaves with 3-foot spikes of white flowers in mid- to late summer; biennial or short-lived perennial. ZONES 5–8.

S. x *sylvestris* **'Snow Hill'** has spikes of pure white blooms through summer on clumps that are 20 inches tall and 12 to 18 inches across. ZONES 4–8.

ALTERNATIVES: For silver sage, *S. officinalis* 'Berggarten'; for 'Snow Hill', *S. verticillata* 'White Rain' or *Veronica spicata* 'Icicle'.

Sedum 'Frosty Morn'

('Frosty Morn' sedum)

Upright clumps about 1 foot tall and wide; blue-green leaves edged in white on thick stems; clustered light pink to white flowers late summer to early fall. ZONES 3–9.

ALTERNATIVES: *Lysimachia punctata* 'Alexander'.

Tradescantia 'Osprey'

('Osprey' tradescantia)

Three-petaled white flowers with pale blue stamens over arching green leaves on 18- to 24-inch stems early summer to early fall; 18-inch-wide clumps. ZONES 5–9.

ALTERNATIVES: The cultivars 'Innocence' or 'Snowcap'.

Verbascum bombyciferum 'Arctic Summer'

('Arctic Summer' mullein; a.k.a. 'Polarsommer' or 'Polar Summer')

A biennial with 2- to 3-foot-wide rosettes of large, fuzzy, silvery leaves in year one, and 5- to 7-foot spikes of yellow flowers in midsummer in year two. ZONES 4–8.

ALTERNATIVES: The cultivar 'Silver Lining' or *V. chaixii* 'Album'.

Verbena 'Snowflurry'

('Snowflurry' verbena)

One-foot-tall, 18 inches or more carpets of toothed green leaves covered with clustered white flowers from mid- or late spring to fall. ZONES 5–10.

ALTERNATIVES: Another white verbena ('Tapien White', 'Temari White', or 'Tukana White').

Veronica spicata

(Speedwell)

Spiky flowers on upright plants. **'Alba'** has white blooms on 12- to 18-inch-tall and -wide plants. *V. spicata* subsp. *incana*; **a.k.a.** *V. incana* (woolly or silver speedwell) has silvery gray leaves and stems topped with spikes of purple-blue blooms; to 1 foot tall and wide. Both flower through summer. ZONES 3–8.

ALTERNATIVES: For 'Alba', try 'Icicle'; for woolly speedwell, try a lamb's ears such as *Stachys byzantina* 'Silver Carpet'.

Pastel Plantings

IF YOU'RE ENAMORED of the traditional English style of gardening, or if you just aren't a fan of bright colors, a bed or border based on pastel-flowered perennials will bring you years of pleasure. These soft colors look great with just about any kind of home, so they're also an excellent choice if you're designing your first perennial garden. You're practically guaranteed to get spectacular results.

Choosing the Right Site

Perennial plantings based on pastel colors are tailor-made for shady sites, because their delicate tints really "pop" there. They're fine for sunny sites as well, although full, intense sun will bleach out pale flowers during the day. The blooms will still look nice in early morning and in the evening, though, so a pastel border is perfect where you'll walk by it as you head out to and come home from work, or around a deck or patio where you relax in the evening.

Think Pink

We like to think of pastels as "comfort colors": They're familiar and safe, and it's almost impossible to made unappealing combinations with them. Although pink flowers are similar to red ones in that they can lean toward either blue (the lilac-pinks) or orange (usually called peach or apricot), pairing different pinks isn't nearly as jarring as different reds can be. And in gardens sited in the shade or viewed at dawn or dusk, these variations are hardly visible anyway. For extra insurance, mix in plenty of "blenders": silvery, gray, and blue foliage, as well as some green flowers, such as bear's foot hellebore (*Helleborus foetidus*), lady's mantle (*Alchemilla mollis*), and the annuals *Nicotiana langsdorfii* and 'Green Envy' zinnias.

Stephanie Says

YOU WANT ROMANCE? You want pretty pastel blooms? You need peonies. Besides their stunning flowers, these long-lived plants offer handsome clumps of good-looking, deep green leaves that make excellent partners for later-flowering perennials. As a bonus, the foliage of many cultivars turns a rich reddish to bronze in fall. Because you'll be choosing them for their blooms, however, and not for their foliage, pay special attention to the flower forms. The big ruffled doubles are a classic favorite for cut flowers, and they're luxuriant in the garden, too, but they need staking to stay upright. If you don't want to bother with stakes or hoops, consider growing single-flowered peonies instead. Their simple but elegant flowers are less likely to be beaten down by bad weather, so they will provide year after year of beauty with practically no work on your part. ✳

Perfect Peonies

Bringing the Outdoors In

WHEN IT COMES TO ROMANCE, a pastel perennial planting sets the stage. Add a pretty pathway accented with a series of rose-covered arbors, and you have a glorious garden that perfectly complements any house. We envisioned this design for a space right outside a sunroom, so you can enjoy it from indoors as well as out. You could add a hedge along the far side of the garden to give the space a sense of enclosure: perhaps the maroon-leaved, white-flowered Diabolo ninebark (*Physocarpus* 'Monlo') to continue the dark-and-light theme, or a row of arborvitae (*Thuja*) to create a dark green backdrop for the lighter blooms.

PLANT LIST

#	Plant	Quantity
1	Achillea 'Martina'	12 plants
2	Aster 'Wood's Blue'	12 plants
3	Calamagrostis x acutiflora 'Karl Foerster'	4 plants
4	Calamintha nepeta 'White Cloud'	12 plants
5	Coreopsis 'Créme Brûlée'	16 plants
6	Dicentra 'King of Hearts'	10 plants
7	Heuchera 'Petite Pearl Fairy'	16 plants
8	Paeonia 'Krinkled White'	1 plant
9	Phlox paniculata 'Eva Cullum'	4 plants
10	Rosa 'Climbing Iceberg'	3 plants
11	Salvia nemorosa 'Caradonna'	6 plants
12	S. nemorosa 'East Friesland'	6 plants
13	Sisyrinchium angustifolium 'Lucerne'	4 plants
14	Stachys macrantha 'Superba'	6 plants
15	Verbascum 'Mont Blanc'	1 plant
16	Vitis vinifera 'Purpurea'	3 plants

PLANTING PLAN

DESIGNER'S CHECKLIST

☐ **Pay special attention to high-visibility plantings.** In sites where you often get up close and personal with your perennials — along a path, by a door, or next to a patio or bench — it's important to choose plants that look good throughout the growing season. Perennials with attractive, long-lasting foliage, such as heucheras, sedums, and low-growing ornamental grasses, provide easy-care beauty whether or not they are in bloom.

☐ **Choose a theme for continuity, then build on it.** To give any design a strong sense of organization, select two or three main colors that will carry through from spring to fall, then add complementary partners to liven things up as the seasons change. This design, for example, relies on base notes of white flowers and maroon foliage, with dashes of pink, yellow, and light and dark blue for variety.

☐ **Repeat features as well as colors.** A single arbor makes a welcoming entrance, but a series of them turns an ordinary path into a feature that's absolutely magical: what designer Doug Kane calls a "journey through the landscape." A cool, shaded path invites you to stroll through to see what's beyond, while you get peeks into the gardens surrounding you as you walk along. Don't have room for multiple arbors? Consider repeating clematis-covered posts on each side of a double border, or use pots of tall annuals at regular intervals to line a path, to draw your eye along the planting.

☐ **Take color cues from furnishings.** If you're designing a garden you'll see mostly from indoors, look around the room to get ideas for color combinations. You might, for instance, have floral-patterned slipcovers or curtains in shades of pink, baby blue, and white, and you could use those three colors as the basis for your plant selections. Repeating indoor colors in your garden will provide a strong visual link to the two spaces and make both look larger. And here's an extra benefit: If you snip blooms to bring indoors, they'll be perfectly color-coordinated with your room.

Achillea 'Martina'

('Martina' yarrow)

Flat-topped clusters of yellow flowers that fade to cream appear through the summer over lacy, deep green leaves; height is 24 to 30 inches, spreads to 18 inches. ZONES 4–8.

ALTERNATIVES: The cultivar 'Alabaster' or 'Anthea'.

Aster 'Wood's Blue'

('Wood's Blue' aster)

Twelve- to 15-inch-tall and -wide mounds of small, green leaves are covered with daisylike, medium blue flowers from late summer well into fall. ZONES 3–8.

ALTERNATIVES: A. novi-belgii 'Professor Anton Kippenburg'.

Calamagrostis x acutiflora 'Karl Foerster'

('Karl Foerster' feather reed grass)

This grass features narrow, upright, 2-foot-wide clumps of green leaves with 4- to 5-foot stems topped in pinkish tan plumes that emerge in midsummer and last well into winter. ZONES 4–8.

ALTERNATIVES: The cultivar 'Overdam', with white-edged green leaves.

Calamintha nepeta 'White Cloud'

('White Cloud' calamint)

Rounded, 1-foot-tall and -wide mounds of small, very aromatic leaves sport clusters of tiny white flowers throughout the summer. ZONES 5–9.

ALTERNATIVES: Creeping baby's breath (Gypsophila repens) or white Carpathian harebell (Campanula carpatica 'White Clips').

Coreopsis 'Crème Brûlée'

('Crème Brûlée' coreopsis)

Soft yellow flowers appear from early or midsummer into fall atop 18- to 24-inch stems; spreads to 2 feet. ZONES 5–9.

ALTERNATIVES: C. verticillata 'Moonbeam'.

Dicentra 'King of Hearts'

('King of Hearts' bleeding heart)

Clusters of rosy pink blooms dangle above mounds of finely cut, blue-green leaves from late spring throughout the summer; clumps are 8 to 12 inches tall and wide. ZONES 3–8.

ALTERNATIVES: The cultivar 'Luxuriant' or 'Zestful'.

Heuchera 'Petite Pearl Fairy'

('Petite Pearl Fairy' heuchera)

Compact, 8-inch-wide mounds of lobed, bronze-purple, silver-mottled leaves send up airy spikes of small pink flowers on 10-inch stems in late spring and early summer. ZONES 5–9.

ALTERNATIVES: The cultivar 'Petite Marbled Burgundy' or another Heuchera or x Heucherella with purple-and-silver leaves.

Paeonia 'Krinkled White'

('Krinkled White' peony)

Snowy white petals surround golden centers in early summer atop sturdy, 30-inch stems clad in lobed, medium green leaves; spread to about 30 inches. ZONES 3–8.

ALTERNATIVES: Any other white peony of your choice.

Phlox paniculata 'Eva Cullum'

('Eva Cullum' phlox)

Thirty- to 36-inch-tall stems bearing narrow green leaves are topped with large clusters of fragrant, medium pink blooms with darker pink centers from mid- to late summer or early fall; spreads to about 2 feet. ZONES 4–8.

ALTERNATIVES: Another pink phlox, such as 'Bright Eyes' or 'Tracy's Treasure'.

Salvia nemorosa

(Perennial salvia)

Spiky, purple-blue flowers appear over medium green leaves from early to midsummer, usually with repeat bloom if you deadhead regularly. 'East Friesland' has deep purple-blue blooms and is about 18 inches tall and wide; 'Caradonna' is similar but has deep purple stems in clumps that are 24 to 30 inches tall and wide. ZONES 4–8.

ALTERNATIVES: S. x sylvestris 'Blue Queen' or 'May Night'.

Sisyrinchium angustifolium 'Lucerne'

('Lucerne' blue-eyed grass)

Grasslike tufts of slender, green leaves sport starry, bright blue, yellow-eyed flowers from late spring into midsummer; height is 6 to 8 inches with a similar spread. ZONES 5–9.

ALTERNATIVES: A pink- or white-flowered dianthus or dwarf fountain grass (Pennisetum alopecuroides 'Little Bunny').

Stachys macrantha 'Superba'

(Big betony)

One-foot-wide clumps of scalloped, deep green leaves send up dense spikes of purplish pink flowers atop 2-foot stems from early summer to early fall. ZONES 5–8.

ALTERNATIVES: Dianthus 'Bath's Pink' or a pink verbena, such as 'Sissinghurst'.

Verbascum 'Mont Blanc'

('Mont Blanc' mullein)

Two-foot-wide rosettes of glossy green leaves give rise to 3- to 4-foot stems featuring spikes of creamy white, yellow-centered blooms from early to late summer. ZONES 5–9.

ALTERNATIVES: V. chaixii f. album.

A Year of Perennials

WHO SAYS GARDENING is just a summertime hobby? True gardeners can find a reason to be outside at just about any time of year. Whether you want to highlight a single season or celebrate your hobby with a glorious year-round garden, this chapter has tips to help you plan a perennial planting that's guaranteed to please.

Perennial Gardens for All Seasons

BACK WHEN HOMEOWNERS had large properties (and a staff to take care of them), a four-season perennial garden was actually four separate borders, each with one period of peak interest. Nowadays, few of us have the time, the space, or the funds to create and maintain multiple single-season plantings, so we tend to combine all of our seasons into one "all-purpose" garden. This approach takes careful planning, but the pleasure such a garden gives all year long will definitely repay the extra effort.

Discovering Multi-Season Perennials

One of the musts for designing any garden is to start with a wish list. In this case, you'll actually need four lists, one to cover each season. Keeping in mind the growing conditions your proposed garden site has to offer (sunlight, soil, and so on), pore through catalogs and books to get ideas of plants you'd like to try for each season.

As you do your research, you'll have an easy time finding perennials that bloom in

Well-chosen perennials, along with shrubs, grasses, and annuals, ensure year-round interest in this large garden.

spring, or summer, or fall, and it's fine to add them to your lists. But for a really great year-round garden, you'll have to dig a little deeper (so to speak) to find perennials that can look good in more than one season. Here are some traits to watch for as you read plant descriptions:

❊ Long bloom season (at least 6 weeks, and ideally more than that, to cover at least two seasons)

❊ Long-lasting seedheads

❊ Attractive stems

❊ Colorful leaves

❊ Evergreen foliage

❊ Showy fall color

As you can see, foliage plays a major role in a four-season border. Flowers come and go, but you have to look at the leaves all the time, so it just makes sense to pay special attention to this feature. And while traits like showy seeds or berries and colorful stems are more often associated with shrubs than perennials, herbaceous plants with these bonus features are definitely worth hunting for.

So when do you know your list is finished? It depends on how big your new border is going to be and how much variety you want it to have. As a general rule, we like to have about a third of the plants for each of the three main growing seasons, plus a few extras for winter interest. If you're not home during a particular season, though — maybe you spend winters in a warm climate, for instance, or summers on the beach — then use more plants for the seasons when you are at home and few or none for the time you're usually gone.

Perennial Partners for the Big Chill

Let's face it: Unless you live where palm trees flourish, it can be difficult to find enough perennials to make a decent showing through the entire year. The solution is simple, though: Look beyond the usual herbaceous perennials.

Dwarf conifers, as well as deciduous shrubs with attractive fruit, showy bark, or interesting stems, are definitely fair game for inclusion in a year-round border. Some of the best multi-season shrubs are bluebeard (*Caryopteris* x *clandonensis*), butterfly bushes (*Buddleia*), elderberries (*Sambucus*), purple cultivars of smokebush (*Cotinus coggygria*), and winterberry hollies (*Ilex verticillata* and hybrids).

Hardy, early-blooming bulbs are invaluable for giving a quick burst of color when you're most desperate to see flowers again. Keep them toward the middle or back of the border, so the emerging perennial foliage will hide the yellowing bulb leaves by late spring. Choose bulbs in the same color scheme you used to whittle down your perennial list, or do something really different (maybe a black-and-white bulb theme, or a red-and-yellow combination) to start your gardening year with a bang.

Even the best-planned perennial gardens may need a little help around the beginning of August, when the summer bloomers have finished their show and the fall bloomers aren't yet ready to do their thing. Plan ahead for the "dog days" by potting up some extra annuals in late spring, either in individual pots or in larger combination pots, and grow them on through the summer. Then, when your border needs some extra color in late summer, or if a perennial dies and leaves a gap, simply fill the space with a pot of annuals.

A Sunny Four-Season Border

THIS SIMPLE BUT SHOWY
BORDER would be ideal along a driveway
or an often used walkway, where you can admire the
colors and textures all year long. To unify the planting, we've
chosen a scheme of four main colors — white, blue, and gold flowers and
deep purple foliage — with a background of leaves in shades of gray, gray-green,
and green. Shown above in fall, this border can still be filled with color even
months after the peak summer bloom if you remove the spent flowers regularly.

PLANTING PLAN

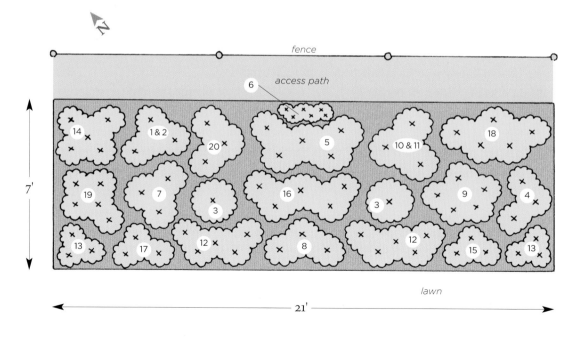

PLANT LIST

1	*Amsonia hubrectii*	3 plants
2	interplanted with *Narcissus* 'Thalia'	12 bulbs
3	*Artemisia* 'Powis Castle'	2 plants
4	*Aster oblongifolius* 'Raydon's Favorite'	3 plants
5	*Calamagrostis* x *acutiflora* 'Karl Foerster'	5 plants
6	*Camassia leichtlinii* 'Blue Danube'	6 bulbs
7	*Coreopsis verticillata* 'Golden Gain'	3 plants
8	*C. verticillata* 'Zagreb'	3 plants
9	*Euphorbia dulcis* 'Chameleon'	5 plants
10	*Heliopsis helianthoides* var. *scabra* 'Golden Plume'	
		3 plants
11	interplanted with *Narcissus* 'Sweetness'	12 bulbs
12	*Heuchera* 'Chocolate Ruffles'	10 plants
13	*Iberis sempervirens* 'Autumn Snow'	6 plants
14	*Iris sibirica* 'Fourfold White'	5 plants
15	*Lavandula angustifolia* 'Blue Cushion'	3 plants
16	*Leucanthemum* x *superbum* 'Becky'	5 plants
17	*Nepeta* x *faassenii* 'Walker's Low'	3 plants
18	*Perovskia atriplicifolia* 'Longin'	5 plants
19	*Salvia nemorosa* 'Caradonna'	5 plants
20	*Sedum* 'Matrona'	3 plants

DESIGNER'S CHECKLIST

☐ **Choose classy grass companions.** Ornamental grasses look great in borders, but their texture is so different that it may look out of place unless you repeat it. One solution is to include several grasses of varying heights throughout the border. Or do what we did here, and echo the fine grass foliage with other narrow-leaved plants, such as Siberian iris (*Iris sibirica*) and bulbs; daylilies (*Hemerocallis*) are fine grass look-alikes too.

☐ **Mix it up.** The real secret to a successful perennial design? We can give it to you in one word: balance. Yes, it's important to repeat colors and textures, but don't get so carried away that you end up using all silver foliage, all spiky flowers, or all anything else. Sure, repetition is usually what first catches your eye — especially if you're looking at the garden from a distance — but it's the subtle interplay of varying heights, foliage textures, flower forms, and bloom colors that gives your garden a sense of depth and sophistication when you see it up close. This is important to remember for any design, but it's especially critical for a four-season garden, as you'll want to site it in a highly visible spot, and it will need to hold its own no matter when you see it.

☐ **Repeat flower and foliage colors.** One of the most common design mistakes is using just one patch of a distinctive color in a border. In this design, for example, a single clump of deep purple foliage would stand out like a sore thumb, so we chose several different purple-leaved plants and used them in different parts of the border. Use this trick when you plan your own gardens, and you'll never go wrong.

☐ **Stay centered.** When you're placing perennials that bloom in bright colors — gold, yellow, orange, red, and white — keep them toward the middle of the border (the middle when looking from side to side, that is). Otherwise, they are likely to draw your eye to the edges of the planting and beyond. You want people to admire your beautiful flower garden, not get distracted by a neighbor's trash cans or your kids' play set.

Amsonia hubrectii
(Arkansas blue star)
Mounded plants (about 3 feet tall and 4 feet wide) sport rounded clusters of pale blue flowers in the late spring over fine-textured, needlelike, bright green leaves that turn bright yellow in fall. ZONES 5–9.
ALTERNATIVES: *A. tabernaemontana*.

Artemisia 'Powis Castle'
('Powis Castle' artemisia)
Two- to 3-foot-tall mounds of lacy, silvery gray, sharp-scented leaves stay on the plant well into winter; spread to 3 feet. ZONES 6–9.
ALTERNATIVES: *A. ludoviciana* 'Valerie Finnis' or southernwood (*A. abrotanum*).

Aster oblongifolius 'Raydon's Favorite'
('Raydon's Favorite' aster)
Dense, rounded mounds of short, slender green leaves are practically smothered with single purple-blue daisies from early fall into mid-fall; height and spread to 3 feet. ZONES 4–9.
ALTERNATIVES: 'October Skies' or another aster.

Calamagrostis x acutiflora 'Karl Foerster'
('Karl Foerster' feather reed grass)
This ornamental grass sends up narrow, upright, 2-foot-wide clumps of green leaves, with 4- to 5-foot stems topped with pinkish tan plumes that emerge in midsummer and last well into winter. ZONES 4–8.
ALTERNATIVES: The cultivar 'Overdam', with white-edged green leaves.

Camassia leichtlinii 'Blue Danube'
('Blue Danube' camassia)
Basal clumps of grasslike green leaves to about 2 feet tall send up 4-foot spikes of starry, purple-blue flowers in late spring. Space bulbs 6 inches apart. ZONES 4–9.
ALTERNATIVES: *C. quamash*.

Coreopsis verticillata
(Thread-leaved coreopsis)
Mounded clumps of needlelike, bright green leaves are topped with rich golden yellow, single flat flowers from early summer to mid-fall (with deadheading). 'Golden Gain' is 18 inches tall and wide. 'Zagreb' is similar, but it's a little shorter and the flowers are a bit more on the yellow side. ZONES 3–9.
ALTERNATIVES: The straight species (*C. verticillata*) for either cultivar.

Euphorbia dulcis 'Chameleon'
('Chameleon' euphorbia)
These rounded mounds about 1 foot tall and wide have maroon leaves and stems topped with tiny, greenish yellow "flowers" in late spring to early summer. Will self-sow. ZONES 4–9.
ALTERNATIVES: *Sedum telephium* subsp. *maximum* 'Atropurpureum' or S. 'Mohrchen'.

Heliopsis helianthoides var. scabra 'Golden Plume'
('Golden Plume' oxeye)
Two- to 3-foot-wide clumps of somewhat coarse, deep green leaves send up sturdy, upright 3- to 4-foot stems featuring double, daisylike, golden yellow blooms all summer (with deadheading). ZONES 3–9.

Heuchera 'Chocolate Ruffles'
('Chocolate Ruffles' heuchera)
This Bressingham Hybrid forms mounds of purplish green to chocolate-brown leaves with ruffled edges, to 1 foot tall and 18 inches across. Airy clusters of tiny white flowers bloom on 18- to 24-inch purple stems in late spring and early summer. ZONES 4–9.
ALTERNATIVES: Any purple-leaved heuchera.

Iberis sempervirens 'Autumn Snow'
('Autumn Snow' perennial candytuft)
One-foot-tall mounds of narrow, deep green leaves look great all year long. Clusters of bright white flowers bloom in late spring and early summer, with some rebloom in fall; spread to 18 inches. ZONES 5–9.
ALTERNATIVES: Any other perennial candytuft cultivar.

Iris sibirica 'Fourfold White'
('Fourfold White' Siberian iris)
Grasslike clumps of slender, arching green leaves display large, pure white blooms, each touched with gold at its heart, in late spring to early summer, followed by interesting upright seedpods that stand well into winter; height and spread from 2 to 3 feet. ZONES 3–8.
ALTERNATIVES: Another white cultivar, such as 'White Swirl'.

Lavandula angustifolia 'Blue Cushion'
('Blue Cushion' English lavender)
One-foot-tall and -wide buns of fragrant narrow, gray-green leaves that last through the winter are accented with spikes of purple-blue flowers from early to late summer atop 18-inch stems. ZONES 5–9.
ALTERNATIVES: Another lavender cultivar.

Leucanthemum x superbum 'Becky'
('Becky' Shasta daisy)
Large, white-petaled, golden-centered daisies bloom atop sturdy, upright 30- to 36-inch stems with deep green leaves; spread to 2 feet. ZONES 4–8.
ALTERNATIVES: The cultivar 'Alaska'.

Narcissus
(Daffodils)

Daffodils form grasslike clumps of narrow, upright green foliage with spring flowers on separate leafless stems. **'Sweetness'** has bright sweetly scented golden yellow blooms, one or two per stem. **'Thalia'** bears two or three richly scented, clear white flowers on each stem. Height of both of these mid-spring daffodils is 1 foot; set the bulbs about 4 inches apart. ZONES 5–9.

ALTERNATIVESS: Other daffodils; there are hosts to choose from.

Nepeta x faassenii 'Walker's Low'
('Walker's Low' catmint)

Low, sprawling mounds of gray-green leaves look good all through the growing season. Spikes of lavender-blue flowers first appear in mid- to late spring, with repeat bloom until frost if you shear them lightly after each flush of bloom; height and spread are 12 to 15 inches. ZONES 4–8.

ALTERNATIVES: 'Blue Wonder' or other cultivar.

Perovskia atriplicifolia 'Longin'
('Longin' Russian sage)

Upright clumps of felted gray stems are clad in silver-frosted green leaves and topped with airy panicles of silvery blue flowers in late summer and early fall; height and spread to 3 feet. ZONES 6–9.

ALTERNATIVES: Any cultivar of Russian sage or caryopteris (Caryopteris x clandonensis).

Salvia nemorosa 'Caradonna'
('Caradonna' sage)

Tidy mounds of rough, medium-green leaves on deep purple stems feature spikes of bright purple-blue flowers from late spring into midsummer (or into fall with regular deadheading); 24 to 30 inches tall and wide. ZONES 4–8.

ALTERNATIVES: S. x sylvestris 'Blue Queen' or 'May Night'.

Sedum 'Matrona'
('Matrona' sedum)

Mounded clumps of upright, deep purple stems with purple-flushed, gray-green leaves produce clusters of pink flowers from late summer into fall, lasting well into winter; 24 to 30 inches tall and 18 to 24 inches across. ZONES 3–9.

ALTERNATIVES: The cultivar 'Purple Emperor'.

Nan's Notebook

WHEN YOU'RE CONSIDERING SHRUB OPTIONS for perennial partners, remember to think about roses too. Don't be put off by the reputation these beautiful plants have of being difficult to grow, because many of them are just as tough and trouble-free as any other landscape shrub. The trick is to look for species and hybrids that thrive for other gardeners in your area, and not to get suckered in by a pretty picture in a glossy catalog. No matter where you live, it is possible to find roses that will give you years of beauty with little or no spraying and no more than average pruning.

Think Rosy Thoughts

In my Pennsylvania garden, one of my favorite perennial partners is red-leaved rose (Rosa glauca). It has red- or pink-tinged, gray-green leaves all through the growing season, accented with single pink flowers in late spring, plus clustered hips that turn orange-red in late summer and last well into winter.

I'm also fond of the floribunda Knock Out ('Radrazz'), which blooms from late spring through the first light frosts and holds its good-looking foliage on deep purple canes through a good bit of the winter. In my garden, it has never shown any disease problems. You seldom hear anyone say much about the fragrance of this rose, but I think it's great — I can sense it from several feet away, and it'll perfume a room if you bring a few blooms indoors. I'll be honest, though: The color of this rose is a challenge. Its buds are sort of orangey red, but the open blooms are definitely on the hot pinkish red side, so companions with either pink or red flowers can clash horribly, and yellow companions, too, may or may not work. Blues are nice, though, as is purple or silver foliage — and you definitely can't go wrong with white-flowered partners. Or go all out by pairing it with orange, violet, blue, and chartreuse for a combo that's guaranteed to stop traffic. ✳

Super Impact for Spring

For most people, the new year begins on January 1, but for gardeners, the new year begins with the first sign of spring and the start of the new growing season. Whether you spend your winters buried in snow or are simply stuck with endless dreary days looking at empty perennial beds, the first blooms of the year are definitely something to celebrate.

Thinking Spring

Of course, cold-climate gardeners aren't the only ones who enjoy a perennial planting of early bloomers. If you live where summers are too hot to make the outdoors enticing, a garden based on spring flowers may be the best way of getting your gardening fix before you retreat indoors to the air conditioner. Spring gardens are also perfect for any space that's heavily shaded by deciduous trees in summer, as woodland wildflowers are naturally adapted to strut their stuff before the trees leaf out and block the sun.

Wherever you live, spring gardens tend to be primarily pastel plantings: pinks, blues, soft yellows, and pale purples, along with lots of white. These colors often look faded and tired in the strong light of summer, but in spring, they never fail to look fresh and cheerful. And because spring pastels rarely appear jarring no matter how you combine them, you're bound to have a gorgeous garden even if you've never planned a perennial garden before in your life.

Extending the Season

In many climates, spring tends to come in one big bang: a few weeks of glorious color, then it's back to shades of green for the rest of the growing season. If you like to wait for mild weather to stroll or sit in your garden, it's fine to fill it with the classic mid- and late-spring lovelies, such as old-fashioned bleeding heart (*Dicentra spectabilis*) and hybrid tulips. But if you enjoy seeking out the very first flowers of the year, make an effort to choose some extra-early bloomers as well, like hellebores (*Helleborus*), scillas, and snowdrops (*Galanthus*). By spreading out the bloom times, you can extend your spring display from just a few weeks to well over 2 months.

Brilliant yellow-greens combined with pinks and lavenders define spring for many gardeners.

A Fantastic
Spring Fling

WANT TO TRY YOUR HAND at a spectacular spring perennial garden? This design links a small tree and a medium-sized shrub to create a half-sun and half-shade planting with plenty of beautiful blooms for the entire spring season, followed by attractive foliage for some summer and fall interest. If you already have trees and shrubs in your yard, it's easy to modify this plan or create your own island bed design; besides adding undeniable beauty, linking individual plants into larger beds cuts down drastically on tedious trimming chores. Keep in mind that you don't have to install this kind of garden all at once. Instead, you could start planting the perennials closest to the shrubs, then gradually expand the beds until they meet.

PLANT LIST

#	Plant	Qty
1	Alchemilla mollis	5 plants
2	Anchusa azurea	3 plants
3	Aquilegia flabellata var. pumila f. alba	3 plants
4	A. 'Magpie'	3 plants
5	Armeria maritima 'Bloodstone'	6 plants
6	Asarum europaeum	8 plants
7	Athyrium niponicum var. pictum	3 plants
8	Aurinia saxatilis	3 plants
9	Carex elata 'Aurea'	3 plants
10	C. muskingumensis 'Oehme'	3 plants
11	Cercis canadensis 'Forest Pansy'	1 plant
12	Delphinium 'Blue Bird'	3 plants
13	Dianthus barbatus 'Sooty'	8 plants
14	D. 'Bath's Pink'	3 plants
15	Dicentra 'Snowflakes'	3 plants
16	D. spectabilis 'Goldheart'	1 plant
17	Digitalis lutea	6 plants
18	Euphorbia amygdaloides var. robbiae	3 plants
19	E. 'Jade Dragon'	3 plants
20	E. polychroma	3 plants
21	Geranium macrorrhizum 'Spessart'	3 plants
22	G. sanguineum 'Album'	3 plants
23	Helleborus × hybridus 'Mrs. Betty Ranicar'	3 plants
24	Heuchera 'Purple Petticoats'	5 plants
25	× Heucherella 'Rosalie'	3 plants
26	× H. 'Sunspot'	3 plants
27	Hosta 'Guacamole'	1 plant
28	H. 'Tokudama Flavocircinalis'	1 plant
29	Iberis sempervirens 'Alexander's White'	3 plants
30	Milium effusum 'Aureum'	3 plants
31	Papaver orientale 'Patty's Plum'	1 plant
32	Phlox divaricata 'London Grove Blue'	3 plants
33	P. stolonifera 'Sherwood Purple'	3 plants
34	Polygonatum odoratum 'Variegatum'	5 plants
35	Pulmonaria 'Little Blue'	3 plants
36	P. saccharata 'Pierre's Pure Pink'	5 plants
37	Smilacina racemosa	3 plants
38	Tiarella 'Cygnet'	3 plants
39	T. 'Tiger Stripe'	3 plants
40	Viburnum carlesii 'Compactum'	1 plant

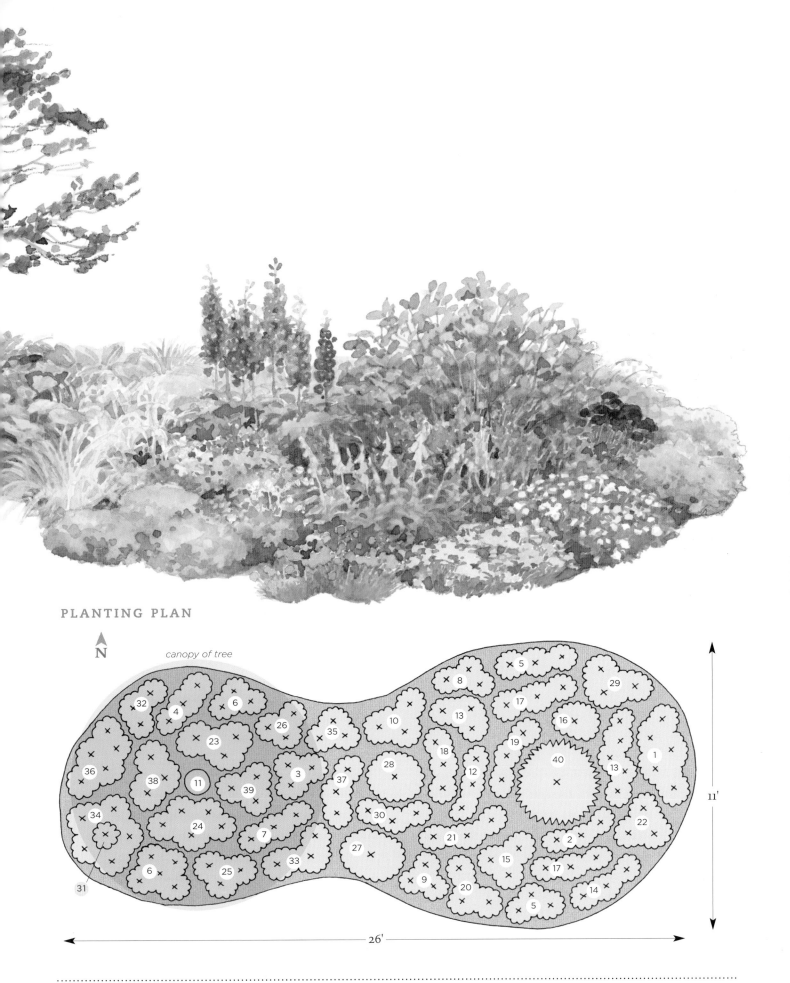

PLANTING PLAN

N

canopy of tree

26'

11'

DESIGNER'S CHECKLIST

☐ **Get twice the beauty from the same space.** Want to have your spring garden do double duty? Make it a spring-and-fall planting instead. This is a great way to get the most from your gardening space if you tend to be away often during the summer. And because some early bloomers leave ugly gaps as they go dormant after flowering, tall and bushy fall bloomers are perfect for keeping the garden looking lush throughout the summer.

☐ **Don't sell your spring garden short.** Few early bloomers are more than 3 feet tall and many of them are significantly shorter, so spring gardens tend to lack vertical interest. Shrubs and small trees can be a big help in giving your garden structure and a more comfortable scale — and add seasonal beauty as well.

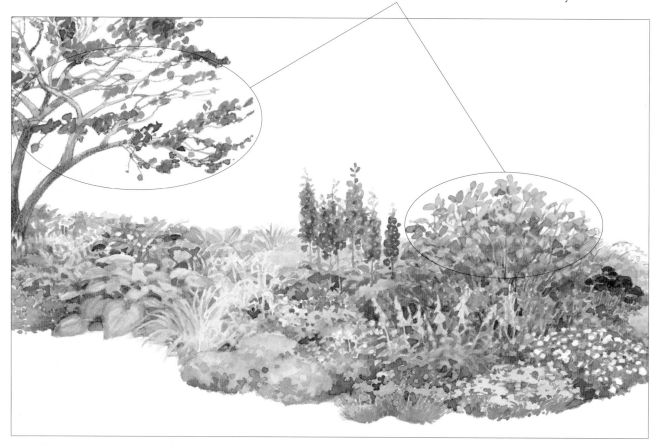

☐ **Plan for the future.** Before you start designing a spring garden, give some thought to how it will look once the main show is over. If you can site it where you won't have to look at it for the rest of the year, your job is easy; go ahead and pick whatever appeals to you for a spectacular early display. Otherwise, be careful to choose perennials that have good summer foliage as well as pretty spring flowers.

☐ **Don't keep your distance.** With their pale colors and delicate forms, spring blooms are best when viewed up close. Whenever possible, then, site a spring garden where you can walk all the way around it: in an island bed, rather than in a border up against a wall or fence. A path through the garden is a plus. A bench is welcome too, because it lets you enjoy the beautiful forms and fragrances at close range.

Beauties for Sun and Light Shade

Alchemilla mollis
(Lady's mantle)

Mounds of scalloped, light green leaves send up airy sprays of tiny, yellow-green flowers from late spring to midsummer; 12 to 18 inches tall and about as wide. Cut back plants by about half in midsummer for a flush of new foliage to enjoy for the rest of the growing season. ZONES 3–9.
ALTERNATIVES: Alpine lady's mantle (*A. alpina*).

Alchemilla mollis

Anchusa azurea
(Italian alkanet)

Eighteen-inch-wide clumps of narrow, hairy green leaves on 3- to 5-foot stems topped with narrow, branching clusters of rich blue blooms in early summer. Tends to be short-lived. ZONES 3–8.
ALTERNATIVES: Blue larkspur (*Consolida ajacis*).

Aquilegia
(Columbines)

These classic late-spring, and early-summer perennials feature nodding blooms accented with spurred petals over clumps of three-lobed, blue-green leaves. *A. flabellata* var. *pumila* f. *alba* (dwarf white fan columbine) is about 8 inches tall and wide with white flowers. ZONES 4–9.
'Magpie' (a.k.a. 'William Guinness') has deep-purple-and-white blooms; about 2 feet tall and 18 inches wide. ZONES 3–8.
ALTERNATIVES: Another columbine with white or purple flowers.

Armeria maritima 'Bloodstone'
('Bloodstone' sea thrift)

Tight, 4- to 6-inch-tall buns of slender, evergreen, grasslike leaves; clustered, deep reddish pink blooms atop 8-inch stems from late spring to early summer; spreads 6 to 12 inches across. ZONES 4–8.
ALTERNATIVES: Another species or cultivar.

Asarum europaeum
(European wild ginger)

Evergreen, 3-inch-tall carpets of rounded, glossy, deep green leaves; rhizomes spread 1 foot or more; insignificant bell-shaped, brownish blooms. ZONES 4–8.
ALTERNATIVES: *Hexastylis shuttleworthii*.

Athyrium niponicum var. pictum
(Japanese painted fern)

Low-spreading mounds of silvery gray fronds on arching maroon stems look good from late spring to frost; about 18 inches tall and 2 feet across. ZONES 4–9.
ALTERNATIVES: Any cultivar ('Silver Falls', 'Ursula's Red') or upright hybrid 'Ghost'.

Aurinia saxatilis
(Basket of gold)

Evergreen, mounded clumps of gray-green leaves; dense clusters of bright yellow blooms in late spring and early summer; 1 foot tall and wide. ZONES 4–8.
ALTERNATIVES: Any basket of gold cultivar or lady's mantle (*Alchemilla mollis*).

Aquilegia 'Magpie'

Carex
(Sedges)

Easy grass relatives prized for foliage. *C. elata* **'Aurea'** (Bowles' golden sedge) has upright or arching, bright yellow blades thinly edged with green in graceful clumps; 18 to 24 inches tall, 18 inches across. ZONES 5–8.
C. muskingumensis **'Oehme'** ('Oehme' palm sedge) produces upright stems that bear horizontal green leaves edged in gold; 2 feet tall and 18 inches across. ZONES 3–8.
ALTERNATIVES: Yellow *Tradescantia* 'Sweet Kate' and blue fescue (*Festuca glauca*).

Delphinium 'Blue Bird'
('Blue Bird' delphinium)

Three- to 4-foot stalks are clad in deeply lobed green leaves and bear spikes of white-centered blue flowers in late spring or early summer; spread to about 2 feet. Best treated as a biennial. ZONES 3–7.
ALTERNATIVES: Annual blue larkspur (*Consolida ajacis*), Italian alkanet (*Anchusa azurea*), or another 3- to 4-foot-tall delphinium cultivar.

Dianthus
(Dianthus, a.k.a. pinks)

Clustered flowers rise above basal clumps of narrow green or blue-green leaves. **'Bath's Pink'** produces 6- to 8-inch-tall clumps of blue-green leaves, with fragrant, soft pink flowers on 1-foot stems from mid- to late-spring to midsummer. About 1 foot wide.
D. barbatus **'Sooty'** ('Sooty' sweet William) is a biennial or short-lived perennial with red-tinged leaves and deep maroon blooms in late spring to early summer; 1 to 2 feet tall and 1 foot across. ZONES 3–8.
ALTERNATIVES: For 'Bath's Pink', another similar-sized species or cultivar, such as cheddar pink (*D. gratianopolitanus*); for 'Sooty', 'Dunnet's Dark Crimson' or *Euphorbia dulcis* 'Chameleon'.

Dicentra

(Bleeding hearts)

These traditional spring favorites produce pink or white heart-shaped blooms.
D. spectabilis 'Goldheart' ('Goldheart' bleeding heart) has bright yellow spring foliage and arching, 3-foot stems with dangling pink hearts in mid- to late spring; clumps are 2 feet across. Cut back the stems lightly in early to midsummer to encourage new growth. ZONES 4–8.
'Snowflakes' is a hybrid that grows in mounds 10 inches tall and wide, with finely cut green foliage and white flowers from mid-spring through much of the summer. ZONES 3–8.

ALTERNATIVES: For 'Goldheart', the common green-leaved *D. spectabilis*; for 'Snowflakes', try 'Langtrees' or *D. eximia* 'Snowdrift'.

Digitalis lutea

(Yellow foxglove)

Spikes of small, tubular, pale yellow blooms rise over glossy, deep green leaves on 2- to 3-foot stems in late spring and early summer; spread to about 1 foot. ZONES 3–9.

ALTERNATIVES: *D. grandiflora.*

Euphorbia

(Spurges)

These early bloomers come in a wide range of sizes. When broken, their leaves and stems exude a milky sap that can be irritating to the skin, so wear gloves when working around them.
'Jade Dragon' is a hybrid that forms dense, shrubby, evergreen clumps of blue-green foliage topped with reddish new foliage, plus large chartreuse bloom clusters from mid- or late spring into summer; height and spread to about 30 inches. ZONES 6–9.
E. polychroma (cushion spurge) forms 12- to 18-inch-tall rounded mounds of medium green leaves topped with bright greenish yellow, flowerlike structures from mid-spring to early summer; spread is 18 to 24 inches. ZONES 4–9.

E. amygdaloides var. robbiae (Robb's wood spurge) forms 1-foot-tall, spreading carpets of evergreen, deep green foliage accented with clusters of chartreuse "flowers" from mid-spring to early summer; height in bloom to 2 feet, spread to 18 inches or more. ZONES 6–9.

ALTERNATIVES: Any other hardy euphorbias.

Geranium

(Hardy geraniums)

These mound-forming perennials come in a variety of sizes, leaf shapes, and bloom colors.
G. macrorrhizum 'Spessart' ('Spessart' bigroot geranium) forms spreading carpets of aromatic, deeply lobed, light green leaves, with deep pink flowers from mid- or late spring well into summer; height to 18 inches and spread to 2 feet. **G. sanguineum 'Album'** (white bloody cranesbill) has starry, deep green leaves and white flowers in late spring and early summer. ZONES 4–8.

ALTERNATIVES: For 'Spessart', try 'Bevan's Variety' or 'Ingwersen's Variety'; for white bloody cranesbill, *G. clarkei* 'Kashmir White'.

Helleborus x hybridus 'Mrs. Betty Ranicar'

('Mrs. Betty Ranicar' Lenten rose)

Evergreen clumps of leathery, deep green leaves arise directly from the ground, with double white flowers atop separate stems in early spring; height and spread to 18 inches. ZONES 5–9.

ALTERNATIVES: Any other Lenten rose or Christmas rose (*H. niger*).

Heuchera 'Purple Petticoats'

('Purple Petticoats' heuchera)

Mounded, 1-foot-tall clumps of dark purple leaves have ruffled edges. Airy clusters of small pinkish white flowers blossom atop 18-inch stems in late spring and early summer; spread is 12 to 18 inches. ZONES 4–9.

ALTERNATIVES: Any other purple-hued heuchera.

x Heucherella

(Heucherella, a.k.a. foamy bells)

Heuchera-like mounds of lobed leaves are accented with 18-inch flower spikes in late spring; foliage clumps are 8- to 12-inches tall and 12- to 18-inches across. **'Rosalie'** has green leaves and pink flowers. **'Sunspot'** has bright yellow foliage with a red star in the center of each leaf, and deep pink flowers. ZONES 5–9.

ALTERNATIVES: For 'Rosalie', any other heucherella; for 'Sunspot', try 'Amber Waves' heuchera or 'Beedham's White' lamium (*Lamium maculatum* 'Beedham's White').

Hosta

(Hostas)

These classic, no-fuss perennials are grown primarily for their foliage, which comes in a variety of shapes, sizes, and colors to fit any shady garden. **'Guacamole'** has chartreuse, edged with green leaves and fragrant, near white flowers on 30-inch stems in late summer. **'Tokudama Flavocircinalis'** has large blue leaves irregularly edged with gold, plus pale lavender flowers atop 2-foot stems in early to midsummer. The foliage clumps of both are 18 inches tall and 4 feet wide. ZONES 3–9.

ALTERNATIVES: Any other hostas in the same color and height range.

Iberis sempervirens 'Alexander's White'

('Alexander's White' perennial candytuft)

Shrubby, 8-inch-tall mounds of narrow, dark green leaves are smothered in clusters of white flowers throughout spring; spread is 12 to 18 inches. ZONES 3–8.

ALTERNATIVES: The straight species (*I. sempervirens*) or another cultivar.

Milium effusum 'Aureum'

(Golden wood millet, a.k.a. Bowles' golden grass)

Tufts of narrow, upright or arching leaves are bright yellow in spring, fading to yellowish green in summer. Loose clusters of tiny, yellow, non-showy flowers in late spring and early summer; height is 12 to 18 inches, spread to 1 foot. ZONES 5–8.

ALTERNATIVES: *Tradescantia* 'Sweet Kate' or golden Hakone grass (*Hakonechloa macra* 'Aureola').

Papaver orientale 'Patty's Plum'

('Patty's Plum' Oriental poppy)
Huge cupped flowers with crinkled, pinkish purple petals and a black center bloom atop 30-inch stems in late spring and early summer; the 2-foot-tall and -wide clumps of toothed leaves die back to the ground by midsummer. ZONES 4–9.

ALTERNATIVES: Another purple, pink, or white Oriental poppy.

Phlox

(Phlox)
Early-flowering phlox are a must-have for the spring garden.

P. divaricata 'London Grove Blue'
('London Grove Blue' woodland phlox) has mid- to late-spring clusters of fragrant, light blue flowers atop 1-foot stems clad in narrow green leaves; foliage height is 6 to 8 inches and spread is to 18 inches. ZONES 4–8.

P. stolonifera 'Sherwood Purple'
('Sherwood Purple' creeping phlox) bears blue-purple flowers atop 6-inch stems in mid- to late spring, over 3-inch-tall carpets of deep green leaves; spread to 1 foot. ZONES 2–8.

ALTERNATIVES: Other cultivars of these species.

Phlox stolonifera 'Sherwood Purple'

Polygonatum odoratum 'Variegatum'

(Variegated Solomon's seal)
Arching maroon stems clad in cream-edged green leaves look good from spring to frost. Small, green-tipped white flowers dangle below the stems in late spring; height to 2 feet, with a spread of 1 to 2 feet. ZONES 4–8.

ALTERNATIVES: Variegated fairy bells (*Disporum sessile* 'Variegatum').

Pulmonaria

(Pulmonarias)
Hairy green or silver-spotted leaves in showy clumps are 10 inches tall and 12 to 18 inches across, typically with clusters of pink buds and blue blooms atop 1-foot stems in early to mid-spring. 'Little Blue' has narrow leaves with silvery white spots. *P. saccharata* 'Pierre's Pure Pink' is noteworthy for its salmon-pink buds and blooms. ZONES 3–8.

ALTERNATIVES: Any cultivar.

Smilacina racemosa

(False Solomon's seal)
Clumps of upright or arching, 30-inch stems are clad in lance-shaped green leaves and topped with plumes of creamy white flowers from mid- to late spring, followed by red berries in summer. ZONES 4–9.

ALTERNATIVES: A white-flowered astilbe, such as 'Deutschland'.

Tiarella

(Foamflowers)
These top-notch shade perennials feature foliage in a wide range of shapes, often with maroon or deep purple markings, plus brushy bloom spikes to 1 foot tall through spring. 'Cygnet' has deeply lobed, dark green leaves with near-black centers; 'Tiger Stripe' has broad, light green leaves with purplish veins. Both have pinkish white flowers and form spreading clumps 6 inches tall and (eventually) 2 feet wide. ZONES 4–9.

ALTERNATIVES: Any cultivar.

Summer Sizzle

COME SUMMERTIME, the temperature isn't the only thing that is heating up; perennial flowers are practically exploding into bloom. Maybe you'd like your gorgeous garden to serve as a setting for a wedding, graduation party, family reunion, or weekend cookouts. Or perhaps as a sun-worshipper, you like nothing better than to spend those long summer days wandering around in your flower gardens. For whatever occasion, here are suggestions for summer gardens guaranteed to fill your life with bright blooms and fabulous foliage.

The primary colors (red, blue, and yellow) in this garden scheme make a bold, cheerful statement.

Getting to Know You

When you're planning a warm-season perennial garden, it's not enough to know that a given plant blooms "in summer." First, the palette of perennials from which to choose for a garden geared to early summer is dramatically different from one slanted toward late summer. And while some summer perennials bloom for just a few weeks, others keep on flowering well into fall. Without a clear idea of accurate bloom times, planning a flower-filled perennial garden of fantastic combinations can be a hit-or-miss proposition.

Once again, the keys to a successful design are to do your homework and to see the plants for yourself. Find out when they typically start flowering, how long they keep going, and what else is in bloom at the same time. Don't rely on plant tags or on the descriptions in general gardening books and magazines, because those are naturally going to reflect the authors' experiences in their own climates. Instead, look for local sources of information, such as authors who have experience gardening in your particular area. Check out display gardens at nearby garden centers and botanical gardens, and make notes of which perennials are blooming each time you visit and which summer combinations you find especially appealing.

Managing Maintenance Needs

Spring gardens tend to be fairly low-maintenance; summer gardens, however, can be as much or as little work as you're willing to put into them. Enjoy spending your summer evenings and weekends puttering around with your perennials? Feel free to experiment with all the latest introductions and hard-to-find rarities you can track down. Want lots of color without a lot of work? Fill your yard with classic, easy-care favorites, such as black-eyed Susans (*Rudbeckia*), ornamental grasses, and sedums. Here are a few more ideas for having a great-looking garden without spending your whole summer on it:

✳ If summer rains tend to be unreliable in your area, stick with perennials that are touted as being drought-tolerant. You'll still need to water them for the first year or two, but after that, they should last through most summers just fine without extra irrigation.

✳ Warm temperatures and high humidity provide ideal conditions for fungi to flourish, so take steps to nip this problem in the bud: Look for disease-resistant cultivars, and space plants properly to avoid overcrowding. If established perennial clumps look crowded, snip out a third to a half of the stems right at ground level in mid- to late spring to allow better air circulation around the remaining shoots; then plan to divide the clump in the fall or the following spring.

✳ In late spring, give the whole planting a careful weeding, water thoroughly if the soil is dry, and spread a 2- to 3-inch-deep layer of chopped leaves, shredded bark, or another organic mulch over the soil. This will drastically cut down on summer weeding and watering chores.

Early-Summer Elegance

IF YOU'VE SPENT ANY TIME AT ALL looking at British gardening books, you've probably drooled over those pictures of double borders packed with lupines, delphiniums, and other early-summer favorites. Well, you may not have the space, time, or budget to create a huge pair of borders for such a short season, but you can still enjoy the effect with this design: a scaled-down set of borders designed to fit in a narrow side yard.

PLANTING PLAN

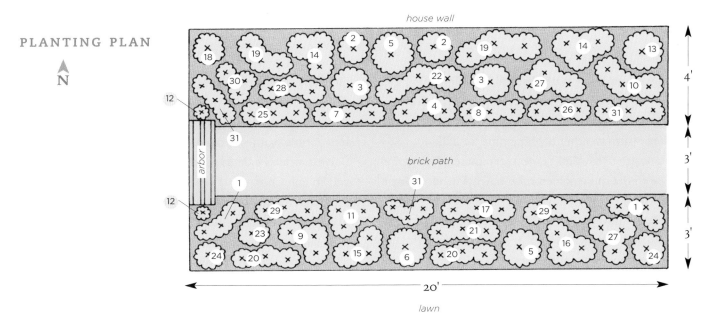

N

PLANT LIST

1	Alchemilla mollis	6 plants
2	Aquilegia vulgaris 'Nora Barlow'	2 plants
3	Artemisia ludoviciana 'Silver Queen'	2 plants
4	Aster x frikartii 'Flora's Delight'	3 plants
5	Baptisia australis	2 plants

6	B. 'Carolina Moonlight'	1 plant
7	Campanula carpatica 'Blue Clips'	3 plants
8	C. carpatica 'White Clips'	3 plants
9	C. lactiflora 'White Pouffe'	3 plants
10	Centranthus ruber	3 plants
11	C. ruber 'Albus'	3 plants
12	Clematis 'Jackmanii'	2 plants
13	Crambe cordifolia	1 plant
14	Delphinium 'King Arthur'	6 plants
15	D. 'Magic Fountain Dark Blue'	3 plants
16	D. 'Magic Fountain Pink'	3 plants
17	Dianthus 'Bewitched'	3 plants
18	Dicentra spectabilis 'Pantaloons'	1 plant
19	Digitalis purpurea f. albiflora	6 plants
20	D. purpurea 'Foxy'	6 plants
21	Geranium clarkei 'Kashmir White'	3 plants
22	G. 'Nimbus'	3 plants
23	G. x oxonianum 'Claridge Druce'	1 plant
24	Iris 'Butter and Sugar'	2 plants
25	Lavandula angustifolia 'Jean Davis'	3 plants
26	L. angustifolia 'Munstead'	3 plants
27	Lupinus 'Gallery White'	6 plants
28	L. 'The Chatelaine'	3 plants
29	Nepeta x faassenii 'Walker's Low'	6 plants
30	Polemonium foliosissimum	3 plants
31	Stachys byzantina 'Big Ears'	9 plants

DESIGNER'S CHECKLIST

☐ **Don't go crazy with daisies.** When planning a summer garden, pay special attention to the flower forms of the perennials you're putting next to each other. Warm weather is prime time for all kinds of composite (daisylike) flowers, and quite a few of them fall into the same golden color range. Put too many of these in one area, and you run the risk of creating a garden of nothing but DYCs (gardening slang for "darn yellow composites"). It's easy to avoid, though: Just watch your color balance, and be sure to mix in lots of spikes and other flower forms.

☐ **Siting a summer garden.** If summers tend to be dry in your area, you might want to put your perennial garden near your house so you don't have to spend lots of time hauling around hoses. Planting summer flowers around a deck, porch, or patio is a wonderful way to enjoy flowers as you relax or entertain; plus, it provides excellent opportunities for watching hummingbirds and butterflies. If, on the other hand, you or your family members are allergic to bees, you'll want to keep flower-based summer gardens away from high-traffic areas and use colorful foliage there instead.

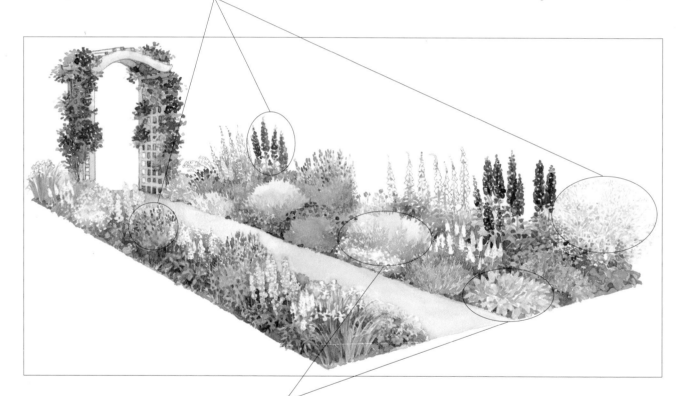

☐ **Have fun with foliage.** Once you have a color scheme in mind, be sure to choose lots of complementary foliage to give your summer bed or border a sense of continuity while the flowers come and go. With rich red, orange, and yellow flowers, foliage in bright greens and moody purples creates a striking backdrop. Silver, blue, and variegated leaves make perfect partners for pastel blooms.

☐ **Anything goes!** In a summer design, just about any color scheme will work, as long as you keep the site in mind. Whites and pastels look cool and refreshing in shady spots and evening gardens; bright colors typically hold up best in sites with full sun.

Alchemilla mollis
(Lady's mantle)

Mounds of scalloped, light green leaves with airy sprays of tiny, yellow-green flowers from late spring to midsummer; 12 to 18 inches tall and about as wide. Cut back plants by about half in midsummer for a flush of new foliage to enjoy for the rest of the growing season. ZONES 3–9.

ALTERNATIVES: Alpine lady's mantle (*A. alpina*).

Aquilegia vulgaris 'Nora Barlow'
('Nora Barlow' columbine)

Double, pomponlike blooms with reddish pink, white-tipped petals rise over clumps of three-lobed, blue-green leaves in late spring and early summer; 2 feet tall and 18 inches wide. ZONES 3–8.

ALTERNATIVES: Another columbine in shades of pink or white.

Artemisia ludoviciana 'Silver Queen'
('Silver Queen' artemisia)

Three- to 4-foot-tall clumps of upright, silvery stems bear silvery white to gray-green foliage; the flowers are not showy. Spreads by rhizomes to 2 feet or more and can be invasive. ZONES 4–9.

ALTERNATIVES: 'Silver King' (equally invasive) or the non-creeping 'Powis Castle'.

Aster x frikartii 'Flora's Delight'
('Flora's Delight' Frikart's aster)

Bushy, 1- to 2-foot-tall and -wide mounds of narrow, dark green leaves are covered from early or midsummer into fall with daisylike blooms that have lilac-blue petals and yellow centers. ZONES 5–9.

ALTERNATIVES: The cultivar 'Mönch'.

Baptisia
(Baptisias)

Bushy, clump-forming perennials have three-parted leaves and spike-like flower clusters in early summer.

B. australis (blue false indigo) grows 4 to 5 feet tall and 3 to 4 feet across, with dark blue flowers followed by long-lasting black seedpods. ZONES 3–9.

Hybrid 'Carolina Moonlight' is similar in size but has butter yellow blooms. ZONES 4–9.

ALTERNATIVES: For blue false indigo, try columbine meadow rue (*Thalictrum aquilegifolium*); for 'Carolina Moonlight', dusty meadow rue (*T. flavum* subsp. *glaucum*).

Campanula
(Bellflowers)

These upright or creeping perennials sport tubular, bell-shaped, or star-shaped blooms, usually in shades of blue.

C. carpatica (Carpathian harebell) grows 8- to 10-inches tall and 12- to 18-inches across, with upward-facing flowers throughout the summer; 'Blue Clips' is blue and 'White Clips', not surprisingly, is white. ZONES 4–7.

C. lactiflora 'White Pouffe' ('White Pouffe' milky bellflower) bears starry white flowers throughout the summer; 1 foot tall and 18 inches across. ZONES 5–7.

ALTERNATIVES: Other bellflower species and cultivars in the same height and color range.

Centranthus ruber
(Red valerian, a.k.a. Jupiter's beard)

Upright to gently sprawling stems are clad in somewhat fleshy green leaves and topped with clusters of small, rosy pink flowers from late spring to early fall (with regular deadheading); 2 to 3 feet tall and wide. **'Albus'** has white flowers. ZONES 5–8.

ALTERNATIVES: For the species, pink 'Kim's Knee High' purple coneflower (*Echinacea purpurea*); for 'Albus', white 'Kim's Mop Head' coneflower.

Crambe cordifolia

Crambe cordifolia
(Crambe, a.k.a. colewort)

Two-foot-tall, 3-foot-wide mounds of broad, crinkled, deep green leaves send up 4- to 6-foot, branched stalks of small, sweetly scented white flowers for a few weeks in early to midsummer. ZONES 5–8.

ALTERNATIVES: Baby's breath (*Gypsophila paniculata*).

Delphinium
(Delphiniums)

Upright stalks are clad in deeply lobed green leaves and topped with spikes of blue, pink, or white flowers in late spring or early summer. **'King Arthur'** has deep purple-blue blooms with white centers; height is 4 to 5 feet, with an 18- to 24-inch spread. **'Magic Fountain Dark Blue'** and **'Magic Fountain Pink'** are 24 to 30 inches tall and 1 foot across. Best treated as a biennial. ZONES 3–7.

ALTERNATIVES: Annual blue larkspur (*Consolida ajacis*), Italian alkanet (*Anchusa azurea*), or another delphinium cultivar.

Dianthus 'Bewitched'

('Bewitched' dianthus)

This dianthus forms 3- to 4-inch-tall clumps of slender, bright silvery blue leaves with 6- to 8-inch stems topped with fragrant, fringed, pale pink blossoms with a red ring and white center in late spring and early summer; spread is 6 to 8 inches. Excellent heat and humidity tolerance. ZONES 3–9.

ALTERNATIVES: Other dianthus species or cultivars of a similar size.

Dicentra spectabilis 'Pantaloons'

('Pantaloons' bleeding heart)

White hearts dangle from arching, 3-foot stems over light green leaves in late spring to early summer; clumps are 2 feet across. ZONES 3–8.

ALTERNATIVES: The cultivar 'Alba'.

Digitalis purpurea

(Common foxglove)

Rosettes of green leaves about 1 foot tall and 1 to 2 feet wide send up stems topped with spikes of tubular blooms in early summer. Best treated as a biennial. **'Foxy'** has maroon-spotted pink, cream, or white flowers on 2- to 3-foot stems; may bloom the first year. **D. purpurea f. albiflora**

Digitalis purpurea

(a.k.a. 'Alba') has white blooms on 3- to 5-foot stems. ZONES 4–8.

ALTERNATIVES: For 'Foxy', try yellow foxglove (*D. grandiflora*) or strawberry foxglove (*D. x mertonensis*); for f. *albiflora*, another tall foxglove.

Geranium

(Hardy geraniums)

These mound-forming perennials come in a wide array of sizes, leaf shapes, and bloom colors. **'Nimbus'** produces loose clumps 18 inches tall and 2 feet across, with white-centered purple flowers over starry green leaves from late spring into fall. *G. clarkei* **'Kashmir White'** has pink-veined white flowers throughout summer over deeply lobed green leaves; 18 inches tall and wide. *G. x oxonianum* **'Claridge Druce'** has five-lobed green leaves and dark-veined, rosy pink blooms from late spring through summer; 2 feet tall and 2 to 3 feet wide. ZONES 4– OR 5–8.

ALTERNATIVES: Other geranium cultivars.

Iris 'Butter and Sugar'

('Butter and Sugar' Siberian iris)

Yellow-and-white flowers in early summer atop 30-inch stems rise from slender, green, grasslike foliage; spread to 2 feet. ZONES 3–8.

ALTERNATIVES: Any Siberian iris (*I. sibirica*).

Lavandula angustifolia

(English lavender)

Shrubby clumps of fragrant, narrow, gray-green leaves that last through winter are accented with aromatic flower spikes from early to late summer. **'Jean Davis'** has light pink blooms; height and spread to about 2 feet. **'Munstead'** has purple-blue flowers; height and spread are 18 to 24 inches. ZONES 5–8 (excellent winter drainage is a must).

ALTERNATIVES: For 'Jean Davis', try 'Dawn to Dusk' catmint (*Nepeta* 'Dawn to Dusk'); for 'Munstead', any other hardy lavender, such as 'Hidcote' or 'Lady'.

Lupinus

(Lupines)

Upright stems are clad in 5- to 7-lobed, green leaves and topped with spikes of pealike blooms in early to midsummer. **'Gallery White'** has white blooms; 18 inches tall and 1 foot wide. **'The Chatelaine'** has pink-and-white flowers on 3-foot stems; 2 feet wide. ZONES 4–7.

ALTERNATIVES: Other lupines or gas plant (*Dictamnus albus*).

Nepeta x faassenii 'Walker's Low'

('Walker's Low' catmint)

Low, sprawling mounds of gray-green leaves look good all through the growing season. Spikes of lavender-blue blossoms first appear in mid- to late spring, with repeat flowers until frost if you shear them lightly after each flush of bloom; height and spread are 12 to 15 inches. ZONES 4–8.

ALTERNATIVES: 'Blue Wonder' or other cultivar.

Polemonium foliosissimum

(Leafy Jacob's ladder)

Ferny, rich green leaves are 1 foot tall and 18 inches across, with 3-foot stems topped with deep blue, bell-shaped blooms in early to midsummer. ZONES 4–8.

ALTERNATIVES: Common Jacob's ladder (*P. caeruleum*).

Polemonium caeruleum

Stachys byzantina 'Big Ears'

('Big Ears' lamb's ears, a.k.a. 'Helene von Stein')

Flat, hairy, gray-green leaves spread to form carpets 8 inches tall and 18 inches wide; seldom flowers. ZONES 4–8.

ALTERNATIVES: Another lamb's ear cultivar or the straight species.

Flowers and Foliage for Fall

FOR MANY A TRUE GARDENER, fall is the most delightful time of year. It's a pleasure to be out on comfortably warm days; cool nights encourage richer colors and longer-lasting blooms. It's a time to enjoy your garden, not just work in it. A fall border of favorites guarantees plenty of beauty for this glorious season, and weeks before as well.

Beyond Chrysanthemums

Gardeners who shop in spring tend to overlook fall-flowering perennials, and no wonder: Late bloomers usually look scrawny in spring sales displays, particularly when next to lush, flower-filled early risers. Some fall perennials don't even emerge until late spring — and who buys an empty-looking pot?

By late summer, though, early-flowering perennials have fallen by the wayside, and gardeners who haven't planned ahead find themselves back at the garden center in August and September; almost invariably, a case of "mum-itis" is the result. Using potted chrysanthemums as fillers in empty spaces is a quick-fix, but not an especially attractive one. Incorporating hardy, dependable fall perennials into your designs is a much cheaper, easier, and more effective way to enjoy colorful autumn beds and borders.

Autumn Advantages

Unlike gardens planned for spring or summer, fall plantings look great for most of the growing season, not just when in flower. Granted, they aren't especially colorful until late summer, but they look full, with lots of attractive foliage. For an extra season of impact from a fall garden, interplant with lots of crocus, daffodils, and other spring bulbs. Just as the bulbs are dying back, the perennials will emerge and hide yellowing bulb leaves; dormant bulbs won't mind being shaded at all.

Really big plants tend to shine at this time of year, many of them easily reaching 4, 5, 6 feet, or even taller. Walking amid these eye-high beauties is an unforgettable experience.

Plan ahead for a final blast of fiery color in your autumn garden.

Surround Yourself with Fall Flowers

WHO HAS TIME to sit down and relax in spring or summer? But by fall, the kids are back in school, the main rush of yard work is done, and the weather's perfect, making this a good time to sit back and get the most out of a pretty garden. This design wraps around a sunny, elevated deck, so it's meant to be looked down upon; that's why the shorter plants are to the inside of the border and the taller plants are around the outer edge (the opposite of how you'd normally arrange them). Remember to allow about 18 inches of space between the edge of the deck and the edge of the garden, so you can sneak in for either deck or garden maintenance without trampling your plants.

PLANTING PLAN

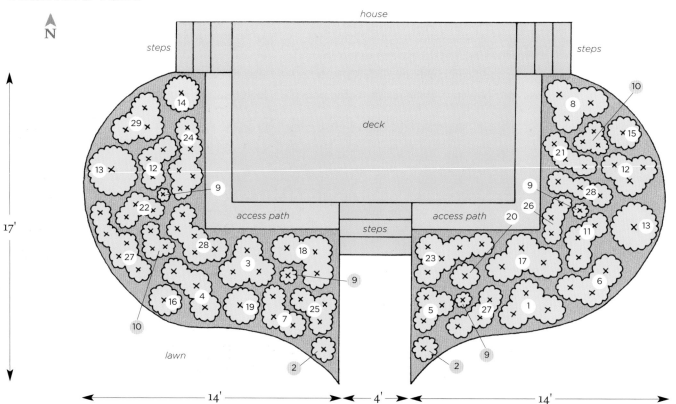

PLANT LIST

1	*Aconitum carmichaelii* 'Arendsii'	3 plants
2	*Amsonia tabernaemontana*	2 plants
3	*Anemone* × *hybrida* 'Andrea Atkinson'	3 plants
4	*Aster laevis* 'Bluebird'	3 plants
5	*A. lateriflorus* 'Prince'	3 plants
6	*A. tataricus* 'Jindai'	3 plants
7	*Boltonia asteroides* 'Snowbank'	3 plants
8	*Chrysanthemum* 'Mei-Kyo'	3 plants
9	*Colchicum autumnale*	4 corms
10	*Crocosmia* 'Emily McKenzie'	6 corms
11	*Helenium* 'Coppelia'	3 plants
12	*Hemerocallis* 'Autumn Minaret'	6 plants
13	*Miscanthus sinensis* 'Zebrinus'	2 plants
14	*Nipponanthemum nipponicum*	1 plant
15	*Panicum virgatum* 'Hänse Herms'	1 plant
16	*P. virgatum* 'Heavy Metal'	1 plant
17	*Pennisetum alopecuroides* 'Hameln'	3 plants
18	*P. alopecuroides* 'Moudry'	3 plants
19	*Perovskia atriplicifolia*	1 plant
20	*P.* 'Little Spires'	1 plant
21	*Phlox paniculata* 'Robert Poore'	3 plants
22	*Physostegia virginiana* 'Miss Manners'	3 plants
23	*Rudbeckia fulgida* var. *fulgida*	5 plants
24	*Sedum* 'Autumn Fire'	5 plants
25	*S.* 'Mohrchen'	3 plants
26	*S.* 'Vera Jameson'	3 plants
27	*Solidago rugosa* 'Fireworks'	8 plants
28	*S. sphacelata* 'Golden Fleece'	8 plants
29	*Vernonia noveboracensis*	3 plants

DESIGNER'S CHECKLIST

☐ **The many colors of autumn.** A fall garden gives you the widest possible palette to choose from of any seasonal garden: bright whites, pretty pastels, and rousing hot colors too. The choice is up to you, of course, but keep in mind that using reds, oranges, golds, and purples in your perennial garden will echo the spectacular fall colors of many deciduous trees and shrubs, thereby tying together the whole landscape.

☐ **Gotta have grasses!** If you omit ornamental grasses from your fall designs, you're missing out on much of the beauty of this season. Warm-season grasses, such as switch grass (*Panicum virgatum*), are in their glory now, with showy flower plumes and seedheads; many also offer fabulous fall foliage color. And as temperatures drop, cool-season grasses, such as blue fescue (*Festuca glauca*), put out new growth, adding a fresh touch to tired-looking plantings.

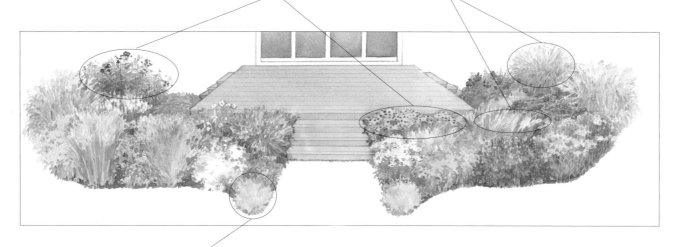

☐ **Don't forget about foliage.** Sure, shrubs and trees get all the press for their showy fall foliage, but many perennials have splendid autumn color as well. Bright yellow, rich red, coppery orange, warm maroon, and plum purple: If woody plants can do it, perennials can too.

☐ **Spread the wealth.** In a short-season area, figure on getting 4 to 6 weeks of flowers from your fall garden — from mid- or late August until late September (or the first heavy frost). In much of the country, the show lasts to mid- or late October; in the deeper South, you may even have flowers for your Thanksgiving table. Paying attention to early-, mid-, and late-fall-flowering perennials gives you the longest possible display. Pinching back many late-flowering perennials by about half in early summer will delay flowering and help ensure fall blooms (instead of late-summer ones) in hot climates.

☐ **A bright idea.** Consider adding a few fall-flowering bulbs to the mix. They tend to be tricky to use in three-season borders, because you must allow room for their spring leaves and fall flowers, then cope with gaps left when top growth disappears in summer. For this reason, it's generally best to plant meadow saffron (*Colchicum autumnale*), fall crocus (*Crocus speciosus*), spider lilies (*Lycoris*), and other late-blooming bulbs and corms where they can come up through low-growing companions, such as plumbago (*Ceratostigma plumbaginoides*), or around a daylily (*Hemerocallis*), where the bulb flowers can easily pop up through daylily leaves.

Fall Favorites for Sun

Aconitum carmichaelii 'Arendsii'
('Arendsii' monkshood)
Upright stems with lobed, dark green leaves; spikelike clusters of hooded, deep blue flowers from late summer to mid-fall; 3 to 4 feet tall, 18 inches wide. ZONES 3–7.
ALTERNATIVES: 'Spark's Variety', 'Royal Velvet' New York aster (*Aster novi belgii* 'Royal Velvet').

Amsonia tabernaemontana
(Willow amsonia)
Shrubby, 2- to 3-foot-tall stems; narrow, deep green leaves turn bright yellow in fall; clusters of starry, pale blue flowers in early summer; 18 inches wide. ZONES 3–9.
ALTERNATIVES: Arkansas bluestar (*A. hubrectii*).

Anemone x hybrida 'Andrea Atkinson'
('Andrea Atkinson' Japanese anemone)
Three-lobed, medium green leaves on 3-foot, branching stems; pure white, yellow-centered flowers in early and mid-fall; clumps spread to 2 feet. ZONES 5–8.
ALTERNATIVES: 'Honorine Jobert' or 'Whirlwind'.

Aster
(Asters)
Classic fall favorites with daisylike flowers on branching stems.
A. laevis 'Bluebird' ('Bluebird' smooth aster) has purple-blue, yellow-centered flowers in early to mid-fall over blue-green leaves on 3-foot stems; spread to 2 feet. ZONES 4–8.
A. lateriflorus 'Prince' ('Prince' calico aster) has slender, upright stems with narrow, dark purple leaves featuring masses of tiny, pinkish white, daisylike flowers in late summer to early fall; 3 feet tall and 18 to 24 inches wide. ZONES 4–8.
ALTERNATIVES: For 'Bluebird' and 'Jindai', other asters; for 'Prince', 'Lady in Black'.

A. tataricus 'Jindai' ('Jindai' Tatarian aster) forms 2-foot-tall carpets of lance-shaped green leaves; sturdy, 4- to 5-foot stems bear light purple, yellow-centered flowers in mid- to late fall; spreads to 3 feet. ZONES 3–8.

Boltonia asteroides 'Snowbank'
('Snowbank' boltonia)
Upright, 4- to 5-foot stems are clad in narrow, blue-green leaves and topped with yellow-centered, white, daisylike blooms from late summer well into fall; clumps are 18 to 30 inches across. ZONES 4–9.
ALTERNATIVES: 'Wedding Lace' New England aster (*Aster novae-angliae* 'Wedding Lace').

Chrysanthemum 'Mei-Kyo'
('Mei-Kyo' hardy mum)
Bushy, 2-foot-tall clumps of lobed green leaves send up lavender-pink, yellow-centered double flowers from mid- to late fall; spread to 3 feet. ZONES 5–9.
ALTERNATIVES: 'Color Echo' or 'Sheffield', or *Dendranthema* 'Pink Bomb' or 'White Bomb'.

Colchicum autumnale
(Meadow saffron)
Straplike, 1-foot-long green leaves in spring die back to ground by midsummer; 6-inch-tall, narrow-petaled pink blooms rise directly from ground in early fall. Plant corms 4 inches deep and 6 inches apart. ZONES 4–9.
ALTERNATIVES: Another *Colchicum* species or hybrid; fall-flowering crocus (*Crocus speciosus*).

Crocosmia 'Emily McKenzie'
('Emily McKenzie' crocosmia, a.k.a. montbretia)
Clumps of upright, sword-shaped green leaves with 24- to 30-inch stems; clusters of bright orange, maroon-marked flowers in late summer to early fall. Plant corms

3 inches deep, 5 inches apart. ZONES 6–9.
ALTERNATIVES: Another later-flowering crocosmia, such as 'Solfaterre' ('Lucifer' usually blooms too early).

Helenium 'Coppelia'
('Coppelia' sneezeweed)
Masses of daisylike flowers with coppery orange petals in late summer and early fall on sturdy, 3-foot stems with narrow green leaves; 18 inches wide. ZONES 4–8.
ALTERNATIVES: 'Moerheim Beauty'.

Hemerocallis 'Autumn Minaret'
('Autumn Minaret' daylily)
Fragrant, narrow-petaled, orange-yellow blooms on 5-foot stems from mid- or late summer to early fall, over 2- to 3-foot-tall and -wide clumps of slender, arching green leaves. ZONES 3–9.
ALTERNATIVES: Another late-flowering daylily hybrid ('Autumn King' or 'Autumn Prince') or *Helianthus* 'Lemon Queen' (cut back by half in early summer to delay bloom until early fall).

Miscanthus sinensis 'Zebrinus'
(Zebra grass)
Slender, arching green leaves with yellow bands grow in large clumps (4 to 5 feet tall, 4 feet across); brownish, whisklike plumes in mid- to late fall. ZONES 5–9, but probably best only in ZONES 5 and 6, where chance of it self-sowing is minimal.
ALTERNATIVES: Porcupine grass (*M. sinensis* 'Strictus') or cultivars of switch grass (*Panicum virgatum*), such as 'Dallas Blues' and 'Northwind'.

Nipponanthemum nipponicum
(Montauk daisy, a.k.a. *Chrysanthemum nipponicum*, Nippon daisy)
White daisies bloom in mid- to late fall atop shrubby clumps of upright stems clad in bright green leaves; height and spread to 2 feet. ZONES 5–9.
ALTERNATIVES: *Dendranthema* 'White Bomb'.

Panicum virgatum

(Switch grass)

A clump-forming, native grass with upright green or blue-green foliage in summer; fall color; airy flower plumes in late summer and fall. 'Hänse Herms' has green leaves that turn deep reddish purple in fall; 6 feet tall, 2 to 3 feet wide. 'Heavy Metal' forms narrowly upright, 3-foot-tall clumps of slender blue-gray leaves that turn yellow in fall; clumps are 2 feet across. ZONES 5–9.

ALTERNATIVES: Other switch grass cultivars.

Pennisetum alopecuroides

(Fountain grass)

Eighteen- to 24-inch-tall and -wide mounds of slender, arching, rich green foliage turns yellow in fall; brushy flower spikes to 3 feet tall from late summer through fall. 'Hameln' has greenish spikes that mature to tan; the purplish brown flower spikes of 'Moudry' self-sow invasively in warm climates, especially in moist soil and irrigated areas. ZONES 6–9.

ALTERNATIVES: Prairie dropseed (Sporobolus heterolepis).

Perovskia atriplicifolia

(Russian sage)

Shrubby clumps of gray-white stems have deeply cut, silvery green leaves. Purple-blue flowers bloom from late summer into fall; 3 to 4 feet tall, 3 feet wide. 'Little Spires' is more compact than the species: just 2 feet tall and wide. Zones 6–9.

ALTERNATIVES: Any Russian sage or caryopteris (Caryopteris x clandonensis) cultivars.

Phlox paniculata 'Robert Poore'

('Robert Poore' garden phlox)

Large clusters of fragrant, purplish pink flowers bloom from mid- or late summer into fall atop upright, 4- to 5-foot stems with mildew-resistant green leaves; spread to about 2 feet. ZONES 5–8.

ALTERNATIVES: Another mildew-resistant cultivar, such as white 'David' or deep reddish purple 'Nicky'.

Physostegia virginiana 'Miss Manners'

('Miss Manners' obedient plant)

Much less of a spreader than the species, this cultivar truly lives up to its common name. Upright clumps to 30 inches tall but only 1 foot wide are topped with spikes of bright white flowers throughout summer into early fall. ZONES 4–8.

ALTERNATIVES: White-flowered blue lobelia (L. siphilitica 'Alba') or white turtlehead (Chelone glabra).

Rudbeckia fulgida var. fulgida

(Orange coneflower)

One-foot-wide clumps of deep green foliage; upright, 18- to 24-inch stems; golden yellow, brown-centered daisies from late summer to mid-fall. ZONES 3–9.

ALTERNATIVES: R. fulgida var. sullivantii 'Goldsturm' (similar but taller, 24 to 30 inches) and blooms from midsummer to early fall.

Sedum

(Sedums)

Clustered flowers in mid- to late summer atop upright stems over succulent leaves. 'Autumn Fire', 2 to 3 feet tall, 18 to 24 inches wide; blue-green leaves and pinkish red flowers that turn bronze in fall. 'Mohrchen', maroon to purplish green leaves; clusters of pink flowers in late summer to early fall; 18 to 24 inches tall and wide. 'Vera Jameson', clusters of rosy pink flowers over purple- or pink-tinged green leaves late summer and early fall; 10 inches tall, 18 inches wide. ZONES 3/4–9.

ALTERNATIVES: 'Autumn Joy', 'Brilliant', 'Purple Emperor', and other upright sedums.

Solidago

(Goldenrods)

Sprays or plumes of golden, late-summer and fall blooms form atop upright or arching stems with narrow green leaves. S. rugosa 'Fireworks', bright yellow flowers in long, arching sprays; 30–40 inches tall, 24–30 inches wide. ZONES 3–8. S. sphacelata 'Golden Fleece', short clusters of golden yellow flowers late summer to early or mid-fall; deep green leaves; 12–18 inches tall and wide. ZONES 5–9.

ALTERNATIVES: Other goldenrod species or hybrids.

Vernonia noveboracensis

(New York ironweed)

Four- to 6-foot stems clad in narrow green leaves and topped with fluffy-looking clusters of purple flowers from late summer into fall; spread to 3 feet. ZONES 5–9.

ALTERNATIVES: Another ironweed species or Aster tataricus 'Jindai'.

Stephanie Says

WHILE YOU'RE RELAXING AND ENJOYING YOUR FALL GARDEN, take a few minutes to look back at the growing season gone by. Think about what worked and what you'd like to change; about new gardens you'd like to add; about existing plantings that could use some renovation. Early fall is a great time to move or divide perennials that have already flowered for the year. Simply cut back the top growth by about half before digging. Water thoroughly after you move them, and they'll be in prime condition come spring. When you prepare new sites for fall planting, it's fine to dig organic matter into the soil, but hold off on concentrated fertilizers, because you don't want to encourage a flush of top growth at this time of year. *

Winter Wonderlands

IT'S A SIMPLE MATTER TO HAVE a gorgeous spring, summer, or fall garden, but creating a great-looking winter garden is definitely a challenge. It's not that it's difficult to find suitable plants; it's more that you need to change the way you look at your garden. Instead of relying on lush foliage and bold splashes of color to create excitement, winter gardens derive most of their impact from the interplay of plant forms: arching dried leaves, spiky seed clusters, and other remnants of the past growing season. If you're willing to develop an appreciation for the subtle beauty of stems and seedheads — and you can resist the urge to chop down everything after the first frost — give a winter garden a try. You're in for lots of delightful surprises.

Location Is Everything

Choosing the right site will go a long way toward making your winter garden a success. Be aware, however, that even the most carefully planned off-season border won't look perfect all of the time: Leaves, fruits, and seedheads may get tattered by wind, discolored by a hard freeze, smashed flat by ice, or nibbled on by hungry critters. Many good winter plants are quite resilient and can bounce back after rough weather, but it's still probably best to avoid placing this kind of planting in a high-visibility spot, such as by your front door. An ideal site is an area that's not especially noticeable during the growing season, but is easy to see from indoors during the winter. With this kind of location, you'll have plenty of opportunity to enjoy its beauty from a distance, even when you're not tempted to trek out to the yard.

Explore Your Options

Perennials for winter gardens come in two main groups: those with evergreen leaves and those with long-lasting stems and/or seedheads. Actually, "evergreen" is somewhat of a misnomer, because winter foliage comes in a range of colors in addition to green: shades of purple, maroon, blue, silver, gold, and copper, as well. Ever-colorful leaves can look great from fall to spring in mild-winter areas and provide a surprising amount of interest through the off season. In colder climates, though (roughly Zone 6 and north), frozen ground and drying winds can cause just about any leaves to tatter and turn brown. Reliable snow cover through the coldest months prevents this damage, but that won't do you much good, as you won't be able to see through the snow.

In these tough-winter areas, you'll have a more effective winter garden if you rely on perennials with good seedheads, as well as ornamental grasses, shrubs, and evergreens. These plants look spectacular when touched with frost, glazed in ice, or dusted with light snow, and they create intriguing (albeit temporary) "sculptures" under a heavier snowfall. These kinds of effects are unpredictable; as Stephanie likes to say, "Serendipity rules in the winter garden!" But if you keep your eyes open, you'll find yourself amazed at how even the most ordinary-looking plants can be transformed into something magical.

A Study in Subtlety

THIS SIMPLE BUT STUNNING winter border is an excellent choice for a sunny side yard, where you could enjoy the evergreen foliage, attractive seedheads, and showy stems of these sturdy perennials and shrubs from the window of your kitchen, family room, or home office. For even more interest, place a few panels of trellising behind the shrubs to provide a beautiful background for the entire planting. Have a bigger space to fill? Add a few winter-flowering shrubs or small trees, such as witch hazel *(Hamamelis)*, on each side of the border, then fill the space beneath them with winter perennials that appreciate summer shade: Christmas fern *(Polystichum acrostichoides)*, hellebore *(Helleborus)*, and hardy cyclamen *(Cyclamen)*, for example.

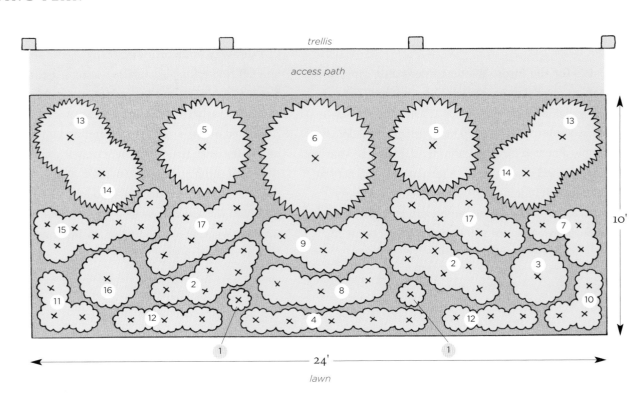

N

trellis

access path

10'

24'

lawn

PLANT LIST

1	*Arum italicum* 'Marmoratum'	2 plants
2	*Aster novae-angliae* 'Purple Dome'	10 plants
3	*Baptisia australis*	1 plant
4	*Bergenia* 'Bressingham Ruby'	5 plants
5	*Cornus sericea* 'Isanti'	2 plants
6	*Corylus avellana* 'Contorta'	1 plant
7	*Euphorbia amygdaloides* var. *robbiae*	3 plants
8	*Gillenia stipulata*	3 plants
9	*Helleborus foetidus*	3 plants
10	*H. x hybridus*	3 plants
11	*H. niger*	3 plants
12	*Iberis sempervirens*	6 plants
13	*Ilex verticillata* 'Rhett Butler'	2 plants
14	*I. verticillata* 'Scarlett O'Hara'	2 plants
15	*Liatris spicata*	7 plants
16	*Molinia caerulea* subsp. *arundinacea* 'Sky Racer'	1 plant
17	*Rudbeckia maxima*	10 plants

DESIGNER'S CHECKLIST

☐ **It's for the birds.** Winter gardens aren't just fun to look at; their abundant seedheads and dried foliage also provide excellent sources of food and shelter for birds. Want to attract even more winged wonders? Supply a heated birdbath or other dependable source of water, and you'll create an ideal off-season habitat. Continue the theme with some ornamental bird-houses, and your winter garden will provide hours of enjoyable viewing for you — and a happy home for your feathered friends.

☐ **Put away your pruners.** Many classic summer- and fall-flowering perennials — asters, astilbes, cone-flowers (*Echinacea* and *Rudbeckia*), globe thistles (*Echinops*), salvias, sedums, and yarrows (*Achillea*), to name just a few — are also exceptional in winter gardens. However, they'll be there only if you don't do the usual thing and cut them down when the seed-heads start to form. Yes, the garden will look a bit untidy as the growing season goes on, but it'll be worth it when you have lots of fascinating forms to look at through a long winter.

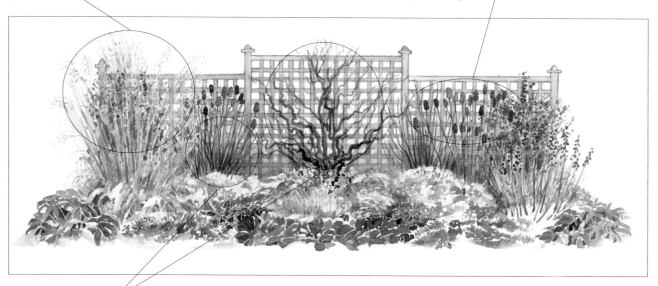

☐ **Build good "bones."** A winter garden lacks the background of lush foliage, so it can really benefit from a good framework of trellises, fences, and small evergreens. Certain deciduous shrubs add excitement, such as the curiously twisted stems of Harry Lauder's walking stick (*Corylus avellana* 'Contorta'), the colorful shoots of red-twig dogwoods (like *Cornus sericea* 'Isanti'), and the bright fruits of winterberry hollies (pair a female *Ilex verticillata* 'Scarlett O'Hara' with a male 'Rhett Butler'). Statues, urns, and other orna-ments become much more prominent at this time of year, as do paved areas and stone walls. Frost-proof pots and planters filled with evergreen boughs are excellent for winter interest too.

☐ **Concentrate your efforts.** If you're not sure you want to commit to a winter garden, it may be tempt-ing to add a few good winter perennials to one of your plantings in the hopes of getting year-round beauty from that border. That can work, but in most cases you're better off planning an area specifically for off-season enjoyment; otherwise, the winter-interest plants may be too scattered to give much impact.

Arum italicum 'Marmoratum'

(Italian arum, a.k.a. 'Pictum')

Arrow-shaped, deep green leaves veined with pale green appear in fall and last through spring before going dormant. (In the cooler parts of its range, the leaves may die back some during the worst weather, but new leaves will appear in late winter.) White-hooded flowers appear among the leaves in spring, developing into spikes of green berries that turn scarlet by fall. Height and spread to 1 foot. ZONES 6–9.

ALTERNATIVES: Another cultivar of this species.

Aster novae-angliae 'Purple Dome'

('Purple Dome' New England aster)

Rounded, 18- to 24-inch-tall and 30-inch-wide clumps of sturdy stems are clad in narrow green leaves and feature bright purple, orange-centered blooms from late summer into mid-fall, followed by puffy seedheads. ZONES 4–8.

ALTERNATIVES: Another compact fall-flowering aster, such as A. novi-belgii 'Alert' or 'Professor Anton Kippenburg'.

Baptisia australis

(Blue false indigo)

Spikelike clusters of dark blue flowers bloom in early summer atop 4- to 5-foot stems clad in three-lobed green leaves, followed by long-lasting black seedpods; spread is 3 to 4 feet. ZONES 3–9.

ALTERNATIVES: Anise hyssop (Agastache) or Siberian iris (Iris sibirica).

Bergenia 'Bressingham Ruby'

('Bressingham Ruby' bergenia)

Dense evergreen clumps of leathery, rich green leaves turn burgundy red in late fall, with clusters of pinkish red flowers from mid- to late spring; height and spread to 1 foot. ZONES 3–8.

ALTERNATIVES: 'Cabernet' or another bergenia.

Euphorbia amygdaloides var. robbiae

(Robb's wood spurge)

One-foot-tall, spreading carpets of evergreen, deep green foliage are accented with clusters of chartreuse "flowers" from mid-spring to early summer; height in bloom to 2 feet, spread to 18 inches. ZONES 6–9.

ALTERNATIVES: Any other hardy euphorbia of your choice.

Gillenia stipulata

(Bowman's root, a.k.a. Porteranthus stipulatus)

Bowman's root produces bushy, 3-foot-tall and 2-foot-wide clumps of reddish stems and lacy green leaves that turn bronze-red in fall. Starry white flowers bloom early to midsummer; small dark seedpods persist well into winter. ZONES 5–9.

ALTERNATIVES: G. trifoliata or globe thistle (Echinops).

Helleborus

(Hellebores)

These early-flowering, evergreen perennials are ideal for winter and spring gardens.

H. foetidus (bear's foot hellebore) has upright stems clad in leathery, deeply cut dark green leaves and boasts clusters of pale green bells from mid- or late winter to mid- or late spring; 18 to 30 inches tall and 18 to 24 inches across. ZONES 4–9.

H. niger (Christmas rose) and H. x hybridus (Lenten rose) have deep green leaves that arise directly from the ground, with saucer-shaped flowers atop separate stems in 18-inch-wide clumps; 1-foot-tall Christmas rose can bloom any time from midwinter to early spring, with white to pinkish flowers; 12- to 18-inch-tall Lenten rose's white, pink, yellow, plum, or red blooms usually appear in late winter or early spring. ZONES 5–9.

ALTERNATIVES: Corsican hellebore (H. argutifolius) and any other hellebores.

Iberis sempervirens

(Perennial candytuft)

Shrubby, 1-foot-tall and -wide mounds of narrow, dark green, evergreen leaves are smothered with clusters of white flowers throughout spring. ZONES 3–8.

ALTERNATIVES: Any perennial candytuft cultivar.

Liatris spicata

(Blazing star)

Upright, 3- to 5-foot stems are clad in slender green leaves and bear dense spikes of fuzzy-looking, purplish pink flowers in late summer and early fall (lasting through much of the winter); spread is 12 to 18 inches. ZONES 4–9.

ALTERNATIVES: Kansas gayfeather (L. pycnostachya) or L. scariosa.

Molinia caerulea subsp. arundinacea 'Sky Racer'

('Sky Racer' purple moor grass)

Slender, upright or arching green leaves in dense clumps to 2 feet tall and 3 feet wide send up 6- to 7-foot stems bearing open clusters of tiny, purplish green flowers in late summer. The whole plant turns bright yellow in fall, then ages to light tan and lasts well into winter. ZONES 5–9.

ALTERNATIVES: The cultivar 'Staefa', 'Transparent', or 'Windspiel', or giant feather grass (Stipa gigantea).

Rudbeckia maxima

(Giant coneflower)

Three-foot-wide clumps of blue-gray leaves send up 5- to 7-foot stems sporting raised, dark cones surrounded by bright yellow petals in late summer and early fall. ZONES 5–9.

ALTERNATIVES: Another species or cultivar of Rudbeckia or Echinacea.

Gardens for Special Effects

FINDING A THEME FOR A NEW GARDEN isn't always as easy as matching particular site conditions, or choosing your favorite colors, or planning for a specific season. Sometimes you're trying to create a certain effect or have a garden with a particular purpose, such as a formal entrance garden or an easy-care island bed. In this chapter, we'll take a look at five unique perennial planting themes and explore the various ways you can make them a part of your own yard.

Minimal-Maintenance Plantings

To PASSIONATE GARDENERS, the idea of planning a "low-maintenance" planting seems pointless, at least at first glance. After all, if you enjoy spending time puttering around in your garden, why would you want a reason to spend less time doing what you love? But when you think about it, we all have one or more gardening tasks that we don't particularly enjoy, be it weeding, deadheading, staking, or edging. The secret to creating an easy-care garden is to minimize the things you don't like to do, so you can spend more time doing the fun stuff.

What Do You Like Least?

Reducing boring gardening chores starts at the design stage. If you're an experienced gardener, you already know what you like and don't like to do, so jot down a list of the yard and garden maintenance tasks you want to minimize. If you're a beginner, chances are you don't have a clue what you'll enjoy and what you won't. Our best advice, then, is to keep your first garden small — somewhere between 20 and 40 square feet. That's plenty of space to get your hands dirty, but not so much that you'll become overwhelmed. As you learn the kinds of care a garden needs, you can fine-tune your plan, or redesign the whole area to meet your needs.

The biggest factor affecting the maintenance needs of any garden is the plants you choose. Here are a few examples of how you can get perennials to do your work for you:

✳ Hate getting stuck with staking? Choose compact cultivars or those selected for their sturdy stems.

✳ To reduce weeding woes, avoid perennials that self-sow heavily.

✳ Don't want to water? Use plants adapted to the natural rainfall in your area.

✳ To minimize deadheading, use plants with small, "self-cleaning" flowers; choose those with attractive seedheads; or rely on perennials that are grown primarily for foliage.

✳ Don't want to bother with dividing every year or two? Choose long-lived perennials that prefer to be left alone.

✳ Hate spraying? Look for perennials that are naturally resistant to the common pests and diseases in your area.

We didn't give you specific examples of plants that fulfill these criteria, because many of these traits depend on your particular climate and growing conditions. For example, a perennial that self-sows in a garden with moist soil may be perfectly well behaved in a dry site. Catalog descriptions provide some clues to low-maintenance features, but seeing how the plants actually grow in your area is by far the better option. A great way to get the real scoop is to visit display gardens at local arboreta and botanical gardens and talk to the people who maintain plantings you find appealing. Or check out books devoted to perennial maintenance, such as *The Well-Tended Perennial Garden,* by Tracy DiSabato-Aust, or *Caring for Perennials,* by Janet Macunovich, to get the lowdown on just how much pampering the perennials you're considering may need to look their best (see Recommended Reading in the Appendix).

Keep It Simple

The amount and type of maintenance a garden needs is also influenced by how you put your plants together and how you get them in the ground. Borders based on masses (roughly speaking, groups of five or more) of a few different perennials are generally much simpler to maintain than are those filled with single clumps or small groupings of many different plants. The more variety there is, the greater the chance that every day, something or another will need some sprucing up.

Growing perennials in masses also makes it easier to match the vigor of the plants. You can combine a bunch of fast growers — like bee balms *(Monarda)*, goldenrods *(Solidago)*, and switch grasses *(Panicum)* — and let them fight it out, or else pair slow growers that will politely share space with each other. If you make the mistake of mixing perennials with very different growth rates, you'll constantly have to dig and divide the thugs to keep them from crowding out less vigorous bedmates. This is one of the most common maintenance problems beginners run into, and one of the trickiest to avoid, because you need experience growing plants before you can predict how fast they'll spread in your conditions — a real catch-22! To improve your odds of choosing plants with similar growth rates, look for clues in catalog descriptions. If you see terms like "vigorous," "great ground cover," and "spreads quickly," keep those plants away from those described as "slow-growing," "tidy," "dainty," or "elegant."

When you prepare the site for planting, it's smart to build up the soil's organic matter with compost, but use chemical fertilizers and manures sparingly, if at all. You don't want to promote a lot of lush growth right away, because that will mean more watering, staking, fertilizing, and dividing in the long run. Building the soil with organic matter and slow-release organic fertilizers produces

Dependable perennial groundcovers, along with shrubs and other perennials, require little maintenance in this striking, hard-working streetside bed.

slower but more balanced plant growth that's less likely to need extra pampering and less prone to pest and disease problems.

Unless you know that your site is evenly moist all year round, consider laying soaker hoses in your new garden (after planting but before mulching). Even drought-resistant plants need a little extra moisture in their first year or two, and soaker hoses are an easy and effective way to water during dry spells. (For more tips on using soaker hoses, see Stephanie Says on page 118.) Whatever you do, don't use commercial plastic or spun-bonded landscape cloth to cover the soil before you plant, thinking that it will eliminate weeding chores. Seeds that drop or blow onto the garden may root in the fabric, making them twice as difficult to pull out. And if you're growing perennials with creeping roots or aboveground runners, weed-blocking fabrics can stop the new shoots from popping up or rooting down, preventing them from forming the thick, dense carpet you'd hoped for.

An Easy-Care Entrance

A GARDEN THAT YOU, your family, and visitors see every day always needs to be at its best. But that doesn't mean you must spend all your free moments fussing at it to keep it perfect, because well-chosen plants can do the work for you. This design relies on perennials with good-looking foliage, good pest and disease resistance, and moderate vigor (strong enough to survive without constant pampering but not so vigorous that they'll crowd out their companions). These low-maintenance perennials also seldom need to be divided — they just look more lush and bloom better year after year.

PLANT LIST

1	*Amelanchier canadensis* Rainbow Pillar	1 plant		13	H. 'June'	1 plant
2	*Astilbe chinensis* 'Pumila'	5 plants		14	*Hydrangea quercifolia* 'Pee Wee'	1 plant
3	*A. simplicifolia* 'Sprite'	5 plants		15	*Iris cristata* 'Alba'	9 plants
4	*Athyrium filix-femina* 'Cristatum'	3 plants		16	*Lamium maculatum* 'Pink Pewter'	9 plants
5	*Brunnera macrophylla* 'Jack Frost'	5 plants		17	*Lysimachia nummularia* 'Aurea'	6 plants
6	*Carex buchananii*	3 plants		18	*Ophiopogon planiscapus* 'Nigrescens'	5 plants
7	*Chrysogonum virginianum*	3 plants		19	*Pachysandra procumbens*	23 plants
8	*Cimicifuga* 'James Compton'	1 plant		20	*Phlox stolonifera* 'Sherwood Purple'	3 plants
9	*Euphorbia amygdaloides* var. *robbiae*	7 plants		21	*Physocarpus opulifolius* Summer Wine	1 plant
10	*Geranium maculatum* 'Espresso'	1 plant		22	*Polygonatum humile*	5 plants
11	*Hexastylis shuttleworthii* 'Callaway'	7 plants		23	*Polystichum acrostichoides*	5 plants
12	*Hosta* 'Blue Cadet'	3 plants		24	*Solidago caesia*	3 plants

PLANTING PLAN

DESIGNER'S CHECKLIST

☐ **Get rid of unneeded lawn.** Lawn care doesn't rank high on most gardeners' "top-10 favorites" list. Replacing grass with perennials in difficult-to-trim spots will make mowing go more quickly, and your yard will look better, too. Just remember that grubs can be a problem where grass was growing, so pick out and destroy these C-shaped, cream-colored beetle larvae if you see them as you prepare the soil and plant; otherwise, they'll feed on the roots of your new perennials.

☐ **All together now.** Instead of mowing and trimming around individual trees and shrubs, create beds that will link several of them, and fill the space with perennial ground covers and bulbs. Besides cutting down on your turf maintenance time, this will protect tender bark from mower and trimmer damage.

☐ **Keep edges simple.** When planning any perennial garden, avoid complicated curves or fussy scallops along edges where the bed is bordered by lawn grass. Smooth curves and straight lines are by far the easiest edges to mow. Add a brick or stone mowing strip, and you'll eliminate trimming chores as well.

☐ **Allow ample elbow room.** At planting time, set out long-lived perennials at the spacing recommended on the label. Yes, they'll look rather sparse initially, so mulch around them to keep down weeds, and fill in with a few annuals if you'd like for the first few years. The perennials will gradually fill their allotted space without becoming overcrowded, and that means you won't have to dig them up and divide them every few years.

Astilbe
(Astilbes)

Although astilbes are typically considered to be shade plants, they can tolerate ample sunshine in sites where their roots never dry out. Their dense clumps of deeply dissected, rich green leaves look great all through the growing season, and their showy flower plumes are attractive long after the blooms have faded. *A. chinensis* 'Pumila' (dwarf Chinese astilbe) blooms in late summer, with 1-foot-tall, pink plumes over spreading carpets of ferny, medium green leaves. *A. simplicifolia* 'Sprite' is 12 to 18 inches tall in bloom, with glossy, deep green leaves. ZONES 4–8.

ALTERNATIVES: Any other pink astilbe cultivars in the same height range, such as 'Hennie Graafland'.

Athyrium filix-femina 'Cristatum'
(Crested lady fern)

Elegant clumps of arching, lacy green fronds look good from late spring to frost; 2 feet tall and 12 to 18 inches across. ZONES 3–8.

ALTERNATIVES: Another fern.

Brunnera macrophylla 'Jack Frost'
('Jack Frost' Siberian bugloss)

Low, broad mounds of silvery, green-veined heart-shaped leaves are accented in mid- to late spring with sprays of small blue flowers; 12 to 18 inches tall and 18 to 24 inches across. ZONES 3–8.

ALTERNATIVES: The cultivar 'Langtrees'.

Carex buchananii
(Leather-leaved sedge)

Upright tufts of slender brown blades form in clumps 18 to 24 inches tall and wide; definitely different and eye-catching! ZONES 6– OR 7–9.

ALTERNATIVES: Bronze sedge (*C. comans* 'Bronze') or red wood rush (*Luzula* 'Ruby Stiletto').

Chrysogonum virginianum
(Green-and-gold)

Six-inch-tall, spreading carpets of fuzzy, deep green leaves are dotted with yellow daisylike flowers from late spring to mid-fall. ZONES 5–8.

ALTERNATIVES: Wild gingers (*Asarum*).

Cimicifuga 'James Compton'
('James Compton' bugbane)

Bushy clumps of deep purple, dissected leaves are 2 feet tall and 18 inches across, accented with foot-long spikes of fragrant, creamy white flowers from late summer into fall. ZONES 4–8.

ALTERNATIVES: *Anthriscus sylvestris* 'Ravenswing'.

Euphorbia amygdaloides var. robbiae
(Robb's wood spurge, a.k.a. *E. robbiae*)

One-foot-tall, spreading carpets of ever-green, deep green foliage send up clusters of chartreuse "flowers" from mid-spring to early summer; height in bloom to 2 feet, spread to 18 inches. ZONES 6–9.

ALTERNATIVES: Red wood spurge (*E. amygdaloides* 'Rubra').

Geranium maculatum 'Espresso'
('Espresso' hardy geranium)

Deeply lobed, dark brown foliage forms mounds 1 foot tall and 12 to 18 inches wide, with light purple flowers in early and mid-spring. ZONES 4–8.

ALTERNATIVES: *G. pratense* 'Hocus Pocus'.

Hexastylis shuttleworthii 'Callaway'
('Callaway' hardy ginger)

Three-inch-tall, evergreen carpets of rounded, silver-marked deep green leaves spread by creeping rhizomes to a foot or more; bell-shaped brownish blooms are not showy. ZONES 5–9.

ALTERNATIVES: European wild ginger (*Asarum europaeum*).

Hosta
(Hostas)

Classic, no-fuss perennials grown primarily for their foliage, which comes in a wide range of shapes, sizes, and colors to fit any shady garden. 'Blue Cadet' forms blue-green mounds 1 foot tall and wide, with pale purple flowers on 18-inch stems in mid- to late summer. 'June' has blue leaves with irregular cream-to-yellow centers, and pale purple flowers on 20-inch stems in early to midsummer; foliage is 18 inches tall and 30 inches across. ZONES 3–8.

ALTERNATIVES: Any other hostas in the same color and height range.

Hosta

Iris cristata 'Alba'
(White crested iris)

Gold-centered white blooms rise in mid-spring among upright, light green leaves that spread by rhizomes to about a foot across; about 6 inches tall. ZONES 3–9.

ALTERNATIVES: Crested iris (*I. cristata*) or white roof iris (*I. tectorum* 'Album').

Lamium maculatum 'Pink Pewter'

('Pink Pewter' lamium)

Clusters of pink blooms in spring over 12- to 18-inch-wide carpets of silver-and-green leaves; height is 6 inches. ZONES 3–8.

ALTERNATIVES: 'Beacon Silver', 'White Nancy', or any other silver-leaved cultivar.

Lysimachia nummularia 'Aurea'

(Golden creeping Jenny)

Ground-hugging mats of trailing stems with rounded, bright yellow leaves are dotted with small, golden yellow flowers in summer; 2 inches tall and 1 to 2 feet across. ZONES 3–8.

ALTERNATIVES: Lamium maculatum 'Aureum' or 'Beedham's White'.

Ophiopogon planiscapus 'Nigrescens'

(Black mondo grass)

Six- to 8-inch-tall tufts of narrow, deep purple-black leaves form clumps that spread to 1 foot; sprays of light pink flowers among the leaves in summer, followed by deep purple berries. ZONES 6–9.

ALTERNATIVES: Luzula 'Ruby Stiletto'.

Lysimachia nummularia 'Aurea'

Pachysandra procumbens

(Allegheny spurge)

Brushy, 4- to 6-inch-tall spikes of white flowers bloom in early spring, followed by whorled, light green leaves that darken with age, developing silvery mottling by fall; the 6- to 8-inch-tall clumps spread slowly to 1 foot. ZONES 5–9.

ALTERNATIVES: Canada wild ginger (*Asarum canadense*).

Phlox stolonifera 'Sherwood Purple'

('Sherwood Purple' creeping phlox)

Blue-purple flowers form atop 6-inch stems in mid- to late spring over 3-inch-tall carpets of deep green leaves; spread to 1 foot. ZONES 2–8.

ALTERNATIVES: P. divaricata 'London Grove Blue'.

Polygonatum humile

(Dwarf Solomon's seal)

Upright, 6-inch-tall stalks bear oblong, bright green leaves accented with small, bell-like white blooms in spring; spreads by rhizomes to form patches about 18 inches across. ZONES 4–9.

ALTERNATIVES: Polygonatum odoratum 'Variegatum'.

Polystichum acrostichoides

(Christmas fern)

Rich green, evergreen fronds are upright when young, gradually becoming more horizontal as they age; 12 to 18 inches tall and across. ZONES 5–9.

ALTERNATIVES: Japanese painted fern (*Athyrium niponicum* var. *pictum*).

Solidago caesia

(Wreath goldenrod)

Narrow, arching wands of golden yellow blooms appear from early to late fall atop slender, purplish stems clad in narrow green leaves; 1 to 3 feet tall and 8 to 12 inches across. ZONES 4–8.

ALTERNATIVES: Autumn fern (*Dryopteris erythrosora*).

Stephanie Says

We've said it before, and I'll say it again: Good-looking leaves are what you should focus on when you want to get the most from your perennial budget. A combination of foliage colors and textures is pleasing all season long, and foliage requires a fraction of the care that flowers do — a perfect recipe for an

Covering Your Bases

easy-care planting. Some perennial producers are now specializing in beautiful, low-growing ground covers that are ideal for low-maintenance beds and borders. The only downside is that these garden gems typically aren't readily available in large quantities; you won't find them sold in flats of 50 for just a few bucks, as you can with standbys like lesser periwinkle (*Vinca minor*). But here's a trick: Look for overgrown pots that are on sale in summer or fall, then snap them up and divide them when you get home. You can often get four or more plants for less than the regular price of one.

Cottage Gardens: Anything Goes

IF GARDENING IS YOUR RULING PASSION, you don't like just looking at plants: You want to be surrounded by them. And that's what a cottage garden is all about — creating a space that you can really live in, with flowers to pick, herbs and vegetables to harvest, fruits to feast upon, and abundant color and fragrance to fill your senses. These beautiful and bountiful plantings are the ultimate in user-friendly gardens.

From Practical to Playful

Way back when, the original cottage gardens were far more practical than pretty. Most were filled with vegetables, herbs, and fruits — productive plants that families needed for day-to-day survival. Over time, though, more and more flowers snuck in, and the classic English cottage garden has evolved from its pragmatic beginnings. Today, there are as many definitions of cottage gardens as there are people who have them. To some, they're a random mix of flowers, or of flowers and herbs; to others, they're a more traditional combination of flowers, herbs, vegetables, and fruits. There are a few things, however, that most cottage gardens have in common:

In an informal cottage garden, you can mix up all kinds and colors of plants that you'd never dare try in a more formal planting.

✳ **A path through the planting.** Most gardens are meant to be admired at a distance, but a cottage garden should be interactive, with ready access to all parts of the planting for easy fragrance-sniffing, flower-picking, and edible-harvesting.

✳ **Volunteers wanted.** In cottage gardens, self-sown seedlings are actively encouraged. The random effect created by these "volunteers" is an important component of the casual cottage-garden experience. So don't be too quick to snip off those dead flowers; let them drop their seeds where they may, then enjoy the results.

✳ **Fun and fanciful accents.** This is the place to allow your creativity free rein. Unique paving, quirky containers, oddball ornaments, and more: It's these personal touches that give a cottage garden its character.

A Cottage Garden — without the Cottage

A TRADITIONAL COTTAGE PLANTING looks most appropriate with a small Colonial-style home, where the house seems to nestle right into the garden. But if this kind of garden appeals to you, don't think you can't have one just because your home is more formal; we have just the plan for you. Based primarily on soft blues, pinks, and yellows and set within a classic "four-square" layout, this design for a full-sun site features an abundance of colorful and fragrant blooms you can enjoy outdoors from late spring or early summer through fall.

PLANTING PLAN

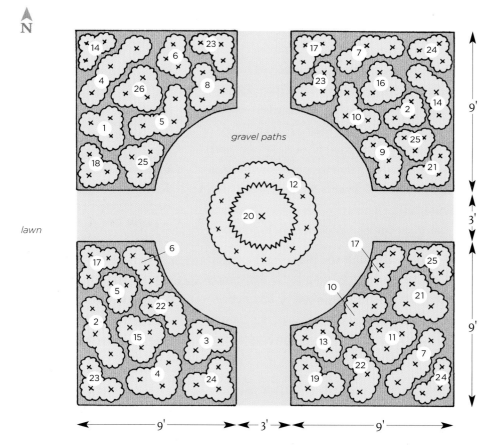

PLANT LIST

1	*Achillea* 'Anthea'	3 plants		14	*L.* x *superbum* 'Snow Lady'	6 plants
2	*A.* 'Moonshine'	6 plants		15	*Phlox paniculata* 'David'	3 plants
3	*Anthemis tinctoria* 'Moonlight'	3 plants		16	*P. paniculata* 'Shortwood'	3 plants
4	*Centranthus ruber*	6 plants		17	*Platycodon grandiflorus* subsp. *mariesii*	9 plants
5	*C. ruber* 'Albus'	6 plants		18	*P. grandiflorus* 'Misato Purple'	3 plants
6	*Coreopsis* 'Sweet Dreams'	6 plants		19	*P. grandiflorus* 'Shell Pink'	3 plants
7	*C. verticillata* 'Moonbeam'	6 plants		20	*Rosa* 'Carefree Wonder'	1 plant
8	*Dianthus* 'Firewitch'	3 plants		21	*Salvia nemorosa* 'East Friesland'	6 plants
9	*D.* 'Little Boy Blue'	3 plants		22	*S.* x *sylvestris* 'Blue Hill'	6 plants
10	*Dictamnus albus*	6 plants		23	*Saponaria* x *lempergii* 'Max Frei'	9 plants
11	*Digitalis purpurea* 'Sutton's Apricot'	3 plants		24	*Scabiosa* 'Butterfly Blue'	9 plants
12	*Lavandula* x *intermedia* 'Grosso'	9 plants		25	*S.* 'Pink Mist'	9 plants
13	*Leucanthemum* x *superbum* 'Little Princess'	3 plants		26	*Sidalcea* 'Party Girl'	3 plants

DESIGNER'S CHECKLIST

☐ **Whimsical ornaments set the tone.** A cottage garden is the place not for formal statues or fancy urns, but rather for fun rustic or homemade accents. Keep an eye out at secondhand shops and yard sales for finds such as old washtubs (they make great planters) and rusty pieces of wrought-iron fencing (excellent for informal plant supports). And don't worry about being tacky: If you think garden gnomes or pink flamingos are amusing, your cottage garden is the place to put them.

☐ **Not just veggin'.** Mixing in edibles with your flowers is a great way to get the most from a small garden space — and that's what a traditional cottage garden is all about. Annual crops of herbs and vegetables like basil, cabbage, cherry tomatoes, eggplant, lettuce, and peppers make quick-growing, colorful fillers for empty spots, while asparagus, artichokes, sages, and rhubarb are ideal as out-of-the-ordinary background or accent plants.

☐ **Don't be fooled.** Despite its casual appearance, a cottage-style garden does need maintenance. Admittedly, there is little or no need for staking, and traditional cottage-garden perennials tend to be fairly rugged when it comes to insect and disease resistance. But like any other garden plants, they'll need fertilizer and water on occasion, as well as dividing when they get too crowded. But the key part is managing all the self-sown seedlings: deciding which flowers you'll allow to set seed and which seedlings you'll allow to remain.

☐ **Be prepared for surprises.** If there's one word to describe a cottage garden, it's *unpredictable*. When you let flowers like foxgloves (*Digitalis*) and gas plant (*Dictamnus*) self-sow, you never know where they'll show up, and in what quantities. It's your job to "edit out" seedlings that come up in inconvenient spots, as well as those that are rather too abundant. If some plants self-sow too freely and appear to be taking over the garden, you may want to deadhead them carefully for a few years to give your other plants a chance to fill in more.

Achillea

(Yarrows)

Flat-topped clusters of bright or pastel blooms are produced all through the summer over clumps of fernlike leaves. **'Anthea'** and **'Moonshine'** have pale yellow blooms and gray-green leaves; 'Anthea' seems to have better heat and humidity tolerance. Both are 18 to 24 inches tall and 12 to 18 inches wide. ZONES 2–9.

ALTERNATIVES: Other yarrows.

Anthemis tinctoria 'Moonlight'

('Moonlight' golden marguerite)

These bushy, 2-foot-tall and -wide clumps of aromatic, deeply divided, medium green leaves showcase light yellow to near white, gold-centered daisies throughout the summer (especially with deadheading). ZONES 3–7.

ALTERNATIVES: The cultivar 'E. C. Buxton' or the hybrid 'Susanna Mitchell'.

Centranthus ruber

(Red valerian, a.k.a. Jupiter's beard)

Upright to gently sprawling stems are clad in somewhat fleshy green leaves and sport clusters of small, rosy pink flowers from late spring to early fall (with regular deadheading); 2 to 3 feet tall and wide. **'Albus'** has white flowers. ZONES 5–8.

ALTERNATIVES: *Dianthus* 'Bath's Pink' for the species; for 'Albus', try *Calamintha nepeta* 'White Cloud' or *Campanula carpatica* 'White Clips'.

Coreopsis

(Coreopsis)

Mound-forming perennials with narrow green leaves are practically smothered in flat-faced, daisylike blooms in early to midsummer; will repeat bloom well into fall if deadheaded.
'Sweet Dreams' grows 12 to 18 inches tall and wide, with pale pink blooms that have a darker pink ring near the center. ZONES 4–9.

C. verticillata **'Moonbeam'** is 18 to 24 inches tall and wide, with butter yellow blooms; **'Zagreb'** is about the same size but has golden yellow flowers. ZONES 3–9.

ALTERNATIVES: Lady's mantle (*Alchemilla mollis*) for 'Sweet Dreams'; 'Crème Brûlée' for 'Moonbeam'.

Dianthus

(Dianthus, a.k.a. pinks)

Clumps of slender, green or blue-green leaves look good all year, with single, semi-double, or double flowers usually in mid- to late spring, sometimes with repeat bloom later in the season. **'Firewitch'** (a.k.a. 'Feuerhexe') has magenta-pink flowers; **'Little Boy Blue'** has white blossoms with pink centers. Both have silvery blue foliage and single flowers; height to 6 inches and spread to 1 foot. ZONES 4–8.

ALTERNATIVES: Other dianthus species or cultivars of a similar size, such as 'Mrs. Sinkins'.

Dianthus plumaris **'Cyclops'**

Dictamnus albus

(Gas plant, a.k.a. burning bush or dittany)

Spikelike clusters of white or pinkish flowers bloom in early summer over clumps of deep green leaves; to 2 feet tall and wide. ZONES 3–8.

ALTERNATIVES: Foxglove penstemon (*Penstemon digitalis*) or white rose campion (*Lychnis coronaria* 'Alba').

Dictamnus albus

Digitalis purpurea 'Sutton's Apricot'

('Sutton's Apricot' foxglove)

Rosettes of green leaves reach 1 foot tall and 1 to 2 feet wide, with 3- to 5-foot stems topped with spikes of tubular, light peachy pink blooms in late spring or early summer. Best treated as a biennial. ZONES 4–8.

ALTERNATIVES: Another tall foxglove.

Lavandula x intermedia 'Grosso'

('Grosso' lavender, a.k.a. lavandin)

Dense, shrubby clumps of fragrant, narrow, silvery green leaves are accented with plump, fragrant flower spikes atop 2- to 3-foot stems from early summer to early fall; spread is 2 feet. ZONES 6–8 (excellent winter drainage is a must).

ALTERNATIVES: Any other hardy lavender, such as 'Hidcote' or 'Munstead', or a catmint (*Nepeta*).

Leucanthemum x superbum

(Shasta daisy)

White-petaled, golden-centered daisies bloom atop upright stems and deep green leaves; 1 to 3 feet tall and 18 to 24 inches across. Most flowers appear in early to midsummer, but deadheading encourages repeat bloom into fall. **'Little Princess'** has 2- to 3-inch-wide flowers on plants to 12 inches tall and 18 inches across; **'Snow Lady'** is similar but a few inches shorter (to 10 inches). ZONES 4–8.

ALTERNATIVES: 'Silver Princess' and 'Snowcap'.

Phlox paniculata

(Garden phlox)

Large clusters of flowers scent the air from mid- or late summer into fall atop upright stems with narrow green leaves. **'David'** bears snowy white blooms atop 36- to 40-inch stems from midsummer to early fall over rich green, mildew-resistant foliage; clumps are 18 inches across.

'Shortwood' has bright pink blooms with a darker eye; grows 4 feet tall and 2 feet across. Both are mildew-resistant. ZONES 4–8.

ALTERNATIVES: For 'David', try the cultivars 'Mt. Fuji', 'White Admiral', or 'World Peace'; for 'Shortwood', use 'Tracy's Treasure' or another pink phlox.

Platycodon grandiflorus

(Balloon flower)

Upright stems clad in medium green to bluish green leaves that turn bright yellow in fall and are topped in late summer with balloonlike buds that open into star-shaped flowers. *P. grandiflorus* subsp. *mariesii* has purple-blue flowers on compact plants (12 to 18 inches tall and wide); **'Misato Purple'** is similar but has more purple in the flowers. **'Shell Pink'** has pale pink flowers on 2-foot stems. ZONES 3–9.

ALTERNATIVES: Other balloon flower selections, such as *P. grandiflorus* f. *apoyama*.

Finding the Right Site

The charm of a cottage garden is in its informality, but the amount of informality you'll be comfortable with depends on your tolerance for controlled chaos. In a highly visible front-yard setting, you may want to go with a design like the one featured on page 202, with soft colors and old-fashioned flowers in carefully planned drifts to evoke the romance of a cottage garden without appearing at all untidy.

In a less visible setting, such as a side or back yard, a free-for-all, unplanned patch of mixed colors could be more to your liking. Or try a compromise: Create a strong framework of geometric beds with well-defined edges to provide a sense of structure, then tuck in whatever strikes your fancy and let the plants sprawl a bit to soften the hard lines. Another option is to use an informal setting, with odd-shaped beds and irregular edges, but then choose a scheme of two or three main colors to visually unify the planting.

Salvia

(Perennial salvias)

Spiky, purple-blue flowers bloom from early to midsummer, often with a repeat show if you deadhead regularly; height and spread from 18 to 36 inches. **S. nemorosa 'East Friesland'** has deep purple-blue blooms; **S. x sylvestris 'Blue Hill'** is a lighter blue; both are 18 inches tall and wide. ZONES 4–8.

ALTERNATIVES: 'Blue Queen' and 'Caradonna'.

Saponaria x lempergii 'Max Frei'

('Max Frei' soapwort)

Low, ground-hugging carpets of slender, deep green leaves have flat, rosy pink flowers atop 1-foot stems, usually from early to mid- or late summer; spreads 1 to 2 feet wide. ZONES 4–8.

ALTERNATIVES: *Calamintha grandiflora*, a hardy geranium, or sea thrift (*Armeria maritima*).

Scabiosa

(Pincushion flower)

Masses of domed blooms are held on wiry stems over dense clumps of plain or deeply toothed green leaves. Bloom is from early or midsummer well into fall (especially with regular deadheading). **'Butterfly Blue'** has lavender-blue flowers, and **'Pink Mist'** is lilac-pink; both have gray-green leaves and grow 1 foot tall and wide. ZONES 3–8.

ALTERNATIVES: For 'Butterfly Blue', any catmint (*Nepeta*); for 'Pink Mist', *Dianthus* 'Bath's Pink'.

Sidalcea 'Party Girl'

('Party Girl' checkerbloom, a.k.a. prairie mallow)

Upright, 3-foot stems are clad in deeply lobed, bright green leaves and topped with spikes of hollyhock-like pink flowers from mid- to late summer (into fall with regular deadheading); spread to 18 inches. ZONES 5–7.

ALTERNATIVES: Strawberry foxglove (*Digitalis* x *mertonensis*) or *Verbascum* 'Pink Domino'.

Formal Borders for Elegance

WHAT BETTER WAY TO SHOWCASE your gardening talents than a formal perennial planting? These elegant and impeccably maintained areas are an ideal choice for a high-traffic area — along a frequently used path, for example, or by a front door — and are a perfect complement to a Victorian- or Colonial-style home.

A Formal Affair

The good looks of a formal garden come at a price, in the form of above-average upkeep. Frequent deadheading, removing discolored leaves, cutting back, fertilizing, watering, and staking are all necessary to maintain an elegant formal design. Don't let your reach exceed your grasp, as they say: It's easy to underestimate just how much time a formal garden will require to look top-notch. Keep in mind, too, that the pretty pictures of formal gardens in books and magazines don't give you the whole story: They often gloss over the expense that went into the construction of those plantings, and the staff of gardeners who care for them!

The key to good planning is really knowing the plants: how big they get, how fast they grow, and how they look throughout the growing season. It is also vital to choose perennials that are naturally suited to the sunlight and drainage your site offers, as well as to your hardiness zone. This is not the place to experiment with plants that may not dependably overwinter in your climate, or with those that normally prefer some shade if you only have full sun. This kind of solid plant knowledge comes from years of hands-on gardening experience, so don't depend solely on information you've gleaned from books and magazines to help you create the garden of your dreams. Instead, start small with perennials you know you can depend on, then expand the planting as you gain confidence with other species and cultivars.

Symmetry and geometry play an important part in a formal garden design.

An Elegant Entrance Garden

MOST FOLKS TYPICALLY THINK of a formal garden as being in a sunny site, and those who have mature trees might even be tempted to cut them down to make room for their dream garden. In truth, though, there are just as many superb perennials for shady sites — and not just the ephemeral beauties that bloom their hearts out in spring and then disappear for the rest of the year. This design for a shaded foundation planting features evergreen foliage, long-lasting flowers, and a variety of contrasting forms to create an unforgettable entry to any home.

PLANT LIST

1	*Aruncus dioicus*	1 plant
2	*Astilbe* 'Peach Blossom'	3 plants
3	*Athyrium niponicum* 'Ursula's Red'	3 plants
4	*Betula nigra* Heritage	2 plants
5	*Brunnera macrophylla* 'Jack Frost'	3 plants
6	*B. macrophylla* 'Variegata'	3 plants
7	*Carex dolichostachya* 'Kaga Nishiki'	3 plants
8	*Cimicifuga* 'Hillside Black Beauty'	3 plants
9	*Geranium pratense* 'Midnight Reiter'	3 plants
10	*Hakonechloa macra* 'Albo-Striata'	5 plants
11	*H. macra* 'All Gold'	3 plants
12	*Heuchera* 'Plum Pudding'	3 plants
13	*Hosta plantaginea*	3 plants
14	*H.* 'Remember Me'	3 plants
15	*H.* 'Sagae'	1 plant
16	*Kirengeshoma palmata*	1 plant
17	*Lamium maculatum* 'Beedham's White'	3 plants
18	*L. maculatum* 'Orchid Frost'	3 plants
19	*Lobelia* 'Ruby Slippers'	5 plants
20	*Luzula* 'Ruby Stiletto'	3 plants
21	*Nyssa sylvatica*	1 plant
22	*Ostrya virginiana*	1 plant
23	*Phlox divaricata* 'London Grove Blue'	3 plants
24	*P. divaricata* 'Plum Perfect'	3 plants
25	*Pulmonaria* 'Blue Ensign'	3 plants
26	*P.* 'Cotton Cool'	3 plants
27	*Styrax japonicus*	1 plant
28	*Thalictrum rochebrunianum* 'Lavender Mist'	5 plants
29	*Tiarella* 'Iron Butterfly'	3 plants
30	*Tricyrtis* 'Empress'	3 plants

PLANTING PLAN

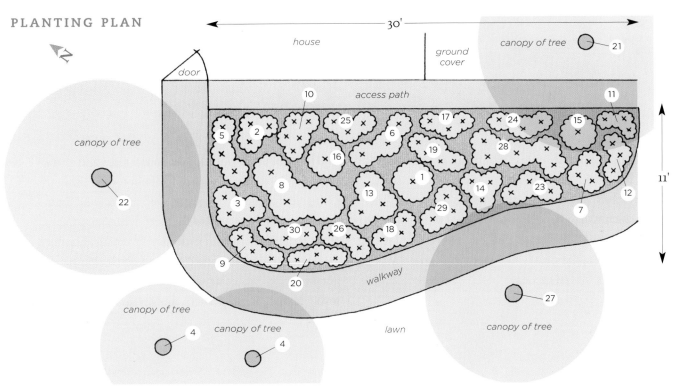

30'

house

ground
cover

canopy of tree　　○—21

door

access path

N

canopy of tree

○
22

11'

5
2
10
25
17
24
6
15
11
16
19
28
12
8
1
7
13
14
23
3
29
30
26
18
9
20

walkway

canopy of tree

4

canopy of tree

4

lawn

canopy of tree

○—27

canopy of tree

DESIGNER'S CHECKLIST

☐ **Be a smart shopper.** High maintenance is a given with formal gardens, but selecting your perennials carefully will make your life a little easier. First, look for descriptive terms like "compact" and "sturdy stems" to minimize staking needs. And if you want to grow phlox, bee balms (*Monarda*), or other perennials that are prone to problems such as powdery mildew and rust, look for cultivars that are selected for disease resistance.

☐ **It bears repeating.** Repetition of colors, flower shapes, and plant forms is important for creating a unified formal design, but don't be too rigid about repeating the exact same plants at regular intervals, or your garden will have a paint-by-the-numbers effect. If you use one clump of 'All Gold' Hakone grass (*Hakonechloa macra*), for example, you might want to place a clump of the white-striped cultivar 'Albo-Striata' farther along the border and a peach-flowered selection at the other end; that will give you the continuity of similar leaf textures but the visual appeal of different colors.

☐ **Be an artful gardener.** Ornaments can make or break a formal garden. It's best to stick with upscale features such as classical urns, statues, or unique pottery, which will enhance the formal feel of the planting. Rustic or whimsical accents such as "fat fannies," goofy gnomes, and plastic flamingos are generally a bad idea in a formal garden.

☐ **Think beyond perennials.** Small trees and shrubs make great partners for perennials in formal designs, giving year-round structure as well as seasonal interest. Just remember to choose them with the same strict criteria you use to pick the perennials: not once-and-done kinds, like forsythias, but those that have good-looking foliage as well as handsome stems, lovely leaves, pretty flowers, and/or showy fruits.

Aruncus dioicus
(Goat's beard)
Four-foot-tall and -wide, shrubby clumps of toothed, medium green leaves give rise to fluffy plumes of creamy white flowers atop 4- to 5-foot stems from early to mid-summer. ZONES 3–8.
ALTERNATIVES: False goat's beard (*Astilbe biternata*) or *A.* 'White Gloria'.

Astilbe 'Peach Blossom'
('Peach Blossom' astilbe)
These dense, 18-inch-wide clumps of deeply dissected, medium-green leaves have 2-foot stems topped with peachy pink flower plumes in midsummer. ZONES 4–8.
ALTERNATIVES: Another 18- to 24-inch-tall astilbe.

Athyrium niponicum 'Ursula's Red'
('Ursula's Red' Japanese painted fern)
Low-spreading mounds of maroon-centered, silvery gray fronds on reddish arching stems look good from late spring to frost; 18 inches tall and wide. ZONES 4–9.
ALTERNATIVES: *A. niponicum* var. *pictum*, 'Silver Falls', or the more-upright hybrid 'Ghost'.

Brunnera macrophylla
(Siberian bugloss)
Low, broad mounds of deep green, heart-shaped leaves are accented with sprays of small blue flowers from early or mid- to late spring; 12 to 18 inches tall and 18 to 24 inches across. 'Jack Frost' has very silvery foliage with green veining; '**Varie-gata**' (a.k.a. 'Dawson's White') has green leaves with a broad, creamy white border. ZONES 3–8.
ALTERNATIVES: Other cultivars, such as 'Looking Glass' for 'Jack Frost' and 'Hadspen Cream' for 'Variegata'.

Carex dolichostachya 'Kaga Nishiki'
(Gold fountain sedge)
Tufts of slender, arching green leaves have yellow margins; the flowers are not showy. About 1 foot tall and 12 to 18 inches across. ZONES 5–9.
ALTERNATIVES: *C. hachijoensis* 'Evergold' or Bowles' golden sedge (*C. elata* 'Aurea').

Cimicifuga 'Hillside Black Beauty'
('Hillside Black Beauty' bugbane)
Bushy clumps of dissected, deep purple-black leaves are about 4 feet tall and 3 feet across, accented with foot-long spikes of fragrant, pinkish white flowers from late summer into fall. ZONES 4–8.
ALTERNATIVES: The cultivar 'Black Negligee' or 'Brunette'.

Geranium pratense 'Midnight Reiter'
('Midnight Reiter' geranium)
Deeply lobed purplish foliage grows in mounds 1 foot tall and 12 to 18 inches wide, with purple-blue flowers from early to midsummer. ZONES 4–8.
ALTERNATIVES: The cultivar 'Hocus Pocus' or 'Victor Reiter Jr.', or *G.* x *oxonianum* 'Katherine Adele'.

Hakonechloa macra
(Hakone grass)
Narrow, arching green leaves form slowly expanding clumps that are 12 to 18 inches tall and eventually about as wide; flowers aren't showy. The leaves of '**Albo-Striata**' are striped with white; '**All Gold**' has yellow foliage. ZONES 6–9.
ALTERNATIVES: The cultivar 'Aureola' for either, and 'Sweet Kate' tradescantia (*Tradescantia* 'Sweet Kate').

Heuchera 'Plum Pudding'
('Plum Pudding' heuchera)
Mounds of lobed, silver-frosted, deep purple leaves grow to 1 foot tall and 18 inches across. Airy clusters of tiny white flowers bloom on purple, 18- to 24-inch stems in late spring and early summer. ZONES 4–9.
ALTERNATIVES: Any purple-leaved heuchera or heucherella.

Hosta
(Hostas)
These classic, no-fuss perennials are grown primarily for their foliage, which comes in a wide range of shapes, sizes, and colors to fit any shady garden. *H. plantaginea* (August lily) has light green leaves in mounds 2 feet tall and 3 feet wide, with fragrant white flowers atop 2- to 3-foot stems in late summer and early fall. '**Remember Me**' has blue-green leaves with a prominent white center splash in each, as well as pale purple midsummer flowers; 1 foot tall and 18 inches across. '**Sagae**' (a.k.a. *H. fluctuans* 'Variegated') produces 2-foot-tall and 4-foot-wide mounds of blue-green leaves irregularly edged with creamy yellow, plus pale lavender flowers atop 4-foot stems in mid- to late summer. ZONES 3–9.
ALTERNATIVES: Any hostas in the same color and height range.

Kirengeshoma palmata
(Yellow waxbells)
Large, shrubby clumps (3 to 4 feet tall and 2 to 3 feet wide) have maplelike green leaves and clusters of nodding yellow bells at the stem tips in late summer and early fall. ZONES 5–8.
ALTERNATIVES: A compact oak-leaved hydrangea (*Hydrangea quercifolia*), such as 'Pee Wee' or yellow-leaved 'Little Honey'.

Lamium maculatum

(Lamium, a.k.a. spotted deadnettle)

Clusters of purplish pink or white flowers bloom in spring over 12- to 18-inch-wide carpets of silver-and-green leaves; height is 6 inches. **'Beedham's White'** has chartreuse leaves and white flowers; **'Orchid Frost'** has silvery foliage and light purplish pink flowers. ZONES 3–8.

ALTERNATIVES: Other lamium cultivars.

Lobelia 'Ruby Slippers'

('Ruby Slippers' lobelia)

Two- to 3-foot spikes of pinkish red flowers bloom from late summer into early fall over low rosettes of green leaves; spread to 1 foot. ZONES 4–8.

ALTERNATIVES: Another hybrid, such as light pink 'Cotton Candy' or reddish pink 'Rose Beacon'.

Luzula 'Ruby Stiletto'

('Ruby Stiletto' woodrush)

Dense mounds of slender evergreen leaves take on reddish tints through the winter and early spring; 1 foot tall and wide. Brown flowers are not showy. ZONES 5–9.

ALTERNATIVES: *L. sylvatica* 'Marginata' or *Carex* 'The Beatles'.

Phlox divaricata

(Woodland phlox)

Mid- to late-spring clusters of fragrant flowers bloom atop 1-foot stems clad in narrow green leaves; foliage height is 6 to 8 inches and spread is to 18 inches. **'London Grove Blue'** has light blue flowers; **'Plum Perfect'** has purple petals with a darker purple center. ZONES 4–8.

ALTERNATIVES: Other cultivars of this species or cultivars of creeping phlox (*P. stolonifera*).

Pulmonaria

(Pulmonarias)

Hairy green or silver-spotted leaves form showy clumps 10 inches tall and 12 to 18 inches across, with clusters of pink buds and blue blooms atop 1-foot stems in early to mid-spring. **'Blue Ensign'** has deep green foliage and brilliant blue flowers; **'Cotton Cool'** has narrow, very silvery leaves and pink-to-blue blooms. ZONES 3–8.

ALTERNATIVES: Any other cultivars.

Thalictrum rochebrunianum 'Lavender Mist'

('Lavender Mist' meadow rue)

Eighteen-inch-tall and -wide clumps of lacy, medium green leaves send up 5- to 6-foot, deep purple stems topped with airy clusters of small, pinkish purple flowers in mid- to late summer. ZONES 5–9.

ALTERNATIVES: A cultivar of Yunnan meadow rue (*T. delavayi*), such as 'Hewitt's Double'.

Tiarella 'Iron Butterfly'

('Iron Butterfly' foamflower)

Foamflower grows in spreading, 6-inch-tall clumps of deeply lobed, dark green leaves with near-black centers. Brushy spikes of pink-tinged white flowers rise to about 1 foot tall and bloom through spring; spreads 1 to 2 feet across. ZONES 4–9.

ALTERNATIVES: Any other cultivar.

Tricyrtis 'Empress'

('Empress' toad lily)

Arching stems clad in glossy green leaves are tipped with purple-spotted, white flowers from late summer to mid-fall; clumps are 2 feet tall and wide. ZONES 5–9.

ALTERNATIVES: Another toad lily.

Graceful Gardens: Always Fashionable

Foliage is king in the formal garden. Each perennial has to hold its own from spring to frost, and good-looking leaves are what you'll count on to fill out the planting as flowers come and go. The perennials you choose must also be vigorous enough to look lush and healthy, but not so vigorous that they will crowd out their companions. Besides creating even more work for yourself, having to divide plants frequently will prevent your design from melding together, as some plants will be well established while new divisions are just getting started. For the same reason, it's smart to use extra-generous spacings when you draw your design and set out the plants; allowing an extra 6 or 8 inches between clumps can add several years to the life of your perennials before they demand to be divided.

Along the same lines, it's wise to evaluate your formal perennial garden soon after planting and make any needed changes as quickly as possible. Replacing established, flowering-size clumps with small plants will make the garden look out of balance for at least a few weeks, and likely for a whole growing season. As much as possible, you want all of the plants to be of a similar age, so they will look their best and put on the prettiest possible show of blooms.

Container Considerations

IF YOU'RE TIRED OF FILLING YOUR POTS and planters with petunias and geraniums, give perennials a try! These garden plants can be just as striking as their annual cousins, and because you don't have to buy new ones each year, they can save you money, too.

* Enjoy seasonal or even year-round color in sites where you can't or don't want to dig: on decks and patios, in paved areas, and above buried wires, for example.

* Try out new combinations by pairing perennials in pots. If effective, move them to the garden; if not, change them next year.

* Grow small perennials in pots to keep them from being crowded by vigorous companions; plant them out once they're larger.

* Pot up perennials that aren't fully cold-hardy in your area, then move them to a sheltered spot or bring indoors during winter.

Have a hankering for tender perennials but don't want to bother planting them in your garden in spring and then digging them up again in fall? Pop them into planters instead, and it's a snap to shift them inside when cold weather threatens.

Container Care 101

Potted plants are the pampered pets of the garden. They need lots of time and attention to look their best, particularly in the form of careful watering. Perennials growing in individual containers (especially in clay pots) may need watering once or even twice a day; larger planters usually last for several days if soaked thoroughly. Mixing water-holding polymers (called hydrogels) into the potting soil before you plant cuts down on watering chores, as does mulching to cover the soil in the pot.

Because roots can't spread to seek nutrients on their own, potted perennials need regular doses of fertilizer. Liquid formulations are quick acting but don't last long; time-release fertilizers provide a small but steady supply of nutrients over a longer period. For best flowering, look for a fertilizer with a higher middle (phosphorus) number, such as 5-15-5. Read the label carefully and follow the application directions to get the best results.

Container-grown perennials benefit from special care over winter. If hardy to at least one zone colder than yours, they should be fine outdoors for the winter; group in a sheltered spot, such as by the house foundation.

Even nonhardy perennials usually benefit from some winter chilling, so store them in a cool but frost-free area, such as an unheated garage or enclosed porch. Water occasionally; provide some light if they have any leaves. If still dormant when spring returns, set them outside when you normally plant perennials. If they have new growth, harden them off as you would indoor-raised annuals, by gradually exposing them to longer periods of outdoors conditions over a week or two.

Containers for Sun and Shade

PLANTING PLAN

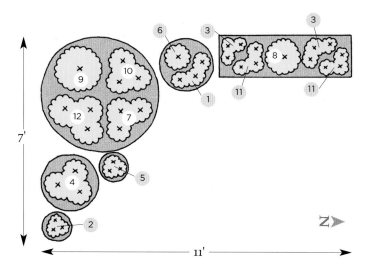

7'

11'

N ▶

PLANT LIST FOR PARTIAL SHADE

1	*Ajuga* Chocolate Chip	3 plants
2	*Bergenia* 'Bressingham Ruby'	3 plants
3	*Carex siderosticha* 'Lemon Zest'	6 plants
4	*Dryopteris erythrosora*	3 plants
5	*Hakonechloa macra* 'Aureola'	3 plants
6	*Heuchera* 'Amber Waves'	1 plant
7	H. 'Bressingham Bronze'	3 plants
8	x *Heucherella* 'Burnished Bronze'	1 plant
9	*Persicaria* 'Brushstrokes'	1 plant
10	*Saxifraga stolonifera* 'Harvest Moon'	3 plants
11	*Tiarella* 'Jeepers Creepers'	6 plants
12	T. 'Tiger Stripe'	3 plants

When you grow perennials in pots, the possibilities are endless. Enjoy spectacular displays that change with the seasons by bringing out potted perennials when they look their best, then moving them out of the way once they're past their prime. Or use perennials with an extended bloom time, good foliage, or both, so they look good throughout the growing season.

PLANT LIST FOR SUN

1	*Caryopteris incana* Sunshine Blue	1 plant
2	*Coreopsis* 'Limerock Ruby'	1 plant
3	*Echinacea purpurea* 'Kim's Knee High'	3 plants
4	*Gaura lindheimeri* 'Crimson Butterflies'	1 plant
5	*Geranium* 'Rozanne'	2 plants
6	*Hemerocallis* 'Penny's Worth'	1 plant
7	*Origanum vulgare* 'Aureum'	3 plants
8	*Pennisetum orientale* 'Karley Rose'	3 plants
9	*Salvia nemorosa* 'Caradonna'	1 plant
10	*Sedum* 'Vera Jameson'	3 plants
11	*Veronica spicata* 'Goodness Grows'	3 plants
12	*V. spicata* 'Royal Candles'	2 plants

PLANTING PLAN

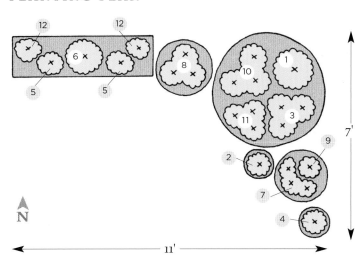

DESIGNER'S CHECKLIST

☐ **Explore your options.** Sure, many perennials look fantastic in traditional terra-cotta containers, but clay pots have their downsides. They dry out quickly, so careful watering is critical, and they may need to be brought indoors in winter to prevent damage from freezing. Concrete, fiberglass, and faux terra-cotta can stay outdoors year-round, and they come in a broad range of colors to complement your home or garden. Feel free to experiment with unusual containers, too, like rusty buckets, clay flue tiles, and other "found" objects; if it has a drainage hole, it's fair game.

☐ **Anything goes!** No one says you have to keep perennials separate from your other favorite container plants. As long as all the plants have the same light requirements and watering needs, you can combine them with annuals, bulbs, dwarf conifers, and even vines. Just like a mixed border in the garden, a mixed container offers months of interest, so you get multi-season or even year-round excitement without needing a lot of space.

☐ **Put pots to work.** Container-grown perennials can do more than just dress up a deck or patio. Potted perennials make terrific temporary fillers in beds and borders, in spots where spring bulbs have died down or early-flowering plants have been cut back. Need to dress up your yard for a wedding, family reunion, or other special gathering? Pop a few pots into existing plantings to really add some zip.

☐ **All shapes and sizes.** For the most interesting display, combine a variety of container sizes — some larger planters holding two, three, or more different plants, along with smaller pots holding one kind of plant each.

Ajuga 'Chocolate Chip'

('Chocolate Chip' ajuga, a.k.a. 'Valfredda')
'Chocolate Chip' forms 2-inch-tall carpets of narrow leaves that are brownish green in deep shade and chocolate brown with more sun; blue-purple flowers appear in spring on 3- to 4-inch stems. ZONES 4–9.
ALTERNATIVES: Dwarf mondo grass (*Ophiopogon japonicus* 'Gyoku-ryu').

Bergenia 'Bressingham Ruby'

('Bressingham Ruby' bergenia)
Dense clumps of leathery, evergreen, rich green leaves turn burgundy red in late fall, with clusters of pinkish red flowers from mid- to late spring; height and spread to 1 foot. ZONES 3–8.
ALTERNATIVES: 'Cabernet' or another bergenia.

Carex siderosticha 'Lemon Zest'

('Lemon Zest' sedge)
Arching, bright yellow leaf blades in clumps 10 inches tall and wide. ZONES 5–8.
ALTERNATIVES: *Liriope muscari* 'Pee Dee Gold Ingot'.

Caryopteris incana Sunshine Blue

(Sunshine Blue caryopteris, a.k.a. 'Jason')
Bushy clumps are 2 to 3 feet tall and wide, with bright yellow leaves and clusters of deep blue flowers in late summer and early fall. ZONES 6–8.
ALTERNATIVES: The cultivar 'Worcester Gold'.

Coreopsis 'Limerock Ruby'

('Limerock Ruby' coreopsis)
Single, gold-centered flowers with velvety, ruby red petals bloom atop bushy clumps of narrow green leaves from early summer into fall; 20 inches tall and wide. Hardiness uncertain; probably ZONES 7–9.
ALTERNATIVES: The cultivar 'Moonbeam'.

Dryopteris erythrosora

(Autumn fern)
New bright copper spring fronds age to a glossy deep green through the summer in clumps 2 feet tall and wide. ZONES 5–9.
ALTERNATIVES: Japanese painted fern (*Athyrium niponicum* var. *pictum*).

Echinacea purpurea 'Kim's Knee High'

('Kim's Knee High' purple coneflower)
Sturdy, upright stems are clad in dark green leaves and topped with bronze-centered daisy-form flowers with rosy pink petals through the summer; 18 to 24 inches tall and wide. ZONES 3–8.
ALTERNATIVES: White 'Kim's Mop Head'.

Gaura lindheimeri 'Crimson Butterflies'

('Crimson Butterflies' gaura)
Bushy clumps of slender stems clad in narrow, reddish leaves are topped with spikelike clusters of bright pink flowers from early summer into fall; 12 to 18 inches tall and wide. ZONES 6–9.
ALTERNATIVES: *Sedum spectabile* 'Autumn Fire' or 'Carl'.

Geranium 'Rozanne'

('Rozanne' geranium)
Single, purplish blue blooms with white centers appear from early summer into fall over bushy clumps of lobed, deep green leaves; 12 to 18 inches tall and 18 to 24 inches across. ZONES 4–8.
ALTERNATIVES: *Campanula carpatica* 'Blue Clips'.

Hakonechloa macra 'Aureola'

(Golden Hakone grass)
Narrow, arching, yellow-and-green-striped leaves form slowly expanding clumps 12 to 18 inches tall and eventually about as wide; flowers are not showy. ZONES 6–9.
ALTERNATIVES: The cultivar 'All Gold' (yellow leaves) or 'Albo-Striata' (striped with white).

Hemerocallis 'Penny's Worth'

('Penny's Worth' daylily)
Clumps of bright green, grasslike leaves showcase bright yellow, trumpet-shaped blooms that appear from midsummer well into fall with regular deadheading; 10 inches tall and wide. ZONES 5–9.
ALTERNATIVES: Another dwarf daylily in the same height range, such as 'Eenie Weenie' or 'Stella d'Oro'.

Heuchera

(Heuchera)
These mound-forming perennials with lovely lobed leaves come in many shades of purple (brown and green, too), often attractively mottled with silver. Airy clusters of small white or pink flowers appear atop wiry stems (18 to 24 inches tall) in late spring and early summer. 'Amber Waves' has golden yellow leaves; 'Bressingham Bronze' has deep reddish purple foliage. Foliage clumps of both are 1 foot tall and 18 inches across. ZONES 4–9.
ALTERNATIVES: For 'Amber Waves', try x *Heucherella* 'Sunspot'; for 'Bressingham Bronze', any purple-hued heuchera.

x Heucherella 'Burnished Bronze'

('Burnished Bronze' heucherella)
Heuchera-like mounds of lobed, deep brown-purple leaves are accented with 18-inch spikes of bright pink flowers in late spring; foliage clumps are 8 to 12 inches tall and 12 to 18 inches across. ZONES 5–9.
ALTERNATIVES: Any purple-leaved heuchera.

Origanum vulgare 'Aureum'

(Golden oregano)
Six- to 12-inch-tall mats of oval, bright yellow leaves grow on trailing stems that spread to 18 inches; clusters of pinkish purple flowers appear atop the stems in summer. ZONES 4–8.
ALTERNATIVES: *Sedum* 'Angelina'.

Pennisetum orientale 'Karley Rose'

('Karley Rose' Oriental fountain grass)
Upright, 18-inch-wide clumps of narrow, rich green leaves are accented with brushy purplish pink spikes atop 3-foot stems from early or midsummer into fall.
ZONES 5- OR 6-9.
ALTERNATIVES: Another fountain grass species or cultivar.

Persicaria 'Brushstrokes'

('Brushstrokes' persicaria, a.k.a. *Tovara* 'Brushstrokes')
Bushy clumps of large, yellowish green leaves are marked with dark maroon, and spikelike clusters of tiny red flowers bloom in mid- to late fall; about 3 feet tall and 2 feet across. ZONES 5-9.
ALTERNATIVES: The cultivar 'Lance Corporal'.

Salvia nemorosa 'Caradonna'

('Caradonna' perennial salvia)
Spiky, purple-blue flowers bloom on deep purple stems over medium green leaves from early to midsummer, usually with repeat bloom if you deadhead regularly; 24 to 30 inches tall and wide. ZONES 4-8.
ALTERNATIVES: S. x sylvestris 'Blue Queen' or 'May Night'.

Saxifraga stolonifera 'Harvest Moon'

('Harvest Moon' strawberry begonia)
Four-inch-tall rosettes of hairy, scalloped, yellow to golden leaves are sometimes tinged with pink. Airy, 18-inch-tall clusters of tiny pinkish flowers appear in midsummer; spreads to 1 foot.
ZONES 6-9.
ALTERNATIVES: Lysimachia nummularia 'Aurea'.

Sedum 'Vera Jameson'

('Vera Jameson' sedum)
Purple stems are clad in purple- or pink-blushed green leaves and topped with clusters of rosy pink flowers from late summer into fall; 8 to 12 inches tall and 18 inches across. ZONES 4-8.
ALTERNATIVES: Another compact sedum species or hybrid, such as 'Purple Emperor' or October daphne (S. sieboldii).

Tiarella

(Foamflowers)
These top-notch shade perennials sport foliage in a variety of shapes, often with maroon or deep purple markings. Brushy spikes to 1 foot tall bloom through spring. Many have attractive reddish leaf tints from fall into winter. 'Jeepers Creepers' has bright green leaves with rounded lobes and prominent dark centers and white flowers; 'Tiger Stripe' has broad, light green, purple-marked leaves and pinkish blooms. Both form spreading clumps 6 inches tall and (eventually) 2 feet wide. ZONES 4-9.
ALTERNATIVES: Any other cultivar.

Veronica spicata

(Spike speedwell)
Blue, pink, or white flower spikes bloom from late spring to midsummer (or later) on upright plants anywhere from 1 to 3 feet tall and 18 to 24 inches across. 'Goodness Grows' has rich blue flowers and 'Royal Candles' has long, deep purple-blue spikes; both bloom from late spring all through summer and grow 1 foot tall and 12 to 18 inches across. ZONES 3-8.
ALTERNATIVES: 'Marcus' salvia (Salvia nemorosa 'Marcus) and Siberian dragon's head (Dracocephalum ruyschianum).

Nan's Notebook

ANOTHER BENEFIT OF POTS AND PLANTERS is that they provide a relatively safe place to grow perennials you wouldn't let loose in your garden — that is, those rampant spreaders that travel quickly by creeping roots. These overactive  perennials will still look pretty when confined in a pot, so if you really want to enjoy them in your garden, containers are your best bet. Just remember to keep the pots on a hard surface, such as brick or paving, or set a saucer under each one, to keep the roots from creeping out of the drainage holes or down over the sides of the pots and into the soil. Clip off faded flowers, too, because they'll still be able to make many unwanted seedlings if you let the seedheads form.

Here's a rundown of some spreading perennials that are good candidates for container growing:

- *Ajuga reptans* (ajuga)
- *Artemisia vulgaris* 'Oriental Limelight' (mugwort)
- *Euphorbia cyparissias* (cypress spurge)
- *Houttuynia cordata* 'Chameleon' (houttuynia)
- *Leymus arenarius* (blue Lyme grass)
- *Lysimachia clethroides* (gooseneck loosestrife)
- *Mentha* (mints)
- *Oenanthe javanica* 'Flamingo' (variegated water parsley)
- *Oenothera speciosa* (showy evening primrose)
- *Phalaris arundinacea* var. *picta* (gardener's garters)
- *Physostegia virginiana* (obedient plant)
- *Pleioblastus viridistriatus* (dwarf greenstripe bamboo)

Naturalistic Plantings

THE IDEA OF A "NATURAL GARDEN" may seem a contradiction in terms. After all, gardens are created and cared for by people — sometimes in direct opposition to what Mother Nature would do on her own. If you enjoy the challenge of growing alpines in Alabama or lupines in Louisiana, you can do it. But if you want to develop a garden that re-creates some of the native habitats where you live, a naturalistic planting could be your cup of tea.

Going Native?

A "natural garden" isn't simply prairie plants grown in sun or woodland wildflowers in shade; rather, it's using tough, vigorous species to create a (mostly) self-sustaining planting. Natural gardens are typically based on native plants (those that are or were found in undisturbed habitats in an area), though not all need be natives. Often, conditions around homes are very different from those in undisturbed places nearby, and plants that once grew where a house currently stands may not be the best choice for current conditions. (Meadow and prairie plants usually do best where the soil isn't especially fertile, for example, so trying to convert a heavily fertilized lawn area into a prairie planting may be disappointing.)

Decisions, Decisions

A successful natural garden starts with observation and research: observe sun and soil conditions your yard offers, and research into perennials naturally adapted to thrive under those conditions. If some of those plants are native to another region, it's up to you whether to include them in your garden.

You'll also decide whether to use cultivars (plants selected for characteristics like flower color, height, or bloom period). "Improved" cultivars and hybrids with double or unusually large flowers or exceptionally compact forms may look out of place in a naturalistic setting. Those selected for their insect or disease resistance, on the other hand, can be valuable for this type of garden. You don't want to spray pesticides in a planting that naturally attracts birds, butterflies, and beneficial insects; resistant cultivars help ensure a nice-looking garden without chemicals.

Local native plant societies are a good source of information about plants and seeds naturally adapted to your climate. For an excellent introduction to naturalistic gardening, look for books by Piet Oudolf (see Recommended Reading, pages 288-289).

To establish a meadow or other naturalistic garden, gardeners often choose native plants, because they thrive in local conditions.

A Meadow-Style Garden

THIS DESIGN, based on Stephanie's own naturalistic garden, is a great option for anyone who wants a meadowlike planting with loads of interest from early summer well into winter. It's separated into two sections, so if you're not ready to commit to a large area right away, try the smaller side first and see how you like it. This design is best suited to a sunny, well-drained site. Have sun but evenly moist to wet soil? Turn back to Solutions for Soggy Sites, starting on page 92, for a wet-site plan featuring lots of moisture-loving natives. Have shade instead? Minimal-Maintenance Plantings, starting on page 194, features a plan for shady areas packed with native foliage and flowering perennials.

PLANT LIST

1	Amsonia hubrectii	4 plants
2	Asclepias tuberosa	3 plants
3	A. verticillata	3 plants
4	Aster laevis 'Bluebird'	3 plants
5	A. oblongifolius 'October Skies'	5 plants
6	Baptisia australis	3 plants
7	Callirhoe involucrata	3 plants
8	Coreopsis verticillata 'Zagreb'	5 plants
9	Eryngium yuccifolium	3 plants
10	Eupatorium maculatum 'Purple Bush'	3 plants
11	Euphorbia corollata	8 plants
12	Gaillardia × grandiflora 'Fanfare'	3 plants
13	Gillenia trifoliata	3 plants
14	Helenium 'Bruno'	3 plants
15	H. 'Coppelia'	5 plants
16	Helianthus 'Lemon Queen'	1 plant
17	Heliopsis helianthoides 'Prairie Sunset'	3 plants
18	Hibiscus 'Kopper King'	3 plants
19	H. moscheutos 'Disco White'	1 plant
20	Monarda 'Jacob Cline'	3 plants
21	M. 'Marshall's Delight'	3 plants
22	Panicum virgatum 'Dallas Blues'	3 plants
23	P. virgatum 'Shenandoah'	3 plants
24	Penstemon digitalis 'Husker Red'	5 plants
25	P. smallii	5 plants
26	Phlox glaberrima 'Morris Berd'	5 plants
27	Physostegia virginiana 'Miss Manners'	3 plants
28	Pycnanthemum muticum	6 plants
29	Rudbeckia fulgida var. fulgida	5 plants
30	R. fulgida var. sullivantii 'Goldsturm'	3 plants
31	Schizachyrium scoparium 'The Blues'	7 plants
32	Solidago rigida	3 plants
33	Sporobolus heterolepis	8 plants
34	Tradescantia 'Mrs. Loewer'	3 plants
35	Veronicastrum virginicum	3 plants

PLANTING PLAN

N

lawn

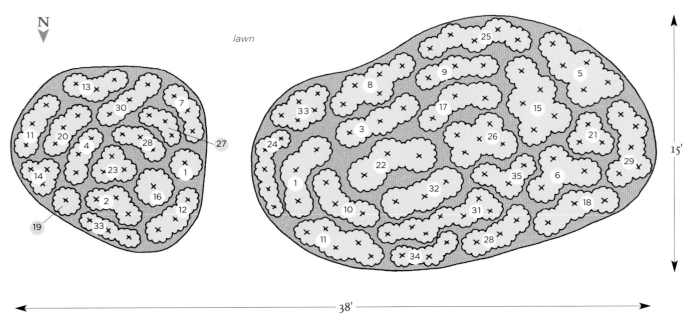

38'

15'

DESIGNER'S CHECKLIST

☐ **Explore all of your options.** When you're selecting perennials for a naturalistic design, traits like height and color are far less important than are vigor, adaptability to your site, wildlife-attracting value, and origin. If you are a purist, you may decide to stick with only native plants, and your own definition of *native* will determine how broad or limited your plant choices will be. If you want the best of all possible worlds, you may opt for a combination of native and nonnative species and cultivars.

☐ **Mix it up.** An abundance of daisylike flowers — asters, coneflowers (*Echinacea* and *Rudbeckia*), sneezeweeds (*Helenium*), sunflowers (*Helianthus*), and the like — is a common sight in sunny naturalistic gardens from midsummer into fall. Although daisies play an important role in these settings by providing resting stops and sustenance for birds and butterflies, you still need to make sure you have grasses and other flower forms, like spikes and clouds, to make the planting visually appealing.

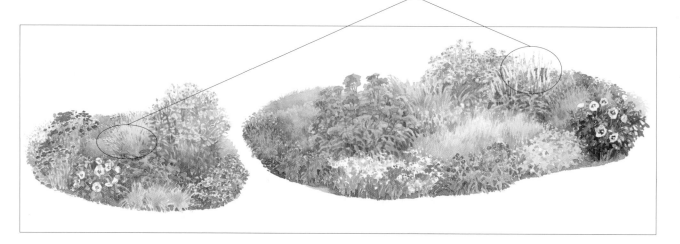

☐ **Expect the unexpected.** No matter how carefully you plan a naturalistic garden, the look will likely change to some extent each year. Over time, grasses tend to hold their own; aggressive spreaders and self-sowers become more dominant; and less vigorous perennials, such as penstemons, may disappear. You can influence the relative success of the flowering perennials by deadheading self-sowers, dividing spreaders, and weeding overabundant seedlings — or simply let them "dance" and enjoy the evolution of your design.

☐ **Meadows need maintenance too.** The more gardenlike your naturalistic planting, the more upkeep it will need. For a seeded meadow or prairie, a single mowing in late winter or early spring (just as you notice some new growth) is generally adequate to keep down weeds. More "gardenesque" areas also benefit from an early spring trim, followed by a thorough weeding, plus some spot weeding (pulling or digging out individual weeds before they set seed) throughout the growing season. Naturalistic gardens don't need watering or fertilizing, and spring mulching is a matter of choice in gardenlike meadow plantings. One bit of maintenance that all benefit from is a good edge between the planting and the surrounding lawn. (Stephanie has had good results with a 4- to 6-inch-deep "trench edge" around her garden.)

Amsonia hubrectii
(Arkansas blue star)
Mounded plants (about 3 feet tall and 4 feet wide) have rounded clusters of pale blue flowers in late spring over fine-textured, needlelike, bright green leaves that turn bright yellow in fall. ZONES 5–9.
ALTERNATIVES: *A. tabernaemontana.*

Amsonia hubrectii

Asclepias
(Milkweeds)
These upright perennials have slender, elongated leaves and clusters of small flowers with reflexed petals; a favorite with bees and butterflies.
A. tuberosa (butterfly weed) usually has orange blooms from midsummer to early fall but may be yellow or reddish instead; 2 to 3 feet tall and 12 to 18 inches across. ZONES 4–9.
A. verticillata (whorled milkweed) has very narrow leaves and greenish white flowers from early summer to early fall; 1 to 2 feet tall; and spreads to 18 inches by creeping roots. ZONES 4–8.
ALTERNATIVES: For butterfly weed, try an orange coneflower *(Rudbeckia)*; for whorled milkweed, *Gaura lindheimeri* or *Gillenia trifoliata.*

Aster
(Asters)
Classic favorites for the fall perennial garden, asters sport daisylike flowers on branching stems.
A. laevis 'Bluebird' ('Bluebird' smooth aster) bears purple-blue, yellow-centered flowers in early to mid-fall over blue-green leaves on 3-foot stems; spread to 2 feet. ZONES 4–8.
A. oblongifolius 'October Skies' ('October Skies' aster) forms mounded, 2-foot-tall and -wide clumps smothered in deep blue, daisylike blooms in early to mid-fall. ZONES 5–9.
ALTERNATIVES: For 'Bluebird', another aster; for 'October Skies', try 'Fanny's Aster', 'Raydon's Favorite', or another aster species or hybrid.

Baptisia australis
(Blue false indigo)
Spikelike clusters of dark blue flowers bloom in early summer atop 4- to 5-foot stems clad in three-lobed, green leaves, followed by long-lasting black seedpods; spread is 3 to 4 feet. ZONES 3–9.
ALTERNATIVES: Anise hyssop *(Agastache foeniculum).*

Callirhoe involucrata
(Purple poppy mallow, a.k.a. winecups)
A low-growing clump-former, winecups sports long, trailing stems clad in deeply cut green leaves and cupped magenta blooms with white centers from early to mid- or late summer; 6 to 12 inches tall and 18 to 30 inches across. ZONES 4–9.
ALTERNATIVES: *Aster novae-angliae* 'Purple Dome'.

Coreopsis verticillata 'Zagreb'
('Zagreb' thread-leaved coreopsis)
Dense mounds of narrow green leaves are virtually smothered in flat-faced, golden yellow blooms in early to midsummer;

will repeat bloom well into fall if dead-headed; 18 to 24 inches tall and wide. ZONES 3–9.
ALTERNATIVES: Another coreopsis of similar size, such as the golden *C. grandiflora* 'Sunray'.

Eryngium yuccifolium
(Rattlesnake master)
Clumps of narrow, spiny-edged, blue-green leaves are anywhere from 1 to 3 feet tall, with sturdy, upright, branching stems bearing small, ball-like clusters of greenish white flowers from midsummer to early fall. ZONES 4–8.
ALTERNATIVES: *Schizachyrium scoparium* 'The Blues'.

Eupatorium maculatum 'Purple Bush'
('Purple Bush' Joe-Pye weed)
This compact (4- to 5-foot-tall) cultivar produces dense clumps of dark, upright stems clad in whorled leaves and topped with clusters of mauve-pink flowers in late summer and early fall; spread is 2 feet. ZONES 5–9.
ALTERNATIVES: The slightly taller cultivar 'Gateway'.

Eupatorium maculatum 'Gateway'

Euphorbia corollata

(Flowering spurge)

Upright, slender, 2-foot stems are clad in oblong green leaves and topped from midsummer to early fall with clusters of petal-like white bracts surrounding yellow-green centers; spread is 12 to 18 inches. ZONES 5–9.

ALTERNATIVES: *Gaura lindheimeri.*

Gaillardia x grandiflora 'Fanfare'

('Fanfare' blanket flower)

Daisylike flower heads with tubular, orange-red florets tipped with yellow will bloom throughout the summer atop 1-foot stems over medium green leaves; spread is 12 to 18 inches. ZONES 3–8.

ALTERNATIVES: The cultivar 'Baby Cole' or 'Kobold' (a.k.a. 'Goblin').

Gillenia trifoliata

(Bowman's root, a.k.a. *Porteranthus trifoliata*)

Bowman's root forms bushy, 3-foot-tall and 2-foot-wide clumps of reddish stems and three-lobed green leaves that turn bronze-red in fall, plus starry white flowers in early to midsummer; small dark seedpods persist well into winter. ZONES 5–9.

ALTERNATIVES: *P. stipulatus* or *Gaura lindheimeri.*

Helenium

(Sneezeweeds)

Masses of dark-centered, daisylike blooms flower in late summer and early fall atop sturdy, 3-foot stems clad in narrow green leaves; spread to about 18 inches. **'Bruno'** has orange-red petals; **'Coppelia'** bears coppery orange blooms. ZONES 4–8.

ALTERNATIVES: Other cultivars, such as 'Mardi Gras' and 'Moerheim Beauty'.

Helianthus 'Lemon Queen'

('Lemon Queen' perennial sunflower)

Upright, 6- to 8-foot-tall stems are clad in rough green leaves and sport lemon yellow blooms from mid- or late summer into fall; clumps are 3 feet across. ZONES 4–9.

ALTERNATIVES: 'Sheila's Sunshine' giant sunflower (*H. giganteus* 'Sheila's Sunshine') or another tall perennial sunflower cultivar.

Heliopsis helianthoides 'Prairie Sunset'

('Prairie Sunset' oxeye)

Masses of maroon-centered, bright yellow daisies bloom in mid- to late summer on 4- to 6-foot deep red stems with dark green leaves; spread to 3 feet. ZONES 4–8.

ALTERNATIVES: Another oxeye cultivar or swamp sunflower (*Helianthus angustifolius*).

Hibiscus

(Mallows)

Shrubby clumps of broad, lobed leaves are accented with large, flat-faced flowers from mid- or late summer to early fall. **'Kopper King'** has burgundy-red leaves and light pink, red-eyed flowers; clumps are 3 to 4 feet tall and 3 feet wide. ZONES 4–9.

H. moscheutos **'Disco White'** ('Disco White' rose mallow) bears white blooms on 2-foot-tall and -wide plants. ZONES 5–9.

ALTERNATIVES: For 'Kopper King', another hybrid or cultivar in the same height range with pinkish or white flowers, such as lavender-pink 'Fantasia' or white 'Everest White'; for 'Disco White', try 'Disco Red' or 'Lord Baltimore'.

Monarda

(Bee balms)

Shaggy-looking flower clusters bloom from mid- to late summer over aromatic green leaves; spread is 2 to 3 feet. **'Jacob Cline'** has large, rich red blooms atop 4- to 5-foot stems; **'Marshall's Delight'** bears bright pink flowers on 3-foot stems. Both show excellent mildew resistance. ZONES 3–9.

ALTERNATIVES: Other bee balms.

Panicum virgatum

(Switch grass)

This clump-forming native grass with upright, green or blue-green foliage sends out airy, purple-tinged flower plumes in late summer and fall. **'Dallas Blues'** grows to 5 feet tall, with broader-than-usual, silvery blue leaves and pinkish plumes; spreads 2 to 3 feet across. **'Shenandoah'** produces upright, 3-foot-tall clumps of slender green leaves with reddish purple tips, turning maroon by fall; clumps are 24 to 30 inches across. ZONES 5–9.

ALTERNATIVES: Other switch grass cultivars.

Penstemon

(Penstemons, a.k.a. beardtongues)

Bushy clump formers with narrow leaves bear tubular flowers in summer. *P. digitalis* **'Husker Red'** ('Husker Red' foxglove penstemon) has rosettes of young maroon-red leaves and red-tinged older leaves, with pink-tinted white flowers from early to mid- or late summer; 2 feet tall and 18 inches across. ZONES 3–9.

P. smallii (Small's penstemon) has purplish pink and white flowers all through the summer; height and spread 1 to 2 feet. ZONES 5–9.

ALTERNATIVES: Hybrids such as 'Apple Blossom' and 'Sour Grapes', or other species, such as hairy penstemon (*P. hirsutus*).

Phlox glaberrima 'Morris Berd'

('Morris Berd' smooth phlox)

Upright stems are clad in very thin, deep green, mildew-resistant leaves and topped with large clusters of fragrant, rosy pink flowers in mid- to late spring; height and spread to 18 inches. ZONES 4–9.

ALTERNATIVES: A pink- or white-flowered cultivar of garden phlox (*P. paniculata*) or meadow phlox (*P. maculata*).

Physostegia virginiana 'Miss Manners'

('Miss Manners' obedient plant)

Much less of a spreader than the species, this cultivar truly lives up to its common name. Upright clumps to 30 inches tall but only 1 foot wide send out spikes of bright white flowers throughout summer into early fall. ZONES 4–8.

ALTERNATIVES: White-flowered blue lobelia (*L. siphilitica* 'Alba') or white turtlehead (*Chelone glabra*).

Pycnanthemum muticum

(Short-toothed mountain mint)

Strongly aromatic leaves are deep green near the base of the plant and silvery white toward the top of the 2- to 3-foot stems, with clusters of tiny pink flowers in midsummer; spreads by creeping roots to 3 feet. ZONES 4–9.

ALTERNATIVES: Another species of mountain mint or *Phlox* 'David'.

Rudbeckia fulgida

(Orange coneflower)

Low clumps of deep green foliage produce upright stems supporting in golden yellow, brown-centered daisies. The variety *fulgida* grows 18 to 24 inches tall and 1 foot wide and flowers from late summer to mid-fall. Variety **R. sullivantii 'Goldsturm'** is similar but a bit taller (24 to 30 inches) and blooms from midsummer to early fall. ZONES 3–9.

ALTERNATIVES: Other varieties of this species.

Rudbeckia fulgida **'Goldsturm'**

Schizachyrium scoparium 'The Blues'

('The Blues' little bluestem)

Dense, 1-foot-tall tufts of narrow, blue-green foliage send up slender, 2- to 3-foot, pinkish stems with inconspicuous flowers in late summer; in fall, the whole plant turns coppery orange, and it stays good-looking through much of the winter. Spread is 12 to 18 inches. ZONES 3–9.

ALTERNATIVES: The straight species.

Solidago rigida

(Stiff goldenrod)

Three- to 5-foot stems carry small green leaves and are topped with clusters of bright yellow flowers in late summer and early fall; spread to 18 inches. ZONES 4–9.

ALTERNATIVES: Another goldenrod, such as *S. rugosa* 'Fireworks'.

Note: Goldenrods are not the cause of fall hay fever. Blame the lighter-weight, windborne pollen of ragweed for that.

Sporobolus heterolepis

(Prairie dropseed)

Rounded mounds of slender, bright green leaves reach 1 foot tall and 12 to 18 inches across. They turn orange in autumn, with 2- to 3-foot stems topped with tiny, cilantro-scented flowers in fall. ZONES 3–8.

ALTERNATIVES: Crinkled hair grass (*Deschampsia flexuosa*) or sideoats grama (*Bouteloua curtipendula*).

Tradescantia 'Mrs. Loewer'

('Mrs. Loewer' tradescantia, a.k.a. spiderwort)

Three-petaled, light blue flowers blossom atop 24- to 30-inch stems over slender green leaves from early summer to early fall; clumps are 18 inches across. ZONES 4–9.

ALTERNATIVES: Another cultivar.

Veronicastrum virginicum

(Culver's root)

Narrow, upright clumps have slender spikes of white blooms from mid- to late summer over whorls of narrow, deep green leaves; 4 to 6 feet tall and 2 feet across. ZONES 3–8.

ALTERNATIVES: 'Ice Ballet' swamp milkweed (*Asclepias incarnata* 'Ice Ballet') has clustered white blooms, rather than spikes, but the height is similar.

Veronicastrum virginicum

A Tale of Two Gardens

Both Nan and Stephanie have experimented with a sunny naturalistic garden. Here's what we've discovered.

NAN'S GARDEN

Nan has a rural property with existing natural meadow areas and enjoys the look of grasses, so she chose to install a seeded meadow instead of turfgrass on top of her sand mound (an above-grade septic leach field).

In any sunny meadow or prairie, warm-season grasses are the backbone from mid-July well into winter. Typically, an established natural meadow is about 65 percent grasses and 35 percent "forbs" (broad-leaved flowering plants). Nan's established meadow areas (former hay-fields) are dominated by about 75 percent grasses, with a few flowers, such as blue-eyed grass (*Sisyrinchium angustifolium*) and goldenrods (*Solidago*).

Now that hay is not being cut each July, more flowers are appearing annually (as are woody weeds such as multiflora rose, which Nan removes by hand, and eastern red cedar seedlings, which she plans to keep). The seed mix for her septic mound meadow (custom-designed for the site by Gary Campbell of Campbell Natural Landscape Design) was 60 percent grasses and 40 percent forbs. By its second summer, it was a veritable blanket of black-eyed Susan (*Rudbeckia hirta*) with some spotted horsemint (*Monarda punctata*). Lots of butterfly weed (*Asclepias tuberosa*) and round-headed bush clover (*Lespedeza capitata*) were coming along, too, and the warm-season grasses were just becoming visible.

Over time, the showy black-eyed Susans will be crowded out by the grasses and longer-lived forbs, giving the area a different look each year. Nan plans to cut her established meadow areas every second or third year in early spring, and her septic mound at the same time annually to keep it looking a bit tidier.

STEPHANIE'S GARDEN

Stephanie lives in a more suburban setting and loves flowers, so she chose a more "gardenesque" natural planting: an island bed filled with a mix of meadow and prairie species and cultivars, with about 80 percent flowers and 20 percent grasses. Unlike Nan's site, which was essentially bare soil, Stephanie started with lawn. She prepared her site by stripping off the sod, then planted "plugs" (small starter plants) in the exposed soil without any further preparation. Tilling and digging bring lots of weed seeds to the surface, so her goal was to keep soil disturbance to a minimum. Weeds were still a problem,

though, so if she were to try this again, Stephanie thinks she would either solarize the soil before planting to kill surface weed seeds or let the weeds sprout and then spray them with herbicide before planting the perennials.

For Stephanie's mini-meadow, yearly maintenance includes cutting down all top growth in early spring, followed by a thorough weeding in spring; she also hand-pulls any large weeds she spots in mid- to late summer. Unlike Nan's seeded meadow, Stephanie's gardenlike planting looks much the same each year, providing a reliable show of bright flowers with distinct blocks of color from carefully chosen perennials planted in large drifts.

Understanding the basics of good design and knowing about a wide range of plants are important for creating a great-looking garden, but developing a pleasing real-life planting is the true test! Every site has its own challenges, which may not be apparent until you actually start digging. When you shop for plants, you may not find the specific cultivars you hoped for, or the sizes your budget allows. And even if all goes according to plan, vagaries of weather may upset the result. We think the secret to joyful gardening is to accept all these challenges, to expect that you'll make changes on the way, and to enjoy every garden as process, not product.

To help inspire you, we designed, installed, and lived with three gardens through two seasons, and captured the experience with words and pictures. We hope that reading about our successes — and yes, our disappointments, too — will help you face your own gardening challenges with a sense of fun and adventure. Read on for some reality gardening!

part three

From Theory to Practice

Building a Border from Scratch

10

OH, THE POSSIBILITIES! Whether you're faced with a boring expanse of turf grass, a patch of unimproved woodland, or a roughly graded site surrounding new construction, creating a garden out of "nothing" can definitely be a daunting experience. But as you can see from the "before-and-after" photographs below and at the left, which were taken just 6 months apart, it's absolutely possible to turn even an expanse of mud and rocks into a flower-filled border — without hiring a landscape crew or taking out a second mortgage to get the job done!

Where Do We Start?

STARTING A BRAND-NEW GARDEN is one of the most challenging design projects, yet it's also one of the easiest. A blank slate calls for a lot of decision making up front, without the helpful clues that existing plantings supply. It also requires more financial investment, because you'll have to buy most (if not all) of the plants needed to fill the garden. When it comes to site preparation, though, things are pretty simple; it's just a matter of getting rid of the grass and weeds that are growing there and then planning the whole site for easy access at planting time.

When we decided to attempt a from-scratch design for this book, Nan's house provided a perfect setting. Its construction was completed late in 2001, and Nan was so busy doing some basic grading during 2002 that she hadn't had time to do much actual gardening. By the spring of 2003, she was ready to get growing, and the front of the house was a natural place to begin.

Site and Soil

The site we chose is a long but relatively narrow strip (about 35 feet long and 4 feet wide) between the front porch and a new path that would lead to both the front door and the side door. It faces southwest and receives full sun from about 10 A.M. until sunset for most of the year. The soil was terrible — heavy clay subsoil that had been backfilled around the foundation and then packed down during the porch construction. Because the whole front of the property sloped down toward the house, Nan's main concern was to intercept runoff before it reached the house. That meant raising the border and the proposed path several inches above the existing grade to create a level area for walking and planting.

Design Considerations

When we sat down to plan this border, we ran through the usual list of questions that a designer would ask a prospective client. Here are some of the points we discussed:

✴ **What's your budget?** Because the border would be in a highly visible site, Nan was willing to invest a fair bit in the project (between $1,000 and $1,500) to install both the border and the path.

✴ **What's your style?** The backdrop for the site — a low stone wall and stained-wood porch against log home construction — set the tone for the garden itself. Nan wanted the border to have a somewhat informal appearance, with lower plants spilling onto the path and taller plants that would lean a bit on each other. Because the border would be visible up close both from the porch and from the path,

NEW SEASON, NEW COLORS!
To add extra interest, we planned this border around two main color schemes. For spring and summer, it's primarily blue and purple with touches of yellow and white; in fall (see page 230), it's mostly yellow with accents of blue and silver.

the planting could be rather intricate; she thought large drifts of just a few different plants would be boring. So we were aiming for something like a cottage garden, but based on only perennials and a few shrubs, what we jokingly called "log cabin casual."

* **How much maintenance?** This wasn't much of an issue for Nan; it was important to her that the border look great, so she was willing to do whatever grooming it would take to keep the plants looking their best. Her only stipulation was to keep staking to a minimum.

* **What season of interest?** The border needed to be attractive all year long, but Nan wanted the emphasis to be on summer and fall interest, as she planned for future gardens in the same area to have the same peak bloom time.

* **Color considerations?** Nan likes bright colors, but because the porch was stained a rusty orange that also contained a bit of pink, flowers in shades of red, orange, and hot pink just didn't seem to work there. Yellows would show beautifully, however. Stephanie suggested white as well, and though white flowers aren't a favorite of Nan's, she was willing to consider them. She thought blue flowers would be a nice complement to the yellow and white, along with some purple foliage to echo the purples that would be planted on the other side of the path.

* **Other thoughts?** If there's one thing the two of us don't have in common, it's the plants we commonly use in our gardens. Knowing Steph's favorites ahead of time, Nan was prepared to ask that the design *not* include daylilies, irises, or peonies; instead, she wanted to use as many ornamental grasses as possible (a lot more than Stephanie would usually consider). And unlike Stephanie, Nan adores tall plants — so no dwarf cultivars for this border.

RISING TO NEW HEIGHTS.
With its distinctly upright habit, 'Karl Foerster' feather reed grass *(Calamagrostis x acutiflora)* did a great job adding height to this narrow border. The 'Goodness Grows' veronica in the foreground, and the repeated masses of 'Caradonna' salvia, also helped to provide vertical accents.

Here's the Plan

FTER SOME LIVELY discussion, we were ready to tackle the actual design. We made a list of possible plants, starting with perennials and grasses that Nan already had and could easily move or divide. Then we added some must-have plants, such as goldenrods and grasses. When we realized most plants on our list were late-summer and fall bloomers, we looked through books and catalogs for others that fit site and color scheme.

For the plan, we felt a scale of ½ inch on paper equals 1 foot in the garden was adequate for detail, but the border was so long, we had to tape together two pieces of paper to draw it. Two lines divided the border lengthwise into thirds, denoting the front, middle, and back.

Starting with the plants Nan already had, we placed the largest first, then added middle and front-of-the-border plants. With the on-hand plants in place, we filled the remaining spaces from the rest of the list, again consulting catalogs for additional ideas. We didn't worry about quantities; we simply sketched rough circles to indicate different plants.

Each time we added a plant, we looked at how the new one worked with those we'd already placed. We made sure not to have one grass next to another grass, for example, or two daisy-flowered or two yellow-flowered perennials next to each other. We made sure we had plants to cover each season as well.

Needless to say, our "finished" plan was pretty rough, with lots of scribbles and crossed-out names, so we redrew it. In the process, we figured out how many plants would be in each drift. Because Nan wanted an immediate effect, we used much closer spacings than usual: roughly 1 foot apart for the back-of-the-border plants and 6 inches apart for those in the middle and front. To double-check that flower and foliage colors were distributed evenly throughout, we filled in each drift with colored pencils. Satisfied with the results, we came up with a shopping list. Now, to get this border into the ground!

A Brand-new Border

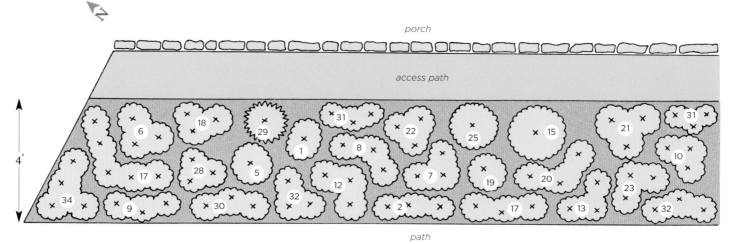

PLANT LIST

1	*Agastache* 'Blue Fortune'	1 plant
2	*Alchemilla mollis*	3 plants
3	*Amsonia hubrectii*	3 plants
4	*Artemisia abrotanum*	1 plant
5	*A.* 'Powis Castle'	1 plant
6	*Calamagrostis* x *acutiflora* 'Karl Foerster'	3 plants
7	*Caryopteris* x *clandonensis* 'Worcester Gold'	3 plants
8	*Centranthus ruber*	3 plants
9	*Coreopsis verticillata* 'Moonbeam'	6 plants
10	*Echinacea purpurea* 'Ruby Star'	3 plants
11	*Eupatorium maculatum* 'Carin'	3 plants
12	*Geranium* 'Brookside'	3 plants
13	*G.* 'Rozanne'	3 plants
14	*G. wlassovianum*	3 plants
15	*Helianthus* 'Lemon Queen'	1 plant
16	*Helleborus* x *hybridus*	3 plants
17	*Heuchera* 'Plum Pudding'	8 plants
18	*Leucanthemum* x *superbum* 'Becky'	3 plants
19	*Molinia caerulea* subsp. *arundinacea* 'Sky Racer'	1 plant
20	*Nepeta* x *faassenii* 'Walker's Low'	3 plants
21	*Panicum virgatum* 'Dallas Blues'	3 plants
22	*P. virgatum* 'Rotstrahlbusch'	6 plants
23	*Penstemon digitalis* 'Husker Red'	3 plants
24	*Persicaria polymorpha*	1 plant
25	*Rosa* 'Darlow's Enigma'	1 plant
26	*Rosa glauca*	3 plants
27	*Rudbeckia fulgida* var. *fulgida*	5 plants
28	*Salvia nemorosa* 'Caradonna'	8 plants
29	*Sambucus racemosa* 'Sutherland Gold'	1 plant
30	*Sedum* 'Purple Emperor'	3 plants
31	*Solidago rugosa* 'Fireworks'	6 plants
32	*Sporobolus heterolepis*	6 plants
33	*Vernonia altissima*	3 plants
34	*Veronica spicata* 'Goodness Grows'	4 plants
35	*Weigela* Wine and Roses	1 plant

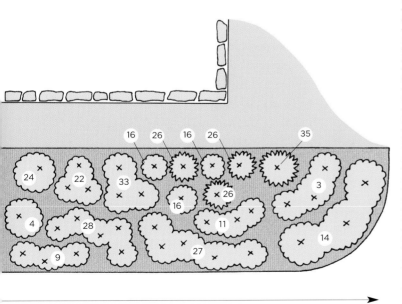

Let's Take a Look

O VERALL, WE WERE THRILLED with how the border performed. The color scheme looked great against the house, and despite some tough weather conditions, there was ample bloom from June well into October. For details, let's look at Nan's gardening notebook.

Mid-April, Year 1

I'm so excited about the border design Stephanie and I came up with — I couldn't wait to get it into the ground! Before that, though, I had a fair bit of site prep to complete. The first order of business was to raise the height of the stone wall behind the border about 6 inches, so I could build up the soil in the border bed and level the planting and path area. Luckily, there's no shortage of

MID-MAY, YEAR 1.
Just a couple of weeks after planting, the access path was still visible - but not for long! If I were to do this over, I'd have made the path a full 2 feet wide, and moved the front of the garden outward to compensate.

stones around here, and it doesn't take long to pile them into a simple dry-stack wall, so that project took just a few hours. Directly in front of the wall, I used a layer of smaller rocks topped with gravel to create a narrow access path between the wall and the back of the border. This path will double as a drain to catch the water from the roof edge, as the porch roof doesn't have gutters.

I also spent some time taking out the few plants I had plunked into this area last fall, as well as removing some scraggly sod that had sprung up where I wanted the new path to be. In the area where the border will be, I left only one plant: a nice 'Darlow's Enigma' rose that was just getting tall enough to be trained on the porch railings. The rest of the odds and ends went into a holding bed out back, and I used the pieces of sod (turned upside down) as the basis for a raised bed I plan to build along the side of the house once this project is done. Now that the site's ready, it's time to go plant shopping — and to pick up the materials for the path, too.

Late April, Year 1

I have to say that shopping for plants is one of my absolute favorite parts of gardening. I picked up most of them in two major shopping sprees: one at an area wholesale perennial producer and one at a small local nursery. A few of the newer cultivars that Stephanie recommended weren't available locally, so I had to track them down on the Web. I managed to find all but one: *Eupatorium purpureum* 'Little Joe' apparently won't be available until fall, so I made do with the cultivar 'Carin' instead. Stephanie tells me it will get quite tall (unlike 'Little Joe'), so I'll have to remember to cut it back each June to keep it from getting out of scale.

Gathering the materials for the new path wasn't nearly as much fun as plant shopping, but with Mom's help it went fairly smoothly. I had gotten the idea from a slide Stephanie used in a presentation she gave to our cottage gardening study group back in February; basically, it was square wooden timbers laid with gravel between them. I love the sound of gravel underfoot, but I don't like the way it shifts around, so I'm hoping the timbers will help hold it in place.

Mom and I were able to find the perfect 4×4×4 timbers at a local home improvement center, so we brought them home and stained them to match the house. I spread a few inches of 2A (modified) gravel over the soil where the path was to go, then we started setting out the timbers 8 inches apart. I filled between them about halfway with more of the modified gravel, then stapled a plastic edging strip along both sides of the path to help steady the timbers and hold the gravel in place. I topped that with some smaller (#7) brown granite gravel that I had on hand.

The entire project (a total of 50 feet of path) took two of us 2 days, but the results were even better than I had hoped. The finished path is a pleasure to walk on, with sturdy footing from the timbers but a nice bit of scrunchy gravel sound. It was definitely worth the effort!

....

Early May, Year 1

Now that the path is complete, it's time to get this garden started! I tilled up the soil in the border-to-be as best I could to break up the compaction, then topped that with about 6 inches of a 50-50 mixture of compost and topsoil to bring it up to the level of the path.

LATE MAY, YEAR 1.
My only disappointment with the path was the sharp-edged, "new" look when it was just finished. But within just a few weeks, the front-of-the-border plants started to spread out, softening the hard line of the path edge.

I raked it smooth, then started adding the plants. First, I brought in those that I needed to move from existing gardens and got them settled into their new home right away. Then I set out the potted perennials. Once I was satisfied they were in the right spots, it was a simple matter to pop them out of their pots and into the loose soil. I didn't even need a trowel! It took just a few hours to get the whole border planted, except for a few empty spots left for a couple of mail-order plants that should arrive any day now.

....

Mid-May, Year 1

The border has been in the ground about 2 weeks now, and it looks terrific already! We've had a few inches of rain and moderate temperatures, so the plants have all settled in quickly — even the late additions that arrived in the mail just a few days ago. The front-of-the-border plants are starting to spill onto the path a bit, and that is really helping to soften the hard lines of the timbers and edging strip.

....

Late May, Year 1

The first blooms are beginning, and the perennials have knit together well; it looks like they've been growing here for years instead of weeks. My only headache is a hungry shrew that has taken up residence in the stone wall. This destructive little critter has been coming out each night and snipping off whole shoots, then dragging them back to its home. Each morning, I see wilted pieces of perennials sticking out of the stone wall at odd intervals. It seems particularly fond of the 'David' phlox. I think I'll replace the clumps it has decimated with new plants, so it doesn't spoil the design.

....

Late June, Year 1

Well, I planted six new clumps of the phlox, but the shrew got at them before I could protect them with chicken wire. It also snacked on a few other plants — especially the switch grasses — but the damage seems be slowing down now that the plants are getting so big. I think I'll just forget about re-replacing the phlox; their companions have filled in so well that there's hardly room for them anyway.

Since the border was planted, we've had rain every 2 to 3 days, at least, and a total of 10 inches of rain for this month alone! With so much moisture, along with the compost-enriched soil and the close spacings we used, I suspect I'm going to have some over-crowded conditions pretty soon. But in the meantime, things are looking really nice, with the 'Moonbeam' coreopsis, 'Caradonna' salvia, red valerian (Centranthus ruber), 'Goodness Grows' veronica, 'Brookside' and 'Rozanne' geraniums, and Persicaria polymorpha all in full flower.

....

Mid-July, Year 1

I finally had to water, for the first time since the border was planted. After so much rain and day after day of cool temperatures, we're finally having some "normal" summer weather, and the plants aren't used to all this heat and sunshine. This seems like a good time to do some serious grooming, so I cut back a few of the perennials that were looking a bit tired, including the 'Brookside' geranium, 'Caradonna' salvia, and 'Moonbeam'

coreopsis. I also did a careful pass through the whole border to get the weeds that sprouted up through the few spots not completely covered by the perennials. All this took about 45 minutes, which is the most time I've spent on the whole border since planting!

....

Mid-August, Year 1

Since early August, we've been back in damp-and-cool-weather mode. On 16 out of the last 18 days, we've had at least a trace of rain! The border is looking fairly "quiet" right now, probably because the plants aren't getting much sun. The 'Rozanne' geranium and 'Goodness Grows' veronica, though, have been real stars so far, flowering nonstop all summer no matter what the weather.

....

Early September, Year 1

A spell of warm weather in late August finally brought out the late bloomers, and now the border is looking terrific. Yellow is definitely the most noticeable theme, with the 'Lemon Queen' helianthus, 'Fireworks' goldenrod (Solidago rugosa), and Rudbeckia fulgida var. fulgida all in their splendor, but there are touches of blue from the geraniums, salvia, and veronica. My only disappointment is that three clumps of boltonia that should have filled the far end of the border dropped all their leaves a few weeks ago and look awful. I think I'll replace them with some monks-hood next spring to get some more blue with all the fall yellows.

....

Early October, Year 1

The garden is still looking nice, even after a rough September. Not only did it stay cool and overcast, but mid-September also brought more than 5 inches of rain in just 2 days, and then a hurricane. I'm amazed at how well the plants have held up, all things considered. Although I had to give the

....

'Lemon Queen' helianthus some help to stand up (I lashed it to the porch railings with baling twine — not pretty, but effective!), none of the other plants flopped horribly. I'm also surprised I didn't have any losses to rot, because the plants are growing so close together. Maybe it's because of the good drainage from the bed being raised above grade?

Mid-November, Year 1

After a few hard frosts — and still *more* rain — the gardening season is pretty much over for this year. I finally got around to planting some bulbs in the border for spring color, mostly 'February Gold' daffodils and blue Siberian squill (*Scilla siberica*) to continue the main yellow-and-blue theme. The perennials are done flowering for now, but there is still a fair bit of color left to enjoy, including the various browns and oranges of the grasses and the purple-leaved heucheras. There is plenty of green as well, from the 'Karl Foerster' feather reed grass (*Calamagrostis* x *acutiflora*), southernwood (*Artemisia abrotanum*), and 'Walker's Low' catmint (*Nepeta* x *faassenii*), plus the bright green basal foliage of the 'Becky' Shasta daisy (*Leucanthemum* x *superbum*) and goldenrod. I've decided to let all the remaining foliage and seedheads stand for the winter, so the border won't look too bare. Nothing now to do but wait for spring!

EARLY OCTOBER, YEAR 1.
I admit it: Staking a plant after it flops, and using light-colored twine to do it, is not a smart idea! From now on, I'll cut the 'Lemon Queen' helianthus back by half in early summer to minimize the need for support. But if it does start to sprawl, I'll use something much less visible, such as black yarn, to tie it up!

LATE MAY, YEAR 2.

'Sutherland Gold' elderberry *(Sambucus racemosa)* is definitely on my Top 10 list of favorite plants! In this setting, it shows up beautifully against the rusty color of the house, and it makes a fantastic contrast to the blues and purples surrounding its base.

Early April, Year 2

Overall, the border plants came through the winter well. Only the red valerian *(Centranthus ruber)* disappeared altogether, and that was no surprise; sometimes I have luck overwintering it, and sometimes it rots out. Two other casualties were the Siberian squill *(Scilla siberica)* bulbs and the 'Rotstrahlbusch' switch grass *(Panicum virgatum)*; both were obvious victims of voles, as evidenced by the tunnels throughout the border. The grass looked fine aboveground, but when I grabbed the old stems to cut them down, the whole clump came up in my hand, leaving a large

hole where the roots used to be! I filled in with fresh soil and replanted with divisions from another clump. Come fall, I'll replace the missing squills with more daffodils, since they were untouched. And next next winter, I'll try cutting all of the top growth down in late fall, so maybe the critters will find a better sheltered place for their winter vacation. Right now, it's too late: I'll just clean up the dead tops that are left, cut back the elderberry to about 1 foot above the ground, and get ready for a great growing season.

Late May, Year 2

So much for spring! After several weeks of July-like temperatures, many of the plants are several weeks ahead of where they should be. Normally, that wouldn't be a problem, but I'm having a garden tour in late June, and I really wanted the border to look its best then, not now! Plus, the fast growth seems to have led to weaker stems than usual, so the plants are starting to flop open. While I hated to do it, I decided to cut back some of the perennials now in full bloom. These included the catmints and 'Caradonna' salvia, which I cut all the way back to the ground. I also sheared back some later-bloomers that were already sprawling out of their allotted space, including the southernwood and the 'Lemon Queen' helianthus; these I cut back by one-half to one-third. Hopefully they'll bush out again soon and look good again in a few weeks!

Mid-June, Year 2

We had midsummer weather in May, and now we're having April weather in June! It's been very cool and rainy, which has been great for planting in other parts of my gardens, but not so ideal for this border: The catmints and salvias that I cut back hard a few weeks ago aren't coming back as quickly as I'd hoped, so I tucked in some additional plants of the slowpokes to fill things out a bit. If I had it to do over for this year, I probably would have cut them back by only half to two-thirds, so they could resprout more easily and be back in bloom sooner. I'll try to remember that next time. Looking ahead, I think I'll need to do some serious moving and dividing next spring, due to the closer-than-recommended spacing I used when I planted last year. But I have lots of other beds to fill now, so no plants will go to waste!

EARLY JUNE, YEAR 2. When I extended the front border around the corner of the house, I used a similar mix of colors and heights to link them. This tall 'Fascination' Culver's root (Veronicastrum) did a great job providing a visual tie between the high porch and the foundation planting.

11 Expanding an Existing Garden

MANY TIMES, increasing the size of a garden you already have is as satisfying as creating an entirely new one. You already know which perennials will thrive in the site and which colors look good there. In addition, you have a good idea of how much maintenance you can handle, and you can use divisions from your existing perennials (if you want) to save money. Besides giving you space to try new plants — always a desirable thing — expanding an existing garden allows you to adjust the plantings edges if needed, and to link it with nearby features such as shrubs and fences. Every expansion will be different, because we all have different starting points, but here's an example of how we handled one particular site.

Where Do We Start?

STEPHANIE'S PROPERTY was a natural place for us to attempt this sample expansion project. She has many established planting areas, but she did have her eye on one particular site — a narrow strip of ground on the other side of a fence that backed the main garden area behind her house. This makeshift garden was a hodgepodge of annuals as well as some divided perennials and bulbs that had not found a permanent home. It had no cohesiveness or design; it just filled a space. Now, this project gave Stephanie the perfect opportunity to turn that awkward space into a beautiful border that would complement her other gardens. Best of all, from Stephanie's point of view, it allowed her to keep her resolve to not install any *new* gardens — because as everyone knows, expanding an *existing* garden area doesn't count!

THE CHALLENGE OF LONG AND NARROW. The board fence that encloses Stephanie's main garden gave us a great starting point for the design. But its low height also provided a challenge: a very long but fairly narrow space.

Site and Soil

Overall, the soil in the area was passable — good enough to support the annuals and decent turf, with average fertility and adequate drainage. Stephanie had never really prepared the existing planted strip as well as she normally would, because she simply had not been sure what she was going to do with the site. The area is backed by a 4-foot-tall fence, so the border definitely needed to be widened to be in scale with its background; that meant some of the turf would have to be removed, and the whole area would need a good dose of organic matter to provide good growing conditions for the new perennials.

We also noted that the site faced south and wasn't shaded by any trees or buildings, so there would be plenty of sun all day long throughout the growing season.

Design Considerations

✳ What's your budget? We figured that $600 to $800 would be enough to fill this rather large space. To keep costs down, we'll use fairly common perennials in the design.

✳ What's your style? Stephanie didn't have any particular style in mind for the area, but it seemed to lean toward a traditional border treatment, due to the solid fence behind the site and the rich green lawn in front.

✳ How much maintenance? Stephanie's bad knees prevent her from bending down for frequent weeding and staking, so she wanted this area to pretty much take care of itself. She doesn't mind pinching off spent flowers, though, so we can plan on getting extended bloom out of perennials that respond well to deadheading

✳ What season of interest? Spring, summer, and fall interest are all important, because Stephanie has many garden visitors all through the growing season. Winter interest isn't an issue; no one sees this area at that time of year.

✳ Color considerations? Stephanie decided that this space would be a perfect spot to try a color-based border, with hot colors on one side and cool colors on the other. She normally doesn't use red or orange flowers in her designs, so this seemed like a good opportunity for her to experiment.

✳ What do you want to keep? Two Knock Out roses were already growing on the site, and Stephanie liked their long bloom season so much that she wanted to keep them where they were. We also decided to keep an existing 'Lochinch' butterfly bush (*Buddleia*).

✳ What do you want to remove? All of the remaining perennials would go, as well as any self-sown annuals.

✳ Other thoughts? Stephanie thinks of this area as her "secret garden," because no one even knows it's there until they walk down a gravel path and step under an archway. She wants to keep it that way, so we'll have to choose fairly short perennials that won't be visible from the other side of the fence.

SOMETHING BORROWED. In another site, this long, narrow border could look skimpy and out of proportion. What makes it work well here is the well-established plantings in the background — what designers call "borrowed scenery."

Here's the Plan

HEATING UP.
Although the aging flowers of the 'Paprika' yarrow (*Achillea*) were a little paler than we had expected, we were pleased with how the "hot color" perennials on this side of the border turned out — particularly the combination of mounded, bright yellow 'Zagreb' coreopsis with the glowing orange spikes of 'Bressingham Comet' kniphofia.

THE SITE IN QUESTION is long and narrow, so we taped together two pieces of blank paper to give us plenty of space to draw. Using a scale of ½ inch on paper to 1 foot in the garden, we sketched in the existing fence and arch, then marked the location of the plants that Stephanie wanted to keep in place. Now it was time to decide how much bigger the new garden should be. The tallest plants need to be less than 4 feet tall so they don't peek up over the fence; thus, making the border about 3 feet wide would keep it in proportion to the site. (Normally, of course, you'd want a few of your perennials to be taller than their backdrop to help "break the line," but in this case it would ruin the secret-garden effect.)

The site naturally divided into two sections, because of an archway set into the fence. To unify the border, we decided to keep it the same width throughout, following the mild curve of the fence. The slightly shorter section was ideal for the bright colors and the softer colors would work well in the longer part. When seen from a distance, both sections would have equal visual weight, because hot colors are quite eye-catching even if there are fewer of them.

Now that we had the outline figured out, we were ready to start placing the plants. We came up with two lists — one for the hot colors (red, orange, gold, and rich purple) and one for the cool colors (pastel pinks, soft yellows, pale purple and blue, and white). Then

we began sketching in the plants, starting with the largest individuals and drifts.

Even though each side of the garden has different colors, we made sure we included some similar plants in each, including lots of grasses and daisy-type flowers, to give a sense of rhythm and balance from the repeated shapes. On the cool side, for example, there is 'Sweet Dreams' coreopsis (*Coreopsis rosea*), a white, daisylike flower with a raspberry eye; 'Becky' Shasta daisy (*Leucanthemum × superbum*), with long-lasting white blooms; and 'Cambodian Queen' chrysanthemum, a large, dark pink, fall-flowering daisy form. Their hot-color counterparts include the single golden daisy forms of 'Zagreb' coreopsis (*Coreopsis verticillata*) and *Rudbeckia fulgida* var. *fulgida*; the red-and-yellow blooms of 'Rotkehlchen' coreopsis (*C. lanceolata*) and 'Fanfare' blanket flower (*Gaillardia × grandiflora*); and the multicolored red-orange-and-yellow flowers of 'Mardi Gras' sneezeweed

(*Helenium*). A bit of deep purple foliage, in the form of 'Stormy Seas' heuchera, also appears on both sides, to contrast with the bright blooms on the hot-color side and add a bit of intensity to the softer side.

Our main challenge came from the existing Knock Out roses Stephanie was eager to keep on the cool-color side; with their reddish pink flowers, they weren't a natural companion for pastel blooms. They do look great with gray and silver foliage, though, as do cool blue and pink flowers, so we included lots of silvery leaves on that end. The existing 'Lochinch' butterfly bush between the two roses also helped to soften the brightness of the roses.

Eventually, all the space on the plan was filled, so it was time to stop. Satisfied with the results, Stephanie figured out her shopping list, grabbed her checkbook, and headed to her favorite wholesale nursery to find the perennials she needed.

SO COOL. Crisp white 'Becky' Shasta daisy (*Leucanthemum × superbum*), along with the soft pinks and blues in the "cool colors" side of this border, provided a welcome contrast to the brighter autumn hues in the main garden on the other side of the fence.

A Garden Expansion

PLANT LIST

1	Achillea 'Paprika'	3 plants
2	Allium senescens var. glaucum	3 plants
3	Anemone 'Pamina'	3 plants
4	Armeria maritima 'Splendens'	3 plants
5	Artemisia 'Powis Castle'	1 plant
6	Aster 'Wood's Purple'	3 plants
7	Aster lateriflorus 'Prince'	3 plants
8	Buddleia 'Lochinch'	1 plant
9	B. davidii 'Black Knight'	1 plant
10	Carex buchananii	1 plant
11	C. muskingumensis 'Oehme'	2 plants
12	Caryopteris x clandonensis 'First Choice'	3 plants
13	Ceratostigma griffithii	1 plant
14	Chrysanthemum 'Cambodian Queen'	3 plants
15	Coreopsis lanceolata 'Rotkehlchen'	3 plants
16	C. 'Sweet Dreams'	3 plants
17	C. verticillata 'Zagreb'	3 plants
18	Crocosmia 'Solfaterre'	3 plants
19	Cryptotaenia japonica f. atropurpurea	1 plant
20	Dianthus 'Essex Witch'	3 plants
21	D. 'Spangled Star'	3 plants
22	D. deltoides 'Nelli'	3 plants
23	Echinacea purpurea 'Kim's Mop Head'	3 plants

24	Eremurus stenophyllus	4 plants
25	Gaillardia x grandiflora 'Fanfare'	1 plant
26	Geranium 'Brookside'	1 plant
27	G. 'Rozanne'	3 plants
28	Helenium 'Mardi Gras'	1 plant
29	Heliopsis helianthoides var. scabra 'Summer Sun'	2 plants
30	Hemerocallis 'Midnight Oil'	3 plants
31	H. 'Norman Lee Hennel'	3 plants
32	H. 'Pandora's Box'	1 plant
33	H. 'Strawberry Candy'	1 plant
34	Heuchera 'Stormy Seas'	6 plants
35	Iris sibirica 'Chilled Wine'	3 plants
36	I. sibirica 'Gull's Wings'	3 plants
37	I. sibirica 'Ruffled Velvet'	2 plants
38	Kniphofia 'Bressingham Comet'	4 plants
39	Lavandula 'Silver Edge'	3 plants
40	Lavatera thuringiaca	1 plant
41	Leucanthemum x superbum 'Becky'	6 plants
42	L. x superbum 'Snowcap'	3 plants
43	Nepeta sibirica 'Souvenir d'André Chaudron'	1 plant
44	Paeonia 'Golden Wheel'	1 plant
45	Pennisetum alopecuroides 'Little Bunny'	5 plants
46	P. alopecuroides 'Moudry'	1 plant

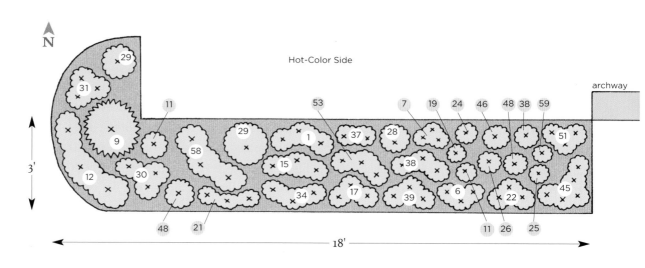

47	*P. orientale* 'Karley Rose'	3 plants
48	*Perovskia* 'Little Spires'	5 plants
49	*Phlox paniculata* 'Blue Paradise'	3 plants
50	*Rosa* Knock Out	2 plants
51	*Rudbeckia fulgida* var. *fulgida*	3 plants
52	*Salvia nemorosa* 'Caradonna'	3 plants
53	*S. nemorosa* 'East Friesland'	3 plants
54	*S. nemorosa* 'Marcus'	3 plants

55	*Scabiosa* 'Butterfly Blue'	2 plants
56	*Sedum* 'Purple Emperor'	1 plant
57	*Stachys byzantina*	3 plants
58	*Stokesia laevis* 'Honeysong Purple'	6 plants
59	*Tradescantia* 'Concord Grape'	1 plant
60	*Verbena* 'Homestead Purple'	3 plants
61	*Veronica spicata* 'Alba'	3 plants

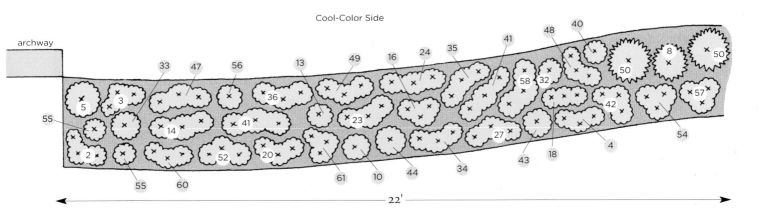

Cool-Color Side

archway

22'

Let's Take a Look

ESPITE NEAR DISASTROUS WEATHER CONDITIONS during the first growing season and the depredations of marauding deer, Stephanie has been pleased with her expanded "secret garden." Most of the plants themselves are fairly ordinary, but arranging them by color produced a truly special effect. For details on how the garden performed during its first two seasons, let's look at Stephanie's notes.

Mid-May, Year 1

Now that the thrill of my perennial shopping spree is fading, it's time to get busy preparing the site. The first step was to dig out the perennials that weren't staying. Then I dug out all of those I wanted to keep for later use in the design and moved them to a holding bed; that way I could improve the soil in the entire border. I had plenty of homemade compost on hand, so I spread a 2-inch-thick layer over the whole border and tilled it in. After leveling the soil with a rake, I set out the pot-ted perennials more or less according to the sketched plan. (I had to make some substitutions because not all of the plants I wanted were available when I went shopping at the nursery.) I made a few adjustments to the shape and size of the clumps of drifts, then planted them, as well as the perennials I had waiting in the holding bed. The plan includes a very special herbaceous peony — the yellow 'Golden Wheel' — but it won't be available until fall; to hold its space, I tucked in some corms of *Acidanthera bicolor*, a tender bulb with

MID-MAY, YEAR 1.
On the paper plan, I had envisioned the border being the same thickness throughout. But when it came time to remove the sod, I decided to widen the far right edge of the border, to help tie it in with the adjacent bed that wrapped around the end of the fence. Remember: It's okay to make changes as you go along!

fragrant white summer flowers. Once I gave the entire site a thorough watering and mulching, I considered it to be "done," or at least as "done" as any garden ever is.

Late June, Year 1

Regular rainfall is usually a blessing for new plantings, but this is too much of a good thing! We've had one of the wettest springs on record, and some perennials that normally would thrive in this site are really suffering. My poor 'Fire Dragon' sun rose (*Helianthemum nummularium*) and *Euphorbia* × *martinii* have gone to the big compost heap in the sky (I replaced them with perennials that tolerate more moisture), along with one plant of 'Marcus' sage (*Salvia* × *superba*). But all is not lost — many of the other perennials have adapted to the damp conditions and are filling in more quickly than I expected. For a first-year border, there are a good number of blooms, and the perennials with golden and purple foliage are adding lots of interest too.

Mid-July, Year 1

When Nan and I had our planning discussion about the style of this garden, I first thought a classic English border would look good in this site. Looking at it now, though, I realize that including lots of the daisy-type flowers that I like so much gives the border a wonderfully relaxed, cottage-garden effect that perfectly suits the setting. And even though I adore the flowers of white and pastel perennials, I have to say that I'm pleased with the exuberant effect of the hot-color part of the garden. I'm proud of myself for breaking out of my normal color comfort zone!

Late July, Year 1

I enjoy growing ornamental grasses as much as the next person, but I also want lots of color, and that's why I often prefer to include daylilies (*Hemerocallis*) in my sunny-site

designs. Their narrow foliage makes a perfect partner for mounding or broad-leaved plants, and their large, showy flowers are anything but subtle. Red, orange, and bright yellow daylilies are all excellent summer choices for a hot-color garden, but in this design I did something different: I chose 'Midnight Oil' and 'Norman Lee Hennel', two hybrids with very dark purple flowers to echo the purple foliage while contrasting with the other

LATE JUNE, YEAR 1.
When you're working with bright yellows, it's easy to fall into the trap of having too many daisy-shaped blooms. But I think the addition of the spiky silvers and blues, as well as the flat-topped yarrow (*Achillea*) flowers, did a great job breaking up the "daisy chain" in this part of the border.

LATE SEPTEMBER, YEAR 1. *Rudbeckia fulgida* var. *fulgida* is one of my favorite perennials for fall color — and you can see why! Blooming a full month later than the more-common cultivar 'Goldsturm', this variety makes a wonderful partner for other fall stars, including Russian sage (*Perovskia*) and ornamental grasses.

bright blooms in this section. I think they look great already, and I'm already looking forward to seeing the display next year, once the plants have had a full season to settle in and can bloom more abundantly.

....

Mid-September, Year 1

I'll be honest — not everything is coming up roses in my newly expanded perennial border. To put it bluntly, I'm very annoyed and extremely frustrated because of a deer problem. It seems like they're getting braver every day, and they're coming closer and closer to the house. In the last few days, they've decimated my 'White Swan' coneflowers (*Echinacea purpurea*), and they've browsed on some of the other perennials, too. At this rate, I won't have anything left for next year! While I investigate other options, such as a deer fence or repellent sprays, I've decided to spread some black plastic bird netting over the border. The netting is hardly visible from a distance, and hopefully it will give the deer a clue that I didn't plant an all-you-can-eat buffet just for them.

....

Late October, Year 1

The rain is still falling, and we've gone through a couple of hurricanes in the past few weeks, but the border is holding its own. The grasses are looking especially good, including 'Little Bunny' fountain grass (*Pennisetum alopecuroides*), a dwarf cultivar with silvery plumes, and 'Moudry', with deep purple-black seedheads. In the cool side of the garden, there's been a particularly pretty vignette with the blue-green foliage and pink plumes of 'Karley Rose' Oriental fountain grass (*P. orientale*) against the semi-double, rosy lavender blooms of 'Pamina' anemone. Even though I hadn't deliberately planned for winter interest in this garden, it looks like I'll have plenty to see if I decide to take a stroll out there; besides the grasses, Siberian iris (*Iris sibirica*),

and torch lily (*Kniphofia*) foliage, there are all kinds of attractive seedheads that will look pretty when dusted with snow.

This growing season may be over, but I've got the perfect remedy for the inevitable winter doldrums: daydreaming about how it will look next year. As I pore over the glossy seed and plant catalogs that are already arriving, I see gardens in my mind's eye, with the possibility of new combinations and new plants to try. I like the idea that any garden is constantly evolving. Once a very parsimonious but wealthy customer asked me when his wife's garden would be completed. "Oh, are you moving?" I asked. "No," he replied. "Has your wife passed away?" "Certainly not!" he retorted. "Well, then, the garden will never be done, and there is no end in sight." I believe all perennial gardens are never finished until we become too old to dig or have been called to the big perennial bed in the great beyond.

My mother used to repeat an interesting saying: "Man plans and God laughs." In the case of perennial gardens, this is a particularly profound statement. Some of the plants die, others perform better than expected, and there's always an unexpected seedling or two that plants itself where I'd never have tried it on my own. So now it's time to close my notes for this year and look forward to the surprises that next spring is sure to bring.

....

Early April, Year 2

After a long, snow-filled winter, it's nice to see so many plants in this border making a return appearance. I lost the *Ceratostigma griffithii*, but that's not a big surprise, since it normally isn't hardy in this area. The winter wet also killed off the 'Silver Edge' lavenders, so I'll need to replace them, too. Overall, I'm lucky not to have had more casualties: The netting I laid over the border kept the deer from browsing over the winter, but a family of rabbits managed to sneak underneath and has

LATE MAY, YEAR 2.

The glorious, hot pink blooms of the Knock Out roses link this outer planting to the inner garden, providing a dash of color to the "cool" end of the border. I always like to add a surprise like this to my designs — it keeps things from getting too predictable!

been snacking on some of the new growth. There's never a dull moment in the garden!

Getting this border ready for spring didn't take much time: All I needed to do was cut back the caryopteris and the butterfly bushes (*Buddleia*), trim the dead growth out of the roses, and cut back all of the grasses. Now I'm ready for things to get growing!

Mid-May, Year 2

I'm really pleased with how the border is shaping up this spring, particularly the plantings on the "cool" side. Most of the color is in the front of the border, with shades of blue and pink predominating. One of the best combinations on the "hot" side is the 'Chilled Wine' Siberian iris (*Iris sibirica*) paired with

the 'Golden Wheel' peony. Both have filled out beautifully in just one year, and the amount of flowering made for a lovely early display.

Early June, Year 2

Thanks to the unusual warm spell we had in May, along with a generous amount of rain, things are looking great in this border. The early-flowering things are still holding on, now that it's cooler again, and the perennials that would normally have waited a few more weeks are already starting to open.

Even without all of the flowers, though, I'd still enjoy the border, thanks to all of the foliage interest. The alliums, crocosmias, daylilies (*Hemerocallis*), kniphofias, and ornamental grasses, for instance, make a wonderful textural contrast to the larger-leaved perennials. And talk about color! The soft silver and gray of 'Powis Castle' artemisia and 'Little Spires' Russian sage, along with the dark-leaved 'Stormy Seas' heuchera, 'Purple Emperor' sedum, and 'Prince' aster (*Aster lateriflorus*), provide a pleasing counterpoint to the soft golden yellows of the 'Worcester Gold' caryopteris and 'Oehme' palm sedge (*Carex muskingumensis*).

So what's my conclusion on the border so far? While some of the combinations didn't work out quite as I had hoped, others surpassed my expectations. And while uninvited creatures treated my prized perennials as their own personal salad bar, I managed to foil them long enough for the plants to get established, so all was not lost. Basically, it reinforced my own philosophy: Enjoy your successes, fix your failures, and just have fun making gardens that you love!

LATE MAY, YEAR 2. I thought this end of the "hot" border needed more pep, so I replaced the 'First Choice' caryopteris with the yellow-leaved cultivar 'Worcester Gold'. It makes a nice echo for the yellow color inside the fence, too.

Reworking an Old Garden

12

F YOU'VE BEEN GARDENING on the same property for more than a few years, you've probably collected gardens the same way other folks collect baseball cards or antique china. It starts with one here, then another over there, and yet another, until you run out of space for new plantings. That doesn't mean you must give up the fun of starting gardens — now it's time to redo the old ones. The first few are probably looking a bit jaded by this time, especially now that you have more experience with plants and gardening in general. Or maybe you've just moved to a house with a garden that needs updating to match your style and plant preferences. Either way, you've got an exciting time ahead of you. Let's take a look at one garden renovation and see how you might approach your project.

Where Do We Start?

F OR OUR "TEST" PROJECT, we decided to redo an old garden at Nan's parents' farm, located right up the road from Nan's new house. The site was the first garden Nan built when she began gardening in the late 1980s, so at this time it's about 15 years old. It looked passable from a distance, but up close, anyone could see that it needed some *serious* help. The original outline of the garden was rather eccentric, with odd angles and an amorphous shape that was intended more to tie together a few existing trees and shrubs than to carry out an aesthetic principle.

In its early years, the sunny half of the garden had been a bed of hybrid tea roses and bearded irises planted in rows; the shady part was a collection of woodland wildflowers and shade-loving plants planted in "drifts of one," as Stephanie likes to say. Over time, the daintiest plants died out, and the tough ones spread freely, and weeds seeded in too. The trees and shrubs had also gotten considerably larger, so what had been full sun years ago now had barely enough light to qualify even as partial shade. Needless to say, the few remaining roses and irises weren't too happy under those circumstances.

Nan has to admit she was kind of embarrassed to look at this old garden with a new critical eye (and a critical co-designer), but she also can come to its defense, believing that even with its flaws, the garden has brought a great deal of pleasure to her parents as well as to passersby over the years. Still, it was clearly time to give this old garden a new look.

Site and Soil

The garden is in a sloping side yard close to the road, and it follows the ground level, so the garden slopes too: mostly toward the road and away from the house. It's located in one of the most difficult sites you can find — under a large silver maple tree. The soil always has been very dry, partly because the dense leafy canopy of the tree extends over the entire area, and partly because of the tree's extensive surface roots. During the growing season, the site receives an hour or so of direct light first thing in the morning, and the outermost part also receives a few hours of afternoon sun; the rest is in full shade from an outbuilding situated on the south side.

A TOUGH SPOT. I wish I could remember why I decided to put a garden here in the first place! This side, especially, is heavily shaded; just a little morning sun gets through. And the soil is very dry, due to the abundant tree roots.

Design Considerations

With any renovation project, the first step is to inventory the site and make a list of what's currently growing there — both good and bad. We put stars next to the plants we wanted to keep in place, check marks next to those we could divide and replant, and minus signs next to those we planned to remove. Then it was time for us to sit down and discuss the key design points.

✱ **What's your budget?** This garden is in a highly visible area, so it was worth spending some money to fix it up. It's fairly large, so it would need lots of perennials; we figured about $800 would cover it. Fortunately, we didn't need to buy any trees, so that expense was spared; there were also lots of existing plants that could be divided and replanted. Besides just a few shrubs and the perennials, the major expense would be trucked-in topsoil to level out the site and to provide some fresh, loose soil so the new plants could get established before the silver maple roots invaded again.

✱ **What's your style?** The area already had a variety of trees and shrubs, so it was a perfect setting for a woodland look. We wanted to eliminate the hodgepodge effect by uniting single, random clumps into natural-looking drifts, just as woodland plants tend to do when they're in an ideal site.

✱ **How much maintenance?** The answer to this one was easy: as little as possible! Nan's mom was willing to look after the planting, but she had plenty of other outdoor work to do. Basic spring cleanup was fine, as were mulching and weeding, but she didn't want to worry about plants that needed frequent division — and definitely no staking or spraying. Her only specific request was that we add a maintenance path through the garden, so she could reach every part either from the path or from the outer edges.

✱ **What season of interest?** In keeping with the woodland theme, we wanted this garden to be a real knockout in spring. Both of Nan's parents enjoy looking for the earliest spring flowers, and the site was also at its sunniest

DOWN THE GARDEN PATH. The original garden here had a small, short access path, but it had long since grown over. In the redesign, we re-established the path and extended it through the whole area. That made it much easier to plant, weed, and groom the "new" garden.

in this season. The second most important consideration was winter interest, primarily from the evergreen foliage of low-growing perennials and ground covers. It was fine for the area to be mostly cool, quiet greens during the summer; the fall interest would come mostly from the colorful foliage of the trees and shrubs.

❋ **Color considerations?** Because this planting is mostly seen from a distance — either from inside the house or from the road — soft colors like blue and lavender were out; they just wouldn't be visible. But hot colors, such as red, gold, and orange, wouldn't fit well with the woodland look we were shooting for. So white flowers were the natural choice, along with some light yellows and pinks, plus lots of silvery and golden foliage to keep things bright even if flowers are lacking.

❋ **What do you want to keep?** The site inventory identified many plants worth keeping, including an 'Arnold Promise' witch hazel (*Hamamelis* × *intermedia*) and a red-leaved Japanese maple (*Acer palmatum*), as well as plenty of spotted lamium (*Lamium maculatum*), giant Solomon's seal (*Polygonatum commutatum*), Allegheny spurge (*Pachysandra procumbens*), pulmonarias, hellebores, hostas, and forget-me-nots (*Myosotis*).

❋ **What do you want to remove?** Obvious candidates for eviction were the poison ivy and multiflora rose seedlings, as well as the English ivy (*Hedera helix*), periwinkle (*Vinca minor*), and Virginia creeper (*Parthenocissus quinquefolia*) that had colonized the shadiest corner. The few remaining hybrid tea roses definitely needed to be put out of their misery, as did a deadlooking summersweet

SENTIMENTAL JOURNEY. **A bright pink azalea definitely wouldn't have been on our list of things to add to this design! But it was already here and had sentimental value, so we kept it in and tried to integrate it as best we could, by adding touches of pink in other parts of the garden.**

(*Clethra alnifolia*) and a leggy mahonia. The most serious problem was *Campanula takesimana,* which had spread throughout the garden. Although it was pretty in bloom (when it deigned to flower), it was too aggressive to be allowed to stay.

In some cases, the decision to keep or remove wasn't easy to make. In one area, there was a fairly large, spindly looking azalea that produced hot pink blooms for a week each May, then just took up space the rest of the year. Nan wanted to keep it, though, because it had sentimental value; her mom had planted it in that spot 40 years ago so that Nan's bedridden grandmother could see it from her window. Stephanie agreed that it was a keeper, but we locked horns on another issue: two dwarf boxwood plants.

Nan argued to keep them because she had rooted them from tiny cuttings back in her college propagation class; Stephanie countered that these two "little green lumps" looked out of place and wouldn't fit with the new theme. We agreed to suspend final judgment on the issue until planting time. (By the way, if you're working with a professional designer on your own renovation project, be open to his or her suggestions about removing old plants, but you shouldn't hesitate to insist on keeping any that you love or that have special meaning for you.)

✳ **Other thoughts?** We both felt that the new planting needed to have more definition, with the plants arranged in distinct drifts, and a more natural-looking shape that would be easier for Nan's dad to mow around. We also wanted to make it more visible from the house but still attractive from the road — a tall order!

Here's the Plan

AFTER MEASURING the existing garden, we taped together four pieces of plain white paper and drew the outline of the garden, at a scale of 1 inch on paper equaling 2 feet in the garden. We drew in the location of the trees and shrubs, too. Our next step was to draw in some gentle curves where the existing outline showed sharp angles or too-tight curves; then we sketched in the maintenance path. The plan was beginning to take shape.

We brainstormed a list of our favorite shade-garden plants, added it to the list of existing "keepers," then roughly sketched in groupings where we thought they would look good. We also added a few more shrubs where we wanted a bit of height, because most of the perennials we hoped to include were less than 2 feet tall (a common situation when you're using lots of early-flowering plants).

At this point, we had a rough but workable plot plan. We decided not to redraw it to scale, instead using the plan to come up with a shopping list with an estimate of how many plants we'd like to have in each drift. That way, Nan could easily make adjustments when she went plant shopping; in case she couldn't find all the plants needed for one drift, she could simply reduce that one and increase another. We also wouldn't know how many of the "keeper" plants we actually had until they were dug up and divided, so we weren't sure how much space to allot to them. Armed with the rough plan and the shopping list, Nan was ready to go.

A Renovated Garden

PLANT LIST

1	*Acer palmatum*	1 plant
2	*A. saccharinum*	1 plant
3	*Alchemilla mollis*	5 plants
4	*Amsonia tabernaemontana*	1 plant
5	*Aquilegia vulgaris* 'Woodside'	5 plants
6	*Aruncus aethusifolius*	5 plants
7	*Astilbe chinensis* 'Pumila'	5 plants
8	*Buxus* sp.	1 plant
9	*Carex oshimensis* 'Evergold'	5 plants
10	*Caryopteris* x *clandonensis* 'Worcester Gold'	3 plants
11	*Centranthus ruber*	3 plants
12	*Cimicifuga* 'James Compton'	3 plants
13	*Clematis* 'Jackmanii'	1 plant
14	*Cornus amomum*	1 plant
15	*Corylus avellana* 'Contorta'	1 plant
16	*Dicentra* 'King of Hearts'	5 plants
17	*Digitalis purpurea* f. *albiflora*	3 plants
18	*Dryopteris erythrosora*	5 plants
19	*Epimedium* x *versicolor* 'Sulphureum'	3 plants
20	*Eupatorium rugosum*	3 plants
21	*Fothergilla gardenii*	3 plants
22	*Hamamelis* x *intermedia* 'Arnold Promise'	1 plant
23	*Helleborus foetidus*	6 plants
24	*H.* x *hybridus*	8 plants
25	*Hemerocallis* 'Autumn Minaret'	5 plants
26	*H.* 'Moon Traveler'	9 plants
27	*Heuchera* 'Pewter Moon'	5 plants
28	*H. villosa* 'Autumn Bride'	5 plants
29	x *Heucherella* 'Burnished Bronze'	5 plants
30	x *H.* 'Silver Streak'	4 plants
31	x *H.* 'Sunspot'	5 plants
32	*Hosta* 'Fortunei Hyacinthina'	3 plants
33	*H.* 'Golden Tiara'	3 plants
34	*H.* 'Krossa Regal'	3 plants
35	*H.* 'Whirlwind'	5 plants
36	*Lamium maculatum* 'Beedham's White'	5 plants
37	*L. maculatum* 'White Nancy'	10 plants
38	*Liriope muscari* 'Variegata'	5 plants
39	*Lysimachia nummularia* 'Aurea'	12 plants
40	*Miscanthus sinensis*	3 plants
41	*Myosotis sylvatica*	24 plants
42	*Osmunda regalis*	3 plants

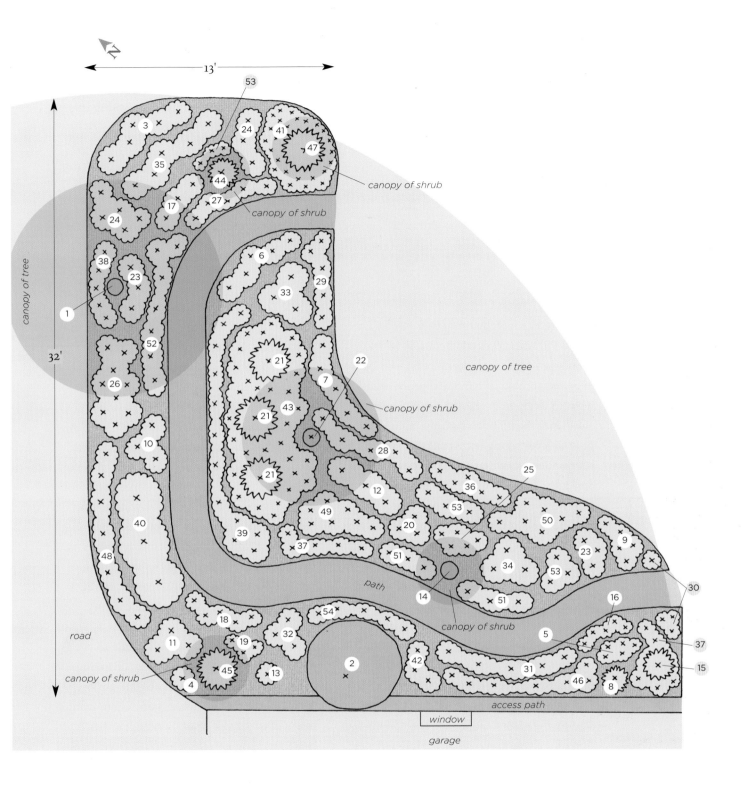

43	*Pachysandra procumbens*	30 plants
44	*Philadelphus coronarius* 'Aureus'	1 plant
45	*Physocarpus opulifolius* Diabolo	1 plant
46	*Polygonatum commutatum*	7 plants
47	*Rhododendron* hybrid	1 plant
48	*Sedum* 'John Creech'	7 plants

49	*Solidago caesia*	7 plants
50	*Tiarella* 'Brandywine'	7 plants
51	T. 'Iron Butterfly'	6 plants
52	T. 'Running Tapestry'	7 plants
53	*Tradescantia* 'Sweet Kate'	9 plants
54	*Viola labradorica*	5 plants

Let's Take a Look

Unlike the border we planned from scratch at Nan's house, renovating this garden called for a lot of flexibility in the site preparation and planting stages. Once it was all installed, however, the results were equally exciting — the area looked 100 times better. Although the garden didn't produce much in the way of flowers during the first year, its pleasing new outline and the overall tidier effect got the thumbs-up from everyone who saw it. For the down-and-dirty details, let's take a look at Nan's notes.

Mid-May, Year 1

After pretty much ignoring this garden for years, I'm really excited about giving it a brand-new look. First, I grabbed a pair of loppers and another of handheld pruners and went to work. I cut out the dead summersweet and the spindly mahonia right at ground level, along with a silky dogwood (*Cornus amomum*) that had gotten way out of control. The witch hazel also needed some help to reveal its original vase-shaped form. And because Stephanie and I had agreed that the azalea should stay, I decided to attempt some renovation to improve the shape. I know the general rule is to take out a third of the old growth every year for 3 years, but as the shrub already looked a little weak, I decided to take out just a few of the straggliest stems this year to see how the plant responds. I think it looks better already! I also gave it a dose of a liquid fertilizer for acid-loving plants. Hopefully, the combination of pruning and regular feeding will encourage some new shoots from the base.

We're having a nice spell of cool, cloudy weather right now, perfect for digging up the plants I want to keep. Luckily, the 50-50 mix of topsoil and compost I ordered arrived the same day I started digging, making a perfect temporary holding area for the transplanted perennials. Keeping Stephanie's objections in mind, I moved the larger boxwood to my house but kept the other one here, because I thought it looked good where it was.

Once I had cleared out all of the keepers, it was time to remove all the remaining plants. Dad isn't susceptible to poison ivy, so I recruited him to pull out all the seedlings I could find, along with one shoot that was climbing its way up the silver maple. After that, I pulled and dug out unwanted stuff for hours. The worst were the periwinkle, English ivy, and campanula, all of which had spread and wound together into a real mess. By the end of the day, I was exhausted, but the site looked great — all clear except for a few patches where I decided the existing plants could stay — and almost ready to plant!

The next morning, I used a spade to cut a new edge around the entire area, changing the curves and angles to match the outline Stephanie and I had decided on. Then, using many of the rocks I had found in the bed itself (and some more scrounged from an old fence line), I built a low, dry-stack wall along the whole outer edge of the garden to level out the planting area and make it more visible from the house. With the remaining small rocks, I outlined the edges of the new path through the garden.

I spent the afternoon hauling wheelbarrows full of soil to fill in behind the wall,

LATE MAY, YEAR 1.
The low stone wall did a great job raising the outer edge of the garden, so it was more visible from the house. It also let me add several inches of fresh topsoil mix, so the newly planted perennials could settle in quickly without immediate competition from the many tree roots.

as well as to add a few inches of fresh soil over the rest of the planting area. I know you have to be careful when changing the grade around existing trees, because you don't want to smother their roots, but I also know how fast those silver maple roots can come up to the surface, so I'm not too worried about doing any harm. The last project of the day was to spread an 18-inch-wide strip of gravel between the garage and the garden, to serve as a drip edge for the garage roof as well as an access path so Mom can get in to water her window box.

Now for the fun part: planting! I had purchased many of the perennials a few weeks ago when I was out shopping for my own garden, so I started the day by setting them out (still in their pots) according to our rough plan. At first, it looked like there would be more than enough, but pretty soon it was obvious that I'd need to go shopping again! Mom and I made the rounds of our favorite nurseries to pick up some more perennials, as well as the few shrubs I hadn't yet purchased. Some of the perennials I wanted weren't available, so I substituted with some other shade lovers I thought could work equally well. Once I added this carload of plants to the site, the garden really started to come together. I made some adjustments to the shape of the groupings, then started planting.

After all of the potted perennials and shrubs were in place, I transplanted the keeper perennials from their holding bed back into their new homes. There was only enough daylight left to allow time for a thorough

watering, so I finished up on the following day with a mulch of compost over the planting area. The last step was spreading two bags of cocoa shell mulch over the path — then the renovation was done. Whew!

Late May, Year 1

My muscles are still aching from all the work this garden needed, but every time I look at it, I'm convinced it was worth every second of effort. The cool, cloudy weather is helping the plants settle in well — even those that had been transplanted to the holding bed and back to the garden have barely wilted. Unfortunately, the little showers that are keeping my own garden well watered aren't helping much here, because the silver maple's leafy canopy intercepts most of the moisture. Still, it's not much bother to water thoroughly every few days, because it gives me a good excuse to admire my handiwork!

Late June, Year 1

The garden doesn't have much happening in the way of flowers now, but it still looks quite pretty, thanks to the different foliage colors and textures. Regular rains during the past few weeks have been heavy enough to make it through the maple leaves and keep the soil moist, so I haven't had to water, but weeding is now an issue. I set out the perennials at their recommended spacings, so they'll need less frequent division in the long run, but it also means there is plenty of space for weeds to pop up this year. Still, they are easy to pull out of the loose soil, so it takes less than a half hour a week to weed the entire area.

So far I've found only one big mistake I made: covering the path with cocoa shell

LATE MAY, YEAR 1. **Besides casting heavy shade and producing lots of surface roots, gardening under a silver maple presents another challenge: hundreds of tree seeds to clean up!**

mulch. I've used it before with no problem, but the constant moisture this month has turned the shells into a slippery, slimy mess that is treacherous to walk on. I spread two bags of bark nuggets over them to provide better footing, and I think that will solve the problem.

....

Late July, Year 1

With little help besides occasional watering and weeding, the plants are all growing well and filling in nicely. The highlight of the month was the dwarf Chinese astilbe (*Astilbe chinensis* 'Pumila') coming into bloom, adding a touch of pink along the inner edge of the garden, while the low-growing 'Moon Traveler' daylilies on the outer edge flaunted their pretty yellow trumpets at folks going by on the road.

....

Mid-August, Year 1

Just as the astilbes were finishing up, the white flower clusters of the *Heuchera villosa* came into flower. We got to enjoy a few blooms from the 'Autumn Minaret' daylily clumps, too, which I didn't expect, as the divisions I planted weren't very large. I think it's also a bit on the too-shady side for them, especially with so much overcast weather. Stephanie and I thought they'd add some welcome late-summer height and color, though, so I'm not giving up on them yet; we'll have to see how they perform next year. I also noticed that the entire drift of yellow corydalis (*Corydalis lutea*) died out, so I replaced it with some dwarf goat's beard (*Aruncus aethusifolius*). That corydalis is a funny little plant; it seems to hate to be moved, but if you can get it going, it seeds all over the place!

....

Early October, Year 1

Even with continued cool and cloudy weather, there is still a fair amount of interest in this garden. The white snakeroot (*Eupatorium rugosum*) started flowering in mid-September, and the wreath goldenrod (*Solidago caesia*) has just begun to bloom; the white and bright yellow flowers look great together. The miscanthus is quite tall now, and I think it looks rather out of scale with the rest of the bed — as well as out of keeping with the woodland theme. On the other hand, we've always enjoyed it in that spot, because it provides a welcome bit of screening from the road, and it looks lovely all winter when backlit by the setting sun. I think I'll leave it for now.

I hope the shrubs and trees in this bed start changing color soon, so we can get some nice photographs for the fall season!

....

Early November, Year 1

The only predictable thing about gardening is its unpredictability. Every other year, the witch hazel, azalea, and Japanese maple in this bed all turned color at the same time, making a spectacular display; this year they took turns, so there was no one time when the garden looked especially showy. I guess it's a good reminder that a garden can look beautiful to you and fulfill all your hopes without being photogenic enough to grace a magazine cover!

Considering the small amount of maintenance this garden has needed, it's given us a great deal of pleasure all through the summer and fall, and we have lots to look forward to next year. I've just planted several bags full of bulbs for spring color — mostly white Siberian squills, 'Thalia' daffodils, and checkered lilies (*Fritillaria meleagris*). In just a few months from now, this garden will really come into its own, just when we're all desperate for some color after the dreary winter months.

In the meantime, there is still a good bit left for us to enjoy for the next few months, including the curious corkscrew stems of

EARLY MAY,
YEAR 2. **The
groundcover perennials
— including lamiums
and foamflowers
(Tiarella) — are really
starting to knit together;
so much less bare soil is
visible this year. Even
without lots of flowers,
the colorful foliage adds
abundant interest.**

the contorted hazel (*Corylus avellana* 'Contorta') and the tan foliage of the miscanthus, plus lots of green from the hellebores and the Allegheny pachysandra (*Pachysandra procumbens*).

Mid-March, Year 2

Taking stock after the snow has disappeared, I'm pleased to find only one major casualty: All five clumps of *Heuchera villosa* 'Autumn Bride' have died out. They should have been perfectly hardy, so I'm not sure why they died. Rather than try again, I think I'll replace

them with some hostas; Mom likes those better anyway.

Otherwise, there's not much to do in the garden to get it ready for the growing season. I cut down the grasses, cleaned up any remaining top growth on the other perennials, and added a fresh layer of bark nuggets to spruce up the path.

Mid-April, Year 2

The Lenten roses (*Helleborus* × *hybridus*) are looking wonderful, and the fresh foliage of the various golden-leaved plants — including

the golden creeping Jenny (*Lysimachia nummularia* 'Aurea') and the variegated columbine (*Aquilegia vulgaris* 'Woodside') — are adding plenty of color. My one disappointment is the bulbs I added last fall. I had hoped the white Siberian squill (*Scilla siberica* 'Alba') and the 'Thalia' daffodils would be blooming together, providing drifts of white that would be echoed in a few weeks by the foamflowers. I should have done my homework better! Apparently 'Thalia' normally blooms fairly late, and combined with the fact that the bulbs were newly planted (many bulbs tend to bloom a little later than usual their first spring), the odds of the blooms coinciding were practically nil. I'll have to look for an earlier-flowering white daffodil for next year.

Mid-May, Year 2

Wow! We had planned for the peak bloom to occur in late spring, and we got it! The foamflowers are absolutely glorious: Besides providing bright drifts of white, their fragrance is noticeable from many yards away. The fothergillas are blooming now too, adding even more white to the mix. Of course, the 'Thalia' daffodils finally made their appearance, just in time to be practically unnoticeable among all the other white flowers!

Along the outer (road-side) edge of the bed, the newer blooms of the Lenten roses are still holding their color well, adding tones of pink and plum as well as more white, beautifully complemented by the sky-blue blooms from a scattering of forget-me-nots (*Myosotis sylvatica*). The bright yellow leaves of golden mock orange (*Philadelphus coronarius* 'Aureus'), along with the emerging yellow-and-green leaves of 'Whirlwind' hosta in that same area, are providing a fantastic finishing touch to that corner. I think my parents are finally getting used to all of the cars stopping in front of their house to look at the garden!

Mid-June, Year 2

Well, things are pretty quiet here once again, now that the peak bloom season is past. But the garden itself is still quite interesting, thanks to the interplay of foliage textures and colors. We're having another fairly rainy year, so the plants have filled in much more quickly than I expected. Still, I don't foresee having to do much division or renovation in the next year or two: just a little "editing" to nip back the too-exuberant spreaders and give the slower growers a bit more space. I can tell that the tree roots are already re-invading the area, but now that the perennials are so well settled in, I think they will be able to hold their own.

Late July, Year 2

Another important lesson from the garden: No matter how carefully you plan it on paper, it will inevitably come up with some surprises of its own. I noticed some pink in the west-facing corner of the garden when I drove by today, so I stopped and was amazed to find several clumps of purple coneflower (*Echinacea purpurea*) blooming happily among the miscanthus! I didn't plant them, so I can only guess that the seedlings came along with the 'John Creech' sedum that I moved here from my place last year. I had also forgotten that I'd tucked in a few tiny bulbs of 'Stargazer' lily from a plant swap last year. The stems aren't even strong enough to hold up the huge flowers, but they're leaning gracefully on the Diabolo ninebark (*Physocarpus opulifolius* 'Monlo'), and the shrub's deep purple leaves really show off the pink-and-white lily blooms. Seen all together, this combination of heights, textures, and flower and foliage colors is really lovely. I only wish I could take credit for it! I look forward to seeing what other surprises this garden will provide us with in the years to come.

appendix

USDA Hardiness Zone Map

The United States Department of Agriculture (USDA) created this map to give gardeners a helpful tool for selecting and cultivating plants. The map divides North America into 11 zones based on each area's average minimum winter temperature. Zone 1 is the coldest and Zone 11 the warmest. Recently, the zones were further divided into "a" and "b", with "a" being the colder portion. To locate your zone, refer to the map here, or use the Zone Finder on the National Gardening Association's website (www.nationalgardening.com), which identifies zones by zipcode.

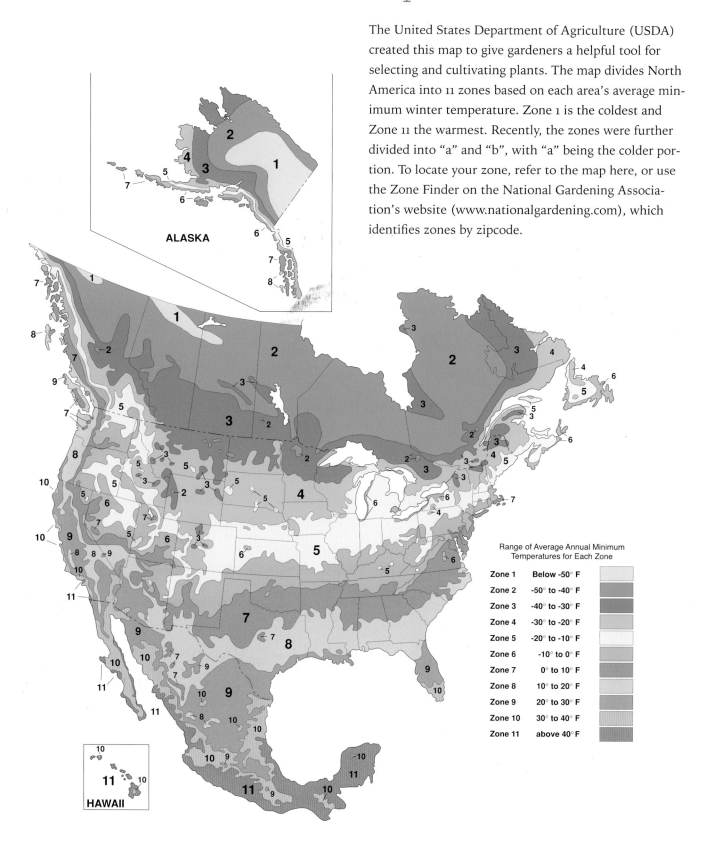

ALASKA

HAWAII

Range of Average Annual Minimum Temperatures for Each Zone

Zone 1	Below -50° F
Zone 2	-50° to -40° F
Zone 3	-40° to -30° F
Zone 4	-30° to -20° F
Zone 5	-20° to -10° F
Zone 6	-10° to 0° F
Zone 7	0° to 10° F
Zone 8	10° to 20° F
Zone 9	20° to 30° F
Zone 10	30° to 40° F
Zone 11	above 40° F

Planning Chart

Ready to plan your new perennial garden? This illustrated chart highlights the key features of all the perennials we used in the designs in part 2, Putting Perennials to Work (pages 88–227). We combined bloom color with time of flowering, so that you can simply scan the Bloom Season columns to find plants that bloom at the time and in the color you want. We've provided quick reference for Foliage Color, as well. (Note that where no symbols appear under Bloom Season, the plant is a grass, fern, or other plant grown mainly for its foliage.) To simplify matters, we divided Height into three categories: low (L:up to about 20 inches tall), medium (M:roughly 20 to 36 inches tall), and tall (T:more than 36 inches tall). If you find a plant that seems to fit your needs, refer to the columns with Light, Soil, and Zone (USDA hardiness zone) ranges to make sure it will thrive in your area. For more detailed information, the "Page" reference indicates where you'll find descriptions of each of these perennials.

LIGHT
- ○ Full Sun
- ◑ Part Shade
- ● Full Shade

SOIL (MOISTURE)
- ◇ Dry
- ◈ Average
- ◆ Moist

BLOOM SEASON
- yellow
- orange
- pink
- red
- green
- blue
- purple
- brown
- white

FOLIAGE COLOR
- yellow
- green & white
- green & yellow
- green
- gray or blue
- white
- brown
- purple or red

Range indicated by ✳ in appropriate color

Genus Species/Cultivar	PAGE	Zone	Light	Soil	Bloom Season (Spring / Summer / Fall)	Height L M T	Fol. Color
Acanthus							
spinosus	129	5-9	Full Sun, Part Shade	Average	purple, summer	M	green
Achillea							
'Anthea'	129, 205	2-9	Full Sun	Dry, Average	yellow, summer	M	gray or blue
'The Beacon'	145	4-8	Full Sun	Dry, Average	red, summer	M	green
'Coronation Gold'	145	3-9	Full Sun	Dry, Average	yellow, summer	M	gray or blue
'Martina'	157	4-8	Full Sun	Dry, Average	yellow, summer	M	green
'Moonshine'	129, 205	2-9	Full Sun	Dry, Average	yellow, summer	M	gray or blue
Aconitum							
carmichaelii 'Arendsii'	185	3-7	Full Sun, Part Shade	Average, Moist	blue, fall	M	green
Agastache							
'Blue Fortune'	129	6-9	Full Sun	Average	blue, summer	M	green
'Red Fortune'	129	6-9	Full Sun	Average	pink, summer	M	green
Ajuga							
Chocolate Chip	217	4-9	Full Sun, Full Shade	Average	blue, spring	L	purple or red
Alcea							
rosea 'Chater's Double White'	151	3-8	Full Sun	Average	white, summer	T	green
Alchemilla							
mollis	123, 171, 179	3-9	Full Sun, Full Shade	Average	green/yellow, summer	L	green

Genus Species/Cultivar	PAGE	Zone	Light	Soil	Bloom Season	Height L M T	Fol. Color
Allium							
senescens var. *glaucum*	117	4–8			Summer		
thunbergii 'Ozawa'	117	4–8			Fall		
Amsonia							
hubrectii	165, 223	5–9			Spring		
tabernaemontana	185	3–9			Spring		
Anchusa							
azurea	171	3–8			Summer		
Anemone							
x *hybrida* 'Andrea Atkinson'	185	5–8			Fall		
sylvestris	151	4–9			Spring		
Anthemis							
'Susanna Mitchell'	151	3–7			Summer		
tinctoria 'Moonlight'	205	3–7			Summer		
Aquilegia							
flabellata var. *pumila* f. *alba*	171	4–9			Spring		
vulgaris 'Nora Barlow'	179	3–8			Summer		
'Magpie'	171	3–8			Summer		
Armeria							
maritima 'Bloodstone'	171	4–8			Summer		
maritima 'Rubrifolia'	117	4–8			Summer		
Artemisia							
ludoviciana 'Silver Queen'	179	4–9			Summer		
'Powis Castle'	165	6–9			Summer		
Arum							
italicum 'Marmoratum'	191	6–9			Spring		
Aruncus							
aethusifolius	105	4–8			Summer		
dioicus	211	3–8			Summer		
Asarum							
europaeum	171	4–8			Spring		
Asclepias							
tuberosa	223	4–9			Summer		
verticillata	223	4–8			Summer		

Genus Species/Cultivar	PAGE	Zone	Light	Soil	Spring	BLOOM SEASON Summer	Fall	HEIGHT L M T	Fol. Color
Aster									
x *frikartii* 'Flora's Delight'	179	5–9							
laevis 'Bluebird'	185, 223	4–8							
lateriflorus 'Lady in Black'	139	5–8							
lateriflorus 'Prince'	185	4–8							
novae-angliae 'Purple Dome'	191	4–8							
novae-angliae 'September Ruby'	145	4–8							
oblongifolius 'October Skies'	129, 223	5–9							
oblongifolius 'Raydon's Favorite'	165	4–9							
pringlei 'Monte Cassino'	151	4–8							
tataricus 'Jindai'	185	3–8							
'Wood's Blue'	157	3–8							
Astilbe									
chinensis 'Pumila'	199	4–8							
'Deutschland'	97	4–8							
'Diamont'	97	4–8							
'Ellie'	105	4–8							
'Peach Blossom'	211	4–8							
simplicifolia 'Sprite'	199	4–8							
Athyrium									
filix-femina 'Cristatum'	199	3–8							
niponicum var. *pictum*	105, 171	4–9							
niponicum 'Ursula's Red'	211	4–9							
Aurinia									
saxatilis	171	4–8							
Baptisia									
australis	179, 191, 223	3–9							
'Carolina Moonlight'	179	4–9							
Bergenia									
'Bressingham Ruby'	191, 217	3–8							
Boltonia									
asteroides 'Snowbank'	151, 185	4–9							
Brunnera									
macrophylla 'Jack Frost'	211, 199	3–8							
macrophylla 'Variegata'	211	3–8							

Genus Species/Cultivar	PAGE	Zone	Light	Soil	Spring	Summer	Fall	HEIGHT L M T	Fol. Color
Calamagrostis									
x acutiflora 'Avalanche'	123	4–8	◯◐	◈		✳✳✳✳✳✳		T	◩
x acutiflora 'Karl Foerster'	157, 165	4–8	◯◐	◈		✳✳✳✳✳✳		T	◼
Calamintha									
nepeta 'White Cloud'	157	5–9	◯◐	◈		✳✳✳✳		L	◼
Callirhoe									
involucrata	223	4–9	◯	◇◈		✳✳✳		L	◼
Camassia									
leichtlinii 'Blue Danube'	165	4–9	◯	◇◆	✳			T	◼
quamash 'Orion'	97	4–8	◯	◇◆	✳			L	◼
Campanula									
carpatica 'Blue Clips'	179	4–7	◯	◈		✳✳✳		L	◼
carpatica 'White Clips'	179	4–7	◯	◈		✳✳✳✳		L	◼
lactiflora 'White Pouffe'	179	5–7	◯	◈		✳✳✳✳		L	◼
Carex									
buchananii	123, 199	7–9	◯	◈	✳✳			L	◼
dolichostachya 'Kaga Nishiki'	211	5–9	◐◑	◈	✳✳			L	◩
elata 'Aurea'	97, 171	5–8	◯◐	◆	✳✳			L	◻
muskingumensis 'Oehme'	171	3–8	◯◐	◇◆	✳✳			L	◩
siderosticha 'Lemon Zest'	217	5–8	◐◑	◈	✳✳			L	◻
Caryopteris									
x clandonensis 'Dark Knight'	111	5–9	◯	◈		✳✳		M	◼
x clandonensis 'Longwood Blue'	111	5–9	◯	◈		✳✳		M	◼
x clandonensis 'Worcester Gold'	139	5–9	◯	◈		✳✳		M	◻
incana Sunshine Blue	217	6–8	◯	◈		✳✳		M	◻
Centranthus									
ruber	179, 205	5–8	◯	◈		✳✳✳✳✳		M	◼
ruber 'Albus'	179, 205	5–8	◯	◈		✳✳✳✳✳		M	◼
Ceratostigma									
plumbaginoides	111	5–9	◯◐	◈			✳✳✳	L	◼
Chelone									
lyonii 'Hot Lips'	97	3–9	◯◐	◇◆			✳✳	T	◼
Chrysanthemum									
'Mei-Kyo'	185	5–9	◯	◈			✳✳	M	◼
'Sheffield Pink'	129	4–9	◯	◈			✳✳✳	M	◼

Genus Species/Cultivar	PAGE	Zone	Light	Soil	Bloom Season			Height L M T	Fol. Color
					Spring	Summer	Fall		
Chrysogonum									
virginianum	199	5–8							
Cimicifuga									
'Hillside Black Beauty'	123, 211	4–8							
'James Compton'	199	4–8							
Colchicum									
autumnale	185	4–9							
Coreopsis									
'Creme Brulee'	157	5–9							
lanceolata 'Sunburst'	145	4–9							
'Limerock Ruby'	217	7–9							
'Sweet Dreams'	205	4–9							
verticillata 'Golden Gain'	165	3–9							
verticillata 'Moonbeam'	111, 205	3–9							
verticillata 'Zagreb'	111, 165, 205, 223	3–9							
Crambe									
cordifolia	151, 179	5–8							
Crocosmia									
'Emily McKenzie'	185	6–9							
Crocus									
speciosus f. albus	151	3–8							
Delphinium									
'Blue Bird'	171	3–7							
'King Arthur'	179	3–7							
'Magic Fountain Dark Blue'	179	3–7							
'Magic Fountain Pink'	179	3–7							
Dianthus									
barbatus 'Sooty'	171	3–8							
'Bath's Pink'	171	3–8							
'Bewitched'	180	3–9							
'Firewitch'	205	4–8							
'Little Boy Blue'	205	4–8							
'Mountain Mist'	117	3–8							
'Mrs. Sinkins'	151	5–9							

Genus Species/Cultivar	PAGE	Zone	Light	Soil	Spring	Summer	Fall	HEIGHT L M T	Fol. Color
Dicentra									
'King of Hearts'	157	3–8							
'Snowflakes'	172	3–8							
spectabilis 'Goldheart'	123, 172	4–8							
spectabilis 'Pantaloons'	180	3–8							
Dictamnus									
albus	205	3–8							
Digitalis									
lutea	172	3–9							
purpurea f. albiflora	180	4–8							
purpurea 'Foxy'	180	4–8							
purpurea 'Sutton's Apricot'	205	4–8							
Dryopteris									
erythrosora	123, 217	5–9							
Echinacea									
purpurea 'Kim's Knee High'	111, 217	3–8							
purpurea 'Magnus'	129	3–8							
purpurea 'Ruby Star'	111, 129	3–8							
purpurea 'White Swan'	151	3–9							
Eryngium									
yuccifolium	223	4–8							
Eupatorium									
coelestinum 'Cory'	130	5–9							
maculatum 'Gateway'	97	4–8							
maculatum 'Purple Bush'	223	5–9							
Euphorbia									
amygdaloides var. robbiae	172, 191, 199	6–9							
corollata	224	5–9							
dulcis 'Chameleon'	139, 165	4–9							
'Jade Dragon'	172	6–9							
polychroma	172	4–9							
Gaillardia									
x grandiflora 'Dazzler'	145	3–8							
x grandiflora 'Fanfare'	224	3–8							

Genus Species/Cultivar	PAGE	Zone	Light	Soil	Spring	Summer	Fall	L M T	Fol. Color
Gaura									
lindheimeri 'Crimson Butterflies'	217	6–9				✻✻✻✻			■
Geranium									
'Brookside'	111	5–8				✻✻✻✻			■
clarkei 'Kashmir White'	180	5–8				✻✻✻✻			■
macrorrhizum 'Spessart'	172	4–8				✻✻✻			■
maculatum 'Espresso'	199	4–8			✻✻				■
'Nimbus'	123, 179–80	5–8				✻✻✻✻✻			■
x oxonianum 'Claridge Druce'	180	5–8				✻✻✻✻			■
'Philippe Vapelle'	123	5–8				✻✻✻✻			■
pratense 'Midnight Reiter'	211	4–8				✻✻			■
'Rozanne'	111, 217	4–8				✻✻✻✻			■
sanguineum 'Album'	172	4–8				✻✻			■
Gillenia									
stipulata	191	5–9				✻✻		T	■
trifoliata	224	5–9				✻✻		T	■
Gypsophila									
paniculata 'Bristol Fairy'	151	3–7				✻✻✻		T	■
repens 'Alba'	117	3–9				✻✻✻		L	■
repens 'Rosea'	117	3–9				✻✻✻		L	■
Hakonechloa									
macra 'Albo-striata'	211	6–9					✻✻		■
macra 'All Gold'	211	6–9					✻✻		■
macra 'Aureola'	123, 217	6–9					✻✻		◨
Helenium									
'Bruno'	224	4–8					✻✻	T	■
'Coppelia'	185, 224	4–8					✻✻	T	■
Helianthus									
'Lemon Queen'	130, 224	4–9					✻✻✻	T	■
'Low Down'	117	6–9					✻✻	L	■
Heliopsis									
helianthoides 'Prairie Sunset'	130, 224	4–8					✻✻	T	■
helianthoides var. scabra 'Golden Plume'	165	3–9					✻✻✻	T	■
helianthoides var. scabra 'Goldgreenheart'	145	2–9					✻✻✻	M	■

Genus Species/Cultivar	PAGE	Zone	Light	Soil	Bloom Season (Spring / Summer / Fall)	Height (L M T)	Fol. Color
Helleborus							
foetidus	124, 191	4–9	◑●	◇	Spring	L	■
x *hybridus*	191	5–9	◑●	◇	Spring	L	■
x *hybridus* 'Mrs. Betty Ranicar'	172	5–9	◑●	◇	Spring	L	■
niger	191	5–9	◑●	◇	Spring	L	■
Hemerocallis							
'Autumn Minaret'	185	3–9	○	◇	Summer	T	■
'Double Cutie'	112	5–9	○	◇	Summer	L	■
'Happy Returns'	112	5–9	○	◇	Summer	L	■
'Pardon Me'	124	4–9	○	◇	Summer	L	■
'Penny's Worth'	217	5–9	○		Summer	L	■
'Royal Occasion'	139	3–9	○	◇	Summer	M	■
Heuchera							
'Amber Waves'	139, 217	4–9	◑	◇	Summer	L	▨
'Bressingham Bronze'	217	4–9	○◑	◇	Summer	L	■
'Harmonic Convergence'	112	4–9	○◑	◇	Summer	L	■
'Chocolate Ruffles'	124, 165	4–9	○◑	◇	Summer	L	■
'Montrose Ruby'	112	4–9	○◑	◇	Summer	L	■
'Petite Pearl Fairy'	157	5–9	○◑	◇	Summer	L	■
'Plum Pudding'	139, 211	4–9	○◑	◇	Summer	L	■
'Purple Petticoats'	172	4–9	○◑	◇	Summer	L	■
x Heucherella							
'Burnished Bronze'	217	5–9	◑	◇◆	Spring/Summer	L	■
'Rosalie'	172	5–9	◑	◇◆	Spring/Summer	L	■
'Sunspot'	124, 172	5–9	◑	◇◆	Spring/Summer	L	▨
Hexastylis							
shuttleworthii 'Callaway'	199	5–9	◑●	◇◆	Spring	L	■
Hibiscus							
'Kopper King'	97, 224	4–9	○	◇◆	Summer	T	■
moscheutos 'Disco White'	224	5–9	○	◇◆	Summer	M	■
moscheutos 'Lord Baltimore'	145	5–9	○	◇◆	Summer	T	■
Hosta							
'Blue Cadet'	124, 199	3–8	◑●	◇◆	Summer	L	■
'Guacamole'	172	3–9	◑●	◇◆	Summer	M	◩
'June'	199	3–8	◑●	◇◆	Summer	L	◩

Genus Species/Cultivar	PAGE	Zone	Light	Soil	Spring	Summer	Fall	Height (L M T)	Fol. Color
montana 'Aureomarginata'	124	3–8							
'Patriot'	105	3–9							
plantaginea	211	3–9							
'Remember Me'	211	3–9							
'Sagae'	211	3–9							
'Tokudama Flavocircinalis'	172	3–9							
Iberis									
sempervirens	191	3–8							
sempervirens 'Alexander's White'	172	3–8							
sempervirens 'Autumn Snow'	165	5–9							
Imperata									
cylindrica 'Rubra'	139, 145	5–9							
Iris									
'Butter and Sugar'	180	3–8							
cristata 'Alba'	199	3–9							
'Immortality'	151	4–9							
pallida 'Argentea Variegata'	151	5–9							
pseudacorus 'Variegata'	97	3–9							
sibirica 'Fourfold White'	152, 165	3–8							
Kirengeshoma									
palmata	124, 211	5–8							
Kniphofia									
'Springtime'	146	5–9							
Lamiastrum									
galeobdolon 'Herman's Pride'	105	3–9							
Lamium									
maculatum 'Beedham's White'	212	3–8							
maculatum 'Orchid Frost'	212	3–8							
maculatum 'Pink Pewter'	200	3–8							
maculatum 'Purple Dragon'	105	3–8							
Lavandula									
angustifolia 'Blue Cushion'	165	5–9							
angustifolia 'Jean Davis'	180	5–8							
angustifolia 'Munstead'	180	5–8							
x intermedia 'Grosso'	205	6–8							

Genus Species/Cultivar	PAGE	Zone	Light	Soil	Bloom Season: Spring	Summer	Fall	Height L M T	Fol. Color
Leucanthemum									
x *superbum* 'Becky'	152, 165	4–8	○	◇		summer		M	■
x *superbum* 'Little Princess'	112, 206	4–8	○	◇		summer		L	■
x *superbum* 'Snowcap'	112, 152	4–8	○	◇		summer		L	■
x *superbum* 'Snow Lady'	206	4–8	○	◇		summer		L	■
Liatris									
spicata	191	4–9	○	◇		summer		T	■
Lilium									
'Pink Pixie'	117	4–8	○	◇		summer		M	■
Lobelia									
'Ruby Slippers'	212	4–8	○◑	◇◆		summer		M	■
siphilitica 'Blue Select'	97	3–8	○◑	◇◆		summer		M	■
Lupinus									
'The Chatelaine'	180	4–7	○	◇		summer		M	■
'Gallery White'	180	4–7	○	◇		summer		L	■
Luzula									
'Ruby Stiletto'	212	5–9	◑●	◇◆		summer		L	■
Lychnis									
chalcedonica 'Alba'	152	4–8	○	◇		summer		T	■
Lysimachia									
nummularia 'Aurea'	200	3–8	○◑	◇◆		summer		L	▨
punctata 'Alexander'	97	4–8	○◑	◇◆		summer		M	◪
Mazus									
reptans	105	3–9	○◑	◇◆	spring			L	■
Milium									
effusum 'Aureum'	172	5–8	◑	◇◆				L	▨
Miscanthus									
sinensis 'Ferner Osten'	130	5–9	○	◇◆			fall	T	■
sinensis 'Morning Light'	152	5–9	○	◇◆			fall	T	◪
sinensis 'Variegatus'	130	4–9	○	◇◆			fall	T	◪
sinensis 'Zebrinus'	185	5–9	○	◇◆			fall	T	◪
Molinia									
caerulea subsp. *arundinacea* 'Sky Racer'	191	5–9	○◑	◇◆			fall	M	■
Monarda									
'Jacob Cline'	146, 224	3–9	○◑	◇◆		summer		T	■

Genus Species/Cultivar	PAGE	Zone	Light	Soil	Spring	BLOOM SEASON Summer	Fall	HEIGHT L M T	Fol. Color
'Marshall's Delight'	224	3-9							
Narcissus									
'Sweetness'	166	5-9							
'Thalia'	166	5-9							
Nepeta									
x *faassenii* 'Blue Wonder'	118	4-8							
x *faassenii* 'Snowflake'	152	4-8							
x *faassenii* 'Walker's Low'	180, 166	4-8							
racemosa 'Little Titch'	118	5-8							
Nipponanthemum									
nipponicum	185	5-9							
Oenothera									
fruticosa 'Fireworks'	146	3-9							
fruticosa 'Summer Solstice'	130	3-9							
Ophiopogon									
planiscapus 'Nigrescens'	200	6-9							
Origanum									
laevigatum 'Hopleys'	130	6-9							
vulgare 'Aureum'	217	4-8							
Pachysandra									
procumbens	200	5-9							
Paeonia									
'Krinkled White'	157	3-8							
Panicum									
virgatum 'Dallas Blues'	224	5-9							
virgatum 'Hänse Herms'	186	5-9							
virgatum 'Heavy Metal'	186	5-9							
virgatum 'Northwind'	146	4-9							
virgatum 'Shenandoah'	139, 224	5-9							
Papaver									
orientale 'Patty's Plum'	173	4-9							
Pennisetum									
alopecuroides 'Hameln'	118, 186	6-9							
alopecuroides 'Little Bunny'	152	5-9							
alopecuroides 'Moudry'	186	6-9							

Genus Species/Cultivar	PAGE	Zone	Light	Soil	Spring	Summer	Fall	Height (L M T)	Fol. Color
Pennisetum (continued)									
orientale 'Karley Rose'	130, 218	6–9	○	◇		✳✳✳✳		L	■
Penstemon									
digitalis 'Husker Red'	225	3–9	○	◇◆		✳✳✳		L	■ (dark)
smallii	225	5–9	○	◇		✳✳✳		L	■
Perovskia									
atriplicifolia	130, 186	6–9	○	◇◆		✳✳		L	■
atriplicifolia 'Longin'	166	6–9	○	◇◆		✳✳		L	■
'Little Spires'	186	6–9	○	◇◆		✳✳		L	■
Persicaria									
'Brushstrokes'	218	5–9	○◑	◇◆			✳✳	L	■
polymorpha	130	4–9	○	◇◆		✳✳✳		T	■
Phlox									
divaricata 'London Grove Blue'	173, 212	4–8	◑●	◇◆	✳✳			L	■
divaricata 'Plum Perfect'	212	3–8	◑●	◇◆	✳✳			L	■
glaberrima 'Morris Berd'	225	4–9	○	◇◆	✳✳			L	■
paniculata 'Becky Towe'	124	4–8	○	◇◆		✳✳✳		M	◪
paniculata 'David'	152, 206	4–9	○	◇◆		✳✳✳		M	■
paniculata 'Eva Cullum'	157	4–8	○	◇◆		✳✳✳		M	■
paniculata 'Little Boy'	130	4–8	○	◇◆		✳✳✳		M	■
paniculata 'Robert Poore'	186	5–8	○	◇◆		✳✳✳		T	■
paniculata 'Shortwood'	130, 206	4–8	○	◇◆		✳✳✳		T	■
paniculata 'Starfire'	146	4–8	○	◇◆		✳✳✳		M	■ (dark)
stolonifera 'Sherwood Purple'	173, 200	2–8	○	◇◆	✳✳			L	■
Physostegia									
virginiana 'Miss Manners'	97, 186, 225	4–8	○◑	◇◆		✳✳✳✳		L	■
Platycodon									
grandiflorus subsp. mariesii	205–06	3–9	○	◇		✳✳		L	■
grandiflorus 'Misato Purple'	206	3–9	○	◇		✳✳		L	■
grandiflorus 'Shell Pink'	206	3–9	○	◇		✳✳		L	■
Polemonium									
foliosissimum	180	4–8	○◑	◇		✳✳		L	■
Polygonatum									
humile	200	4–9	◑●	◇	✳✳			L	■
odoratum 'Variegatum'	173	4–8	◑●	◇	✳✳			M	■

Genus Species/Cultivar	PAGE	Zone	Light	Soil	Spring	Summer	Fall	HEIGHT L M T	Fol. Color
Polystichum									
acrostichoides	200	5–9							
Potentilla									
tridentata	152	2–8							
Primula									
veris	97	4–8							
Pulmonaria									
'Blue Ensign'	212	3–8			✳✳				
'Cotton Cool'	212	3–8			✳✳				
'Little Blue'	173	3–8			✳✳				
saccharata 'Pierre's Pure Pink'	173	3–8			✳✳				
'Silver Streamers'	105	3–8			✳✳				
Pycnanthemum									
muticum	225	4–9							
Rudbeckia									
fulgida var. fulgida	186, 225	3–9							
fulgida var. sullivantii 'Goldsturm'	112, 225	3–9							
maxima	146, 191	5–9							
Salvia									
argentea	152	5–8							
nemorosa 'Caradonna'	157, 166, 218	4–8				✳✳✳			
nemorosa 'East Friesland'	112, 157, 206	4–8				✳✳✳			
nemorosa 'Marcus'	118	3–8				✳✳✳			
x sylvestris 'Blue Hill'	206	4–8				✳✳✳			
x sylvestris 'May Night'	112	4–8				✳✳✳			
x sylvestris 'Snow Hill'	152	4–8							
Sanguisorba									
menziesii	146	4–8				✳✳✳			
Saponaria									
x lempergii 'Max Frei'	206	4–8							
Saxifraga									
stolonifera 'Harvest Moon'	218	6–9				✳			
Scabiosa									
'Butterfly Blue'	206	3–8				✳✳✳✳✳			
'Pink Mist'	206	3–8				✳✳✳✳✳			

Genus Species/Cultivar	PAGE	Zone	Light	Soil	Bloom Season			Height (L M T)	Fol. Color
					Spring	Summer	Fall		
Schizachyrium									
scoparium 'The Blues'	225	3–9	○	◇◈	• • •	• • •	✳✳✳	M	▦
Sedum									
'Autumn Fire'	131, 186	3–9	○	◇◈	• • •	✳✳ •	• • •	M	▦
'Frosty Morn'	152	3–9	○	◇◈	• • •	• ✳✳	• • •	L	◪
'Matrona'	131, 166	3–9	○	◇◈	• • •	• ✳✳	• • •	M	▦
'Mohrchen'	186	4–9	○	◇◈	• • •	• ✳✳	• • •	L	■
'Ruby Glow'	118	4–8	○	◇◈	• • •	✳✳✳	• • •	L	▦
telephium subsp. *maximum* 'Atropurpureum'	139	5–9	○	◇◈	• • •	• ✳✳	• • •	L	■
'Vera Jameson'	118, 186, 218	4–8	○	◇◈	• • •	• ✳✳	• • •	L	■
Sidalcea									
'Party Girl'	206	5–7	○	◈	• • •	• ✳✳	• • •	T	▦
Sisyrinchium									
angustifolium 'Lucerne'	157	5–9	○	◇◈	• • ✳	✳✳ •	• • •	L	▦
Smilacina									
racemosa	173	4–9	◐●	◇◈	• ✳✳	• • •	• • •	M	▦
Solidago									
caesia	200	4–8	○◐	◈	• • •	• • •	✳✳✳	M	▦
'Crown of Rays'	131	3–8	○	◈	• • •	• • ✳	✳ • •	M	▦
rigida	225	4–9	○	◈	• • •	• • ✳	✳ • •	T	▦
rugosa 'Fireworks'	131, 186	3–8	○	◈	• • •	• • ✳	✳ • •	T	▦
sphacelata 'Golden Fleece'	186	5–9	○	◈	• • •	• ✳ ✳	✳ • •	L	▦
Sporobolus									
heterolepis	225	3–8	○	◇◈	• • •	• • •	✳✳ •	L	▦
Stachys									
byzantina 'Big Ears'	180	4–8	○◐	◇◈	• • •	• • •	• • •	L	▦
macrantha 'Superba'	157	5–8	○◐	◇◈	• • •	✳✳✳✳	• • •	L	▦
Stokesia									
laevis 'Klaus Jelitto'	131	5–9	○	◈	• • •	✳✳✳	• • •	M	▦
laevis 'Silver Moon'	131	5–9	○	◈	• • •	• ✳✳✳	• • •	M	▦
Tanacetum									
vulgare 'Isla Gold'	139	4–8	○◐	◇◈	• • •	• ✳✳✳	• • •	M	▦
Thalictrum									
rochebrunianum 'Lavender Mist'	212	5–9	○	◇◈	• • •	• ✳✳	• • •	T	▦

Genus Species/Cultivar	PAGE	Zone	Light	Soil	Spring	Summer	Fall	HEIGHT L M T	Fol. Color
Thymus									
serpyllum 'Pink Chintz'	118	4–8						L	■
serpyllum 'Snowdrift'	118	4–8						L	■
Tiarella									
'Cygnet'	173	4–9						L	■
'Dark Star'	105	4–9						L	■
'Iron Butterfly'	212	4–9						L	■
'Jeepers Creepers'	218	4–9						L	■
'Oakleaf'	105	4–9						L	■
'Tiger Stripe'	173, 218	4–9						L	■
'Winterglow'	124	3–8						L	■
Tradescantia									
'Mrs. Loewer'	225	4–9						M	■
'Osprey'	152	5–9						M	■
'Sweet Kate'	139	4–9						L	■
Tricyrtis									
'Empress'	212	5–9						M	■
hirta 'Alba'	124	4–9						M	■
Verbascum									
bombyciferum 'Arctic Summer'	152	4–8						T	■
'Mont Blanc'	157	5–9						T	■
Verbena									
'Snowflurry'	152	5–10						L	■
Vernonia									
noveboracensis	186	5–9						T	■
Veronica									
spicata 'Alba'	152	3–8						L	■
spicata 'Blue Fox'	112	3–8						L	■
spicata 'Goodness Grows'	118, 218	3–8						L	■
spicata 'Icicles'	112	3–8						L	■
spicata subsp. incana	152	3–8						L	■
spicata 'Royal Candles'	218	3–8						L	■
Veronicastrum									
virginicum	97, 225	3–8						T	■

Recommended Reading

STEPHANIE'S FAVORITES

Over time, I've collected literally hundreds of gardening books. They're almost as addictive as plants! But when I sat down to prepare this list, I found only a handful that I really couldn't do without. Here are some of my favorites:

Armitage, Allan M. *Herbaceous Perennial Plants: A Treatise on Their Identification, Culture, and Garden Attributes* (Second Edition). Champaign, IL: Stipes Publishing, LLC., 1997.

> I love Allan's descriptions, combinations, and complete honesty about the merits of each plant. He also likes humorous stories and comments, which I happen to like as well. I wore out one second edition and am on a new copy.

Brickell, Christopher, and Judith D. Zuk, Editors-in-Chief. *The American Horticultural Society A-Z Encyclopedia of Garden Plants.* New York, NY: DK Publishing, Inc., 1997.

> This book was a gift from my son; it's one I use often. It has wonderful illustrations of all sorts of plants, both mundane and weird. The information is short and to the point for a quick reference.

Griffiths, Mark, et al. *The Royal Horticultural Society Shorter Dictionary of Gardening: A Comprehensive and Essential Reference.* London, England: Macmillan Publishing Co., 1998.

> A brief version of plant listings and technical terms, and a good cross-reference for information and nomenclature. So if you are not quite sure of the terminology in something you're reading, this is a good book to have at your fingertips.

Jelitto, Leo, and Wilhelm Schacht. *Hardy Herbaceous Perennials.* Portland, OR: Timber Press, 1985.

> For those who want to know all of the nitty-gritty details about perennials, this two-volume set tells where plants were originally found, indicates who hybridized particular selections, and cites minute differences between cultivars.

Jekyll, Gertrude (revised by Graham Stuart Thomas). *Wood and Garden.* Salem, NH: Ayer Company, 1983.

> All Miss Jekyll's books have been reprinted, as well as editions about her life and work. Many of today's ideas on garden design and plant use came from this lady. Some plant names have changed, but much that she wrote about is still valid in today's gardening world. I've seen many concepts presented as new that are just tweaks of what she wrote more than 75 years ago. Considering that Gertrude was a bachelorette, her writing is very romantic and inspiring. I like to go back to the source for inspiration.

Oehme, Wolfgang, and James van Sweden with Susan Rademacher Frey. *Bold Romantic Gardens: The New World Landscapes of Oehme and Van Sweden.* Reston, VA: Acropolis Books, 1991.

> I love all of the books by Wolfgang Oehme and James van Sweden, but this is my all-time favorite. It was one of the most exciting books on design to come along since Gertrude gave up the ghost. The concepts in this book broke ground in that they were not depicting the English park or cottage gardening, but a new ideal for American gardening. We owe them a debt of gratitude for showing us how to combine perennials and grasses in our gardens.

Ottesen, Carole. *Ornamental Grasses: The Amber Wave.* New York, NY: McGraw-Hill, 1995.

> This is another fine book that shows how to integrate grasses into the landscape.

Harper, Pamela J. *Color Echoes: Harmonizing Color in the Garden.* New York, NY: Macmillan Publishing Co., 1994.

> The term "color echoes" came from the pen of this great plantswoman. This term caught on and today's garden designers are well-aware of the way we look at color, thanks to the original ideas in this book. For those who need tutoring in the language of color, this is an excellent reference. The prose and pictures both come from Pam Harper, and she includes all kinds of gardens and combinations to illustrate her ideas.

Albert, Susan Wittig. *Indigo Dying.* New York, NY: Berkley Books, 2003.

Nichols, Beverley. *Merry Hall.* Portland, OR: Timber Press, 1998.

> For those not wanting to read serious tomes in the winter, I recommend some fun reading. *Indigo Dying* is one in a series of very good mysteries. The clever woman detective who stars in Wittig's books is a wonderful herbalist who always manages to get involved. There are plants galore in her books, occasionally recipes, and always the fun of trying to figure out "who dunnit." Of course, plants are sometimes either the killer or the cure. Beverley Nichols is a gardening guru whose stories make me smile and laugh out loud with all of the hi-jinx in this weird mélange of English characters. Sometimes the author is downright malicious and vindictive as he describes the trials and tribulations of restoring an old estate. A quick read, but oodles of fun. If you enjoy this one, look for the sequels, too.

NAN'S FAVORITES

I, too, have collected many gardening books over the years; it's an occupational hazard! I use a variety of plant encyclopedias, but my real favorites are the inspirational design-related titles. Here are a few of the books I adore for winter afternoon reading. (I used to keep them for bedtime, but I found that I lost a lot of sleep, because I'd get stirred up with new planting ideas and would stay up too late making notes for next year's gardens!)

Gerritsen, Henk, and Piet Oudolf. *Dream Plants for the Natural Garden*. Portland, OR: Timber Press, 2000.

King, Michael, and Piet Oudolf. *Gardening with Grasses*. Portland, OR: Timber Press, 1998.

Oudolf, Piet, and Henk Gerritsen. *Planting the Natural Garden*. Portland, OR: Timber Press, 2003.

——, with Noel Kingbury. *Designing with Plants*. Portland, OR: Timber Press, 1999.

> If a book has Piet Oudolf's name on it, I will buy it. I'm still very color-oriented in my gardens, but these books have opened my eyes to the exciting possibilities of form and texture as well, particularly for fall and winter. All these books (but especially *Dream Plants*) are fun to read and filled with down-to-earth observations and plain-spoken opinions-definitely not the same old stuff!

Sarah Raven. *The Bold and Brilliant Garden*. Holbrook, MA: Adams Media Corporation, 1999.

> This book completely changed my attitude toward using bright colors in my gardens. After years of treasuring soft colors and harmonious pairings, I'm now having a blast combining bold blocks of hot pinks, purples, yellows, and oranges-strong, contrasting combos I never would have thought to try before. And I find that, instead of being appalled at the "gaudiness," visitors to my garden seem to respond more favorably to these brightly colored plantings than to restrained palettes of soft blues, pinks, and whites. Though these colors aren't for everyone, if you're looking to be inspired by something different, this book is a great start!

Pope, Nori & Sandra. *Color by Design: Planting the Contemporary Garden*. San Francisco, CA: Soma Books, 1998.

> If your color taste runs toward safer combinations, this book is an excellent resource for creating elegant monochromatic borders. The photographs are lovely, and the discussions of color effects are absolutely eye-opening.

www.gardenweb.com

> Sometimes, books simply don't have the timely, site-specific information you need when you're planning your beds and borders. There are currently over 200 forums on GardenWeb, on just about any gardening-related subject you can name, including various plants, garden styles, techniques, and regions. For the best time to divide perennials in your area, suggestions for plants that will thrive on a difficult site, or a real gardeners' honest opinions on the latest perennial introductions, this is the place to come! You can even post pictures of unknown plants to get ID help. Most of GardenWeb is free to everyone, but if you use it often, consider paying the modest membership fee to help support the site. In return, on your member page, you can share information about yourself with other members, post a list of plants and seeds that you'd like to trade, and keep an online garden journal.

Other Handy References

DiSabato-Aust, Tracy. *The Well-Tended Perennial Garden: Planting and Pruning Techniques*. Portland, OR: Timber Press, 1998.

Ellis, Barbara. *Taylor's Guide to Perennials*. Boston, MA: Houghton Mifflin Company, 2001.

Erler, Catriona Tudor. *Poolscaping: Gardening and Landscaping Around Your Swimming Pool and Spa*. North Adams, MA: Storey Books, 2003.

Hayward, Gordon. *Garden Paths: Inspiring Designs and Practical Projects*. Firefly Books, 1997.

—— *Taylor's Weekend Gardening Guide to Garden Paths*. Houghton Mifflin, 1998.

Hodgson, Larry. *Perennials for Every Purpose: Choose the Plants You Need for Your Conditions, Your Gardens, and Your Taste*. Emmaus, PA: Rodale Books, 2000.

Macunovich, Janet. *Caring for Perennials: What to Do and When to Do It*. North Adams, MA: Storey Publishing, 1997.

Ondra, Nancy J. *Grasses: Versatile Partners for Uncommon Garden Designs*. North Adams, MA: Storey Books, 2002.

Phillips, Ellen, and C. Colston Burrell. *Rodale's Illustrated Encyclopedia of Perennials*. Emmaus, PA: Rodale, Inc., 2004.

Please Don't Eat the Delphiniums!

Gardening is supposed to be fun for everyone, and most times it is. But if your yard is frequented by kids and/or pets, you'll probably want to take extra care when selecting and siting your plants to avoid possible health problems. A surprising number of common perennials can be potentially toxic if ingested; others might cause skin reactions if touched, or have sharp or spiny leaves that can scratch, cut, or prick unwary passersby. Here's a brief overview of some of the most common culprits and their possible dangers. This is by no means a comprehensive listing of all potentially harmful perennials, so if you are concerned about this issue, check with your pediatrician, veterinarian, or local poison control center for more information, or investigate online resources on toxic plants using a search program to look for key words such as "toxic" or "poisonous" and "perennials." It's probably not practical to avoid all possible problem plants in your gardens, but it's smart to at least be aware of the potential dangers so you can make informed design choices.

Acanthus spinosus (spiny bear's breeches) — Spiny leaves

Aconitum (monkshoods) — Harmful if eaten, skin irritant

Actaea (baneberries) — Harmful if eaten, skin irritant

Anemone (anemones) — Harmful if eaten

Aquilegia (columbines) — Harmful if eaten

Arisaema (Jack-in-the-pulpits) — Harmful if eaten

Arum (arums) — Harmful if eaten, skin irritant

Asclepias (milkweeds) — Harmful if eaten

Baptisia (false indigos) — Harmful if eaten

Caltha (marsh marigolds) — Harmful if eaten

Colchicum (autumn crocus) — Harmful if eaten

Convallaria majalis (lily of the valley) — Harmful if eaten

Cortaderia (pampas grasses) — Sharp-edged leaves

Delphinium (delphiniums, larkspur) — Harmful if eaten

Dicentra (bleeding hearts) — Skin irritant

Dictamnus albus (gas plant, dittany) — Skin irritant

Digitalis (foxgloves) — Harmful if eaten

Eryngium (sea hollies) — Spiny leaves

Euphorbia (euphorbias, spurges) — Harmful if eaten, skin irritant

Gaillardia (blanket flowers) — Skin irritant

Helenium (sneezeweeds) — Skin irritant

Helleborus (hellebores, Lenten roses) — Harmful if eaten, skin irritant

Hyacinthus (hyacinths) — Skin irritant

Iris (irises) — Harmful if eaten

Lobelia (lobelias, cardinal flowers) — Harmful if eaten

Lupinus (lupines) — Harmful if eaten

Miscanthus (miscanthus, Japanese silver grass) — Sharp-edged leaves

Narcissus (daffodils) — Harmful if eaten, skin irritant

Polygonatum (Solomon's seals) — Harmful if eaten

Pulsatilla (pasque flowers) — Harmful if eaten

Ranunculus (ranunculus, buttercups) — Harmful if eaten, skin irritant

Rudbeckia (rudbeckias, black-eyed Susans) — Skin irritant

Ruta (rue) — Harmful if eaten, skin irritant

Scilla (squills) — Harmful if eaten

Tanacetum (tansy) — Skin irritant

Tulipa (tulips) — Skin irritant

Yucca (yuccas, Adam's needles) — Sharp-pointed leaves

Acknowledgments

I would like to share this book with all of my former students, who taught me as much as I taught them. I would like to express my love and gratitude to all of my Perennial Plant Association family, who helped make my long career possible and provided me inspiration and guidance. Appreciation also to my three friends, Bobbie, Lynne, and Jan, who are my comrades in all sorts of horticultural escapades. I am grateful to my mother and father, who placed a trowel in my hand at six years old and never realized before they died that they had placed my feet on a winding path that led to a long career in this field. Thank you to David Trauptman, who helped us with the original concept for the graphics on pages 26 and 63. And thank you to Dr. Liz Sluzis for getting me my first writing job in horticulture. Thanks to my wonderful editor, Gwen Steege, who is a joy to work with on this book. Thanks to Rob Cardillo, photographer extraordinaire, who makes miracles with his lenses. Last, but not least, thank you to my co-author, who led me by the hand so that this book could get written. I can honestly say she has been friend and mentor through thick and thin. She hides her light under a bushel, but to me she is one of horticulture's brightest undiscovered stars.

— STEPHANIE COHEN

Regardless of whose name is on the cover, the reality is that every book is a group effort: a combination of direct and indirect influences from countless people. Once again, Team Storey — including Gwen Steege, Kent Lew, Cindy McFarland, and Sarah Guare — has come through with a winner, thanks to their consistent ability to combine overall vision with exquisite attention to detail. Lois Lovejoy's skill at turning our rough plot plans into lovely illustrations amazed me to no end and contributed greatly to the beauty of the finished book. And then there's Rob Cardillo, with his uncanny knack for capturing garden images that are both technically top-notch and aesthetically breath-taking. I'd also like to thank all of the nursery owners and growers everywhere — and specifically Kim Bechtle of Still Pond Nursery, Marian Martin of Martin's Greenhouse, and Emma Richards of Richards' Plants — for growing the amazing array of plants that never fail to inspire me. But most of all, I thank my buddy Steph for sticking with me through the years it took to turn her dream into this reality. Working with a co-author is more than just a business arrangement: It's a matter of trust, compromise, and dedication — and a whole lot of fun as well. It's been an unforgettable experience!

— NANCY ONDRA

Garden Design Credits

Alaska Botanical Garden, Anchorage, AK: pp. vii-ix, 174
Beaubaire Garden, Warminster, PA: p. 192
Brookside Gardens, Wheaton, MD: p. 23
Bunting Garden, Swarthmore, PA: pp. 4, 98
Chanticleer Garden, Wayne, PA: pp. 7, 16, 17, 22 left, 22C, 27 bottom left, 30, 33 bottom right, 34, 36, 66, 77, 90, 113, 140, 160, 213
Cohen Garden, Collegeville, PA: pp. 21, 29, 31, 33 top left, 38, 45, 46 right, 68, 78C, 83, 131 top, 134, 158, 219, 227, 242-255
Cole Garden, Gary Keim designer, Owings Mills, MD: p. 6
Colonial Park, East Millstone, NJ: p. 53
Culp Garden, Downingtown, PA: pp. 14, 40, 180 left, 195, 207
Fordhook Farm, Grace Romero designer, Doylestown, PA: pp. vi-vii, 24, 46-47, 49, 63, 64 top, 130, 181
Frelinghuysen Arboretum, Morristown NJ: pp. 33 bottom left, 81 top, 132

Hedrick Garden, Philadelphia, PA: p. 78 left
Hiroshi Garden, Ardmore, PA: p. 64 bottom
Isabella Garden, Piedmont Designs, Gladwyne, PA: pp. 80, 85
Jabco-Henderson Garden, Swarthmore, PA: p. 100
Jerry Fritz Garden Design, Ottsville, PA: pp. 59, 79
Kehlor Garden, Tamaqua, PA: pp. 18, 81 bottom
Krombolz Garden, West Chester, PA: pp. 87 bottom, 167
Landscape Arboretum of Temple Univeristy, Ambler, PA: pp. 2, 22 right, 33 top right, 223 top
Linden Hill Gardens, Ottsville, PA: pp. 10 middle, 48, 52, 69, 76 top
Little and Lewis Garden, Bainbridge Island, WA: p. 87 top
Longwood Gardens, Kennett Square, PA: pp. ii, 25 bottom, 27 top right, 92, 107

Lycknell Garden, Pretty Dirty Ladies designer, Reading, PA: p. 50
Morris Arboretum, Philadelphia, PA: pp. 9, 10 bottom, 20, 54, 55, 72, 82, 84, 125, 147, 199
Muir Garden, Tom Borkowski designer, Fort Washington, PA: pp. 46, 56
Ondra Garden, Pennsburg, PA: pp. 12, 25 top, 37, 61, 75, 101, 131 bottom, 139, 226, 230-241, 256-268
Rayner Garden, Toronto, ON: pp. 60, 119
Reed Garden, Malvern, PA: p. 19
Scott Arboretum, Swarthmore, PA: pp. 32, 42
Sillivan-Smith Garden, Bethlehem, PA: p. 78 right
Thyrum Garden, Wilmington, DE: p. 74
Waterloo Gardens, Devon, PA: pp. 28 top, 146 left
Weinsteiger Garden, Alburtis, PA: p. 201
Wells Medina Nursery, Medina, WA: p. 10 top
Willowwood Arboretum, Morristown NJ: p. 86

Index

Page numbers in **bold** indicate tables; those in *italic* indicate illustrations.